APPLIED POSITIVE PEDAGOGY IN SPORT COACHING

Positive Pedagogy is an athlete-centred, inquiry-based approach that transforms the way we understand learning and coaching in sport and can be successfully employed across a range of different sports and levels of performance. *Applied Positive Pedagogy in Sports Coaching: International Cases* reflects the uptake of Positive Pedagogy by coaches across different countries and sport settings through its complete focus on their experiences of using it and adapting it to their needs and contexts.

Comprising 17 detailed chapters that examine both Team Sports (Part 1) and Individual Sports (Part 2), this book seeks to provide insight into the opportunities and challenges involved in the application of Positive Pedagogy for sport coaching (PPed). Critically, it also identifies any problems the coaches encountered, how they addressed them and what they learned from these experiences.

Acting as a complementary text to the successful *Positive Pedagogy for Sport Coaching*, 2nd edition, *Applied Positive Pedagogy in Sports Coaching: International Cases* is an exciting, applied text that will be vital reading for all practising sports coaches or physical education teachers looking to improve or even transform their professional practice, as well as sports coaching students and researchers.

Richard Light is Professor of Sport Pedagogy in the College of Education, Health and Human Development at the University of Canterbury, New Zealand. He is a prominent figure in research on, and the development of, athlete-centred coaching. Richard's experience as a coach was in school sport as a primary and secondary school teacher. At high-performance level, he coached rugby in Japan and taught martial arts in Australia, where he coached state and national champions in karate and kickboxing.

Stephen Harvey is Professor of Coaching, Health and Physical Education in the Department of Recreation and Sports Pedagogy at Ohio University, USA, and a prominent figure in research on games-based coaching. Stephen is a licensed physical education teacher who has coached a collegiate national championship winning team in women's soccer as well as junior and master's level international field hockey teams. He coaches at a local soccer club and has led coach development sessions for numerous organizations, including USA field hockey and the United States Olympic Committee. Stephen recently qualified as an International Council for Coach Education Coach Developer through participation in the Nippon Sport Science University Coach Developer Academy.

APPLIED POSITIVE PEDAGOGY IN SPORT COACHING

International Cases

Edited by Richard Light and Stephen Harvey

Routledge
Taylor & Francis Group

NEW YORK AND LONDON

First published 2021
by Routledge
52 Vanderbilt Avenue, New York, NY 10017

and by Routledge
2 Park Square, Milton Park, Abingdon, Oxon OX14 4RN

Routledge is an imprint of the Taylor & Francis Group, an informa business

© 2021 Taylor & Francis

The right of Richard Light and Stephen Harvey to be identified as the authors of the editorial material, and of the authors for their individual chapters, has been asserted in accordance with sections 77 and 78 of the Copyright, Designs and Patents Act 1988.

Trademark notice: Product or corporate names may be trademarks or registered trademarks, and are used only for identification and explanation without intent to infringe.

Library of Congress Cataloging-in-Publication Data
Names: Light, Richard, 1951– editor | Harvey, Stephen, editor. | Curry, Christina, author. | Gibson, Kass, author. | Hill, Nick, author. | Jarrett, Kendall, author. | Kuklick, Clayton, author. | Paterson, Juliet, author. | Pill, Shane, author. | Pimenta, Ricardo, author. | Price, Letitia, author. | Razak, Mohammad Shah, author. | Sup, Michael, author.
Title: Applied positive pedagogy in sport coaching : International coaching cases / Richard Light and Stephen Harvey.
Description: New York, NY : Routledge, 2020. |
Includes bibliographical references. |
Identifiers: LCCN 2020014974 (print) | LCCN 2020014975 (ebook) |
ISBN 9780367489816 (hardback) | ISBN 9780367489823 (paperback) |
ISBN 9781003043812 (ebook)
Subjects: LCSH: Coaching (Athletics) | Coaching (Athletics)--Psychological aspects. | Athletes--Psychology.
Classification: LCC GV711 .L48 2020 (print) | LCC GV711 (ebook) |
DDC 796.07/7--dc23
LC record available at https://lccn.loc.gov/2020014974
LC ebook record available at https://lccn.loc.gov/2020014975

ISBN: 978-0-367-48981-6 (hbk)
ISBN: 978-0-367-48982-3 (pbk)
ISBN: 978-1-003-04381-2 (ebk)

Typeset in Bembo
by Taylor & Francis Books

CONTENTS

ILLUSTRATIONS

Figure

Tables

CONTRIBUTORS

Bianca C. de Aguiar completed a PhD at the University of Canterbury in New Zealand on games teaching in secondary schools under the supervision of Professor Richard Light. She has an extensive background in gymnastics in Portugal as a competitor where she competed in artistic gymnastics for eight years and won several national titles. As a coach, she coached acrobatic gymnastics in Coimbra at recreation, development and competition levels, and taught Physical Education, including gymnastics. While undertaking her PhD she worked at Christchurch School of Gymnastics in Canterbury, New Zealand where she coached pre-school, recreation and competitive classes in gymnastics. She now holds a postdoctoral position at Waseda University in Japan.

Christina Curry is a former Head of Health and Physical Education Department at a secondary school for the NSW Department of Education who completed a PhD in 2013 on the implementation of TGfU at an independent secondary school in Sydney, Australia. She is at the Western Sydney University where she was Director of Secondary Education and now teaches and conducts research in Leadership, Health and Physical Education with a focus on Game Sense. She is regularly invited to conduct workshops on Game Sense and Positive Pedagogy for sport coaching and was involved in its early development.

Kass Gibson is a Senior Lecturer in the School of Sport, Health and Wellbeing at Plymouth Marjon University in the UK. His research focuses on the relationships and effects between different ways of knowing, meanings, experiences, and practices in physical activity, sport, physical education, and public health.

Nick Hill is a Physical Education teacher, Athletic Development and Rugby coach who has taught and coached sport in England, Chile and the USA at all levels in schools, universities and adult clubs. He has been developing a player-centred coaching approach for many years with many successes and a range of challenges in different environments and cultures. Since reading about Positive Pedagogy for sport coaching in 2017 and being invited to the 2018 Global Coaching Symposium in 2018 and then 2019 he has increasingly taken a PPed approach to his coaching.

Kendall Jarrett is a Lecturer in Academic Practice at the University of Kent (UK), where he uses his background in sport pedagogy and teacher/coach education to inform his current teaching and research in academic practice and educational leadership. Kendall has 20 years of coaching experience across a range of different sports in a number of different countries. In positions as a head coach, assistant coach, team manager and team masseur, over his sport coaching and administration career, he has worked with teams from junior cricket and basketball levels, through to senior elite field hockey teams at National Championship level.

Clayton Kuklick was an assistant baseball coach with Kutztown University, University of North Carolina-Wilmington, Georgia College and State University, and Shepherd University and head coach of collegiate summer league teams across the USA. He now works as an Assistant Professor in the Master of Arts of Sport Coaching program at the University of Denver where he facilitates coaches' development of learner-centered pedagogical approaches across a range of sports and levels.

Richard Light is Professor of Sport Coaching at The University of Canterbury and a leading figure in the development of athlete centred coaching with a focus on Game Sense and Positive Pedagogy for sport coaching. His coaching background in high performance sport is in rugby which includes professional coaching in Japan and martial arts where he coached several Australian national champions in kickboxing and karate. He has also coached children and young people across a range of sports in schools and community-based sport clubs in Australia.

Juliet Paterson has worked in swimming and athletics development as a primary teacher and P.E. subject lead, over a 17-year period. She is currently, British Triathlon's South West Skills School Lead and authored the BTF 'Triathlon in Schools' programme, co-authored the 'Coaching Children and Young People in Triathlon' programme and edited the Federation's children's coaching development literature. Juliet recently completed a Master's degree with a study on 'Coaching Children and Young People', at Plymouth Marjon University, UK in which she examined the impact of Positive Pedagogy upon her practice and the experiences of junior triathletes, under the supervision of Dr Kass Gibson.

Shane Pill is Associate Professor in Physical Education and Sport at Flinders University, Australia. Shane is a well-established figure and leader in the development of athlete-centred coaching and particularly with Game Sense. He received a 2016

Australian Government award for Outstanding Contribution to Student Learning and is editor of *Perspectives on athlete-centred coaching* published by Routledge in 2018. Shane is regularly invited to speak and demonstrate practice in athlete-centred coaching and was invited to the 2019 Ohio Global Coaching Symposium that focused on Positive Pedagogy for sport coaching where he delivered presentations on PPed.

Ricardo Pimenta was awarded his PhD for a study on why adolescent girls play basketball in a New Zealand secondary early 2019. He moved from Portugal to New Zealand to undertake his PhD with Professor Richard Light with a background as a player and coach of basketball in Portugal and coached club and school basketball in Christchurch, New Zealand for four years. During this time, he also worked as a tutor in the Bachelor of Sport Coaching program that included working on a course on Positive Pedagogy for sport coaching and as a research assistant from 2015–2016 at the University of Canterbury.

Letitia Price is an assistant coordinator for the Ohio University online master's degree in Soccer Coaching. Having previously coached international, representative, collegiate and high school athletes, within the areas of strength and conditioning, soccer and sport performance lifestyle. She is currently undertaking her doctoral degree, with her study entitled, *Women in sport, women's leadership in sport and community sport engagement*, while also coaching the Ohio University field hockey varsity team to where she provides athlete-centred sport science support.

Mohammad Shah Razak was awarded his PhD on 'Moral and Ethical learning in Sports in Secondary Schools' at the University of Canterbury under the supervision of Professor Richard Light and is now Head of the Department of Physical Education at Jurongville Secondary School in Singapore. He has an extensive background in teaching physical education and coaching sport at recreational and competitive levels in Singapore over an eighteen-year period in both primary and secondary schools and worked as a tutor in the Bachelor of Sport Coaching program at The University of Canterbury.

Michael Sup is a Co-Founder and Director of Education at Beyond Pulse. He previously held coaching positions in the UK and the USA. These positions ranged from professional youth soccer academies in England to youth soccer clubs and high schools in the USA. In addition to being a UEFA, USSF and USC licensed coach, Michael also holds a PhD in Curriculum and Instructions from Ohio University.

ACKNOWLEDGEMENTS

We would both like to thank our families for their patience and apologize to them for the time, energy and passion we had to devote to completing what has become a really engaging book. As an edited book we also have to thank all the contributors for agreeing to write a chapter and work with us to make the valuable contributions to the book that they do. Spread across the globe they have all kept to schedule and taken the time to write their reflections on using PPed in ways that provide the insight into and understanding of practice when applying PPed. The style of chapter we sought can be very difficult to write but all the contributors came through with the style and quality of chapters that make this such an effective and innovative book.

INTRODUCTION

Richard Light

Positive Pedagogy for sport coaching (PPed) is a recent addition to athlete/ student–centred approaches to coaching sport and teaching physical education that is distinctive from all other game-based approaches (GBA) because its application is not limited to team games. The first edition (Light and Harvey, 2017b) broke new ground by applying advances in the development of GBA to coaching team sports to coaching individual sports and focusing on skill and/or technique. After theorizing PPed pedagogy and athlete learning, and outlining its pedagogical features, the first edition provided examples of its application in common individual sports such as javelin, gymnastics and swimming that have a strong technical focus, as well as the more technical aspects of other sports such as karate and kayaking. The second edition (Light and Harvey, 2019) updated readers on the ongoing development of the PPed approach and how it can be applied to all sports. In both editions the theory, pedagogy and research discussed was grounded in practice through chapters written by coaches and academics in which they reflected on their experiences of using PPed across a range of sports and both institutional and cultural settings. These insights into the practice of coaches using PPed reflected its flexibility and the ways in which coaches, and teachers, can gradually move toward PPed as they gain understanding and confidence, and as their athletes/students adapt to a new method. They provided examples of how different coaches in different situations, working in different sports, and with dif– ferent experience in working with PPed, adapted it to achieve their aims and purposes. They offered insights into what is possible with PPed and the challenges involved with its implantation and ways of dealing with them without telling readers what to do, when to do it or how.

Both editions of *Positive Pedagogy for Sport Coaching* included examples of coaches using PPed for individual and team sports but the second edition paid a little more attention to examples of coaches implementing PPed. Following close of the heels of the second edition, *Applied Positive Pedagogy in Sport: International Coaching Cases* is completely focused on coaches' experiences of implementing PPed as what we see as a logical development. The 17 chapters in this book on coach implementations of PPed across a range of sports, and in particular cultural and institutional settings, can be seen as an international collection of 'case studies' in PPed that readers can interpret, think about and develop ideas and motivation from to improve their coaching. A number of other books have effectively focused on the presentation of case studies in sport coaching and physical education teaching (see Armour, 2014; Baghurst and Parish, 2017) but none have focused on a particular pedagogical approach as we do in this book. The 17 chapters on coaches' use of PPed in this book and the contexts within which the coaching occurred suggest the beginnings of the influence of PPed on coaches across different countries and sports through its focus on their experiences of using it and adapting it to their needs and particular contexts.

The practical focus of this book makes sense to Stephen and me but we want to emphasize how it assumes prior knowledge of PPed from reading one or both of the first two editions of PPed, or at least one of the journal articles we have written (see Light and Harvey, 2017a). Given the central importance of understanding the philosophical positions of humanism and holism that PPed sits on this should inform coach and teacher decision making. It is essential for readers of this book to have at least a rudimentary comprehension of PPed and its bottom up approach. While 'going in cold' to read the 17 reflective chapters in this book on coach experiences of implementing PPed might be interesting for anyone involved in sport coaching or teaching physical education, it would not provide adequate insights into, or understanding of, PPed without having read the first and/or second editions. These two books fully explain what PPed is, what philosophical positions it sits on, how it operates as a framework to guide practice, how it has been developed and what its core pedagogical features are.

Following this introduction, we include a chapter that outlines the PPed approach but see this more as a reminder about what PPed is rather than a detailed introduction to it. This third book follows on from the first and second editions of *Positive Pedagogy for Sport Coaching* in a logical progression toward the practical issues involved in its implementation and builds on assumed prior knowledge that is necessary to get the most from reading it. It provides examples of how PPed has been used and adapted by a range of coaches, in a variety of sports and in a range of cultural, social and institutional settings. It is modelled on Parts II and III in the second edition of PPed, but with more chapters, more variation in contexts and more detail in the longer chapters. It continues cutting edge development in coaching (and teaching) that builds on the development of advances in coaching team sports with a strong emphasis on providing positive learning and promoting wellbeing. It is a book focused on practice that suggests the beginning of its influence on coaching due to the range of chapters in it and in team sports in particular.

In each of the 17 reflective chapters in this book, coaches provide some background on their experiences and the context within which the coaching was undertaken, and their knowledge of PPed to reflect on their implementation of it over a single session, a cluster of sessions, a season or parts of a season. They identify what went well for them and any problems they encountered, discuss how they addressed them and suggest what they feel they learned from these experiences and in some cases, what they would do differently next time. We provided a basic format for writing the chapters, but a few adapted this to suit unusual situations such as Chapter 2 on a season long conversation on cricket coaching in England at very different levels and Chapters 9 and 11 that draw on empirical research in New Zealand and the UK. As might be expected, the uptake of PPed has been more evident for team sports than in individual sports, which is why I contribute four chapters on my own experiences of coaching individual sports at different times in my career and in the diverse settings of Australia, Japan, Singapore, the UK and New Zealand.

The chapters in this book focus on using PPed to coach rugby, basketball, Australian football, cricket, baseball, football (soccer), striking and fielding games (as a general category), swimming, triathlon, gymnastics, boxing, rock climbing, strength and conditioning, beach sprinting and one chapter on teaching javelin in a Singapore school in physical education. They report on coaching in Australia, New Zealand, Singapore, Japan, the USA and the UK by coaches from Australia, New Zealand, the UK, Singapore, Portugal and the USA across a wide range of age groups and levels of competition. When inviting authors to contribute, we strove to establish a good balance between the experience and background of the contributors, the sports, and the cultural and institutional settings. Shane Pill and I have profiles in researching and writing on sport and physical education pedagogy with seven others such as Kendall Jarrett, Kass Gibson and Christina Curry emerging in the field at different stages of their careers (who also coach). It also includes five coaches who are not academics to provide much needed understanding of how coaches interpret and use athlete-centred coaching such as PPed. For these contributors we provided writing guidance and support but strove to ensure that their chapters are authentic accounts of their experiences.

The Book

Applied Positive Pedagogy in Sport: International Coaching Cases comprises 20 chapters in total, including this introduction, an outline of Positive Pedagogy for sport coaching and a discussion of the collection in 'Concluding thoughts'. The 17 reflective chapters are divided into two parts of: Part 1: Team sports and Part 2: Individual sports.

This Introduction is followed by 'An outline of Positive Pedagogy for sport coaching', a chapter that provides an overall outline of Positive Pedagogy for sport coaching and its core pedagogical features. These are: 1) designing and managing learning experience, 2) questioning, 3) adopting and inquiry-based approach and 4) making learning positive. Part 1 comprises eight chapters of coach reflections on using PPed in team sports with Part 2 comprising nine chapters on individual sports and with two chapters in Part 2 drawing on empirical studies (Chapters 9 and 11).

Part 1: Team sports

Part 1 opens with a chapter by Shane Pill in which he takes us back into his past to recount a session he ran in Australian football that was informed by the Game Sense approach he was first exposed to through the ideas of one of Australia's greatest team sport coaches, Rick Charlesworth. In this chapter, he reflects briefly on his change from a transmission (of knowledge) orientated coach to Game Sense coaching and then focuses on a training session he conducted when working in a semi-professional state league, Australian football program. He outlines how, on reflection, the Game Sense approach he was using and developing reflects so much of a Positive Pedagogy for sport coaching.

As another Australian, but one living in the UK, Kendall Jarrett collaborates with Elliot Wilson and Andy Siddall in Chapter 2 to provide insight into how a season-long conversation about PPed shaped their coaching of cricket at two different levels. They suggest that although sport coaches in England hold largely negative views on CPD (continued professional development), with one working in an elite county cricket system and the other at a local village cricket club, they both 'covert all manner of opportunity to develop their craft', and especially peer-to-peer coaching conversation, that forms the focus of this chapter. It details a season-long coaching conversation that focused on developing their understanding and use of the Positive Pedagogy for sport coaching framework to further their coaching craft. They used questions derived from Light and Harvey's (2017) 'Positive Pedagogy for sport coaching' article to drive their coaching conversations and provide a framework for a season-long, peer-led review and development of their personal coaching practice. They also draw on the critical perspective of colleague, Andy Siddell.

Chapter 3 focuses on coaching basketball in a New Zealand secondary school. Having learned to play and coach basketball in Portugal, Ricardo Pimenta moved to New Zealand to complete a PhD, where he further developed his coaching and was influenced by working as a tutor in a university sport coaching program that emphasized athlete-centred coaching and one course focused on PPed. Here, Ricardo reflects on his use of PPed when teaching girls' basketball in a New Zealand elite, independent high school where his aim was to make learning as positive as possible. He was encouraged to do so by two experiences. The first was what he learned though conducting a PhD study on why adolescent girls enjoyed playing school basketball in which he drew on Antonovsky's Salutogenic Theory and Sense of Coherence (SoC) model (see Antonovsky, 1996), and Martin Seligman's work in Positive Psychology to explain and understand their enjoyment. The second experience that influenced his coaching was that of working as a tutor in a course on athlete-centred coaching.

Since beginning his PhD study, Ricardo has been developing a PPed influenced approach to his coaching informed by the PERMA model (see Seligman, 2012) in particular. In this chapter he reflects on using the PERMA model to increase happiness and enjoyment in adolescent girls' basketball and finishes by explaining how he now structures his training sessions around the five elements of the model which are: Positive emotions, Engagement, Relationships, Meaning and Achievement.

Chapter 4 takes us to the USA where Clayton Kuklick shows how PPed can offer an alternative to baseball's emphasis on pedagogical strategies that incorporate block-like drills in batting practice, bullpen work, and position-specific defensive periods. Despite significant growth in writing and research on GBA, few have paid attention to baseball, which could be due to how tightly structured play is in it. Like the chapter in the second edition of *Positive Pedagogy for sport coaching* (Light and Harvey, 2019) that focused on coaching American football by Tanner Snead, this chapter shows how PPed can be adapted to highly structured sports. In this chapter, Clayton explains how he departed from this traditional approach as a collegiate baseball coach by using PPed. He outlines how he used small-sided games, questioning and inquiry instead of always telling players what to do and using drills. It concludes with reflections and considerations for implementing Positive Pedagogy for sport coaching in baseball to enhance athlete learning, creativity, teamwork, and problem solving.

I wrote the following chapter (Chapter 5) after conducting a workshop on coaching football (soccer) using PPed at a Japanese Women's University. While in Japan and based in Tokyo, I travelled to Kansai (West Japan) to conduct a PPed seminar during October 2019. As one of the three chapters on coaching/teaching in Asia it provides readers with some insight into adapting PPed coaching to the cultural and institutional context but, unlike Chapter 12, I did not encounter any major challenges. In it I outline the progression of activities I used in the workshop and the positive results I felt I achieved and suggest how the particular context of the session contributed to it. In it I also discuss the issue of when and how to focus on technique in PPed.

In Chapter 6 Michael Supp focuses on how he made sport more enjoyable for young people as a way of combating worrying drop-out rates in the US (but not limited to the US). In it he outlines and discusses how he combined PPed and the use of wearable technology to contribute to making youth sport more enjoyable. He outlines how, when using wearable technology in youth soccer (football) he recognized its potential to motivate young players by drawing on Positive Pedagogy to make soccer fun. It shows how he used this unusual combination to develop a strong focus on player-centered learning that fostered inclusive, dynamic and challenging practice environments. The chapter concludes with Michael showing how these features of PPed helped spur the development of a wearable technology tool to help objectively measure coaching performance at the youth level while developing an athlete-centred approach.

Authored by Christina Curry, Chapter 7 reflects on how she made 15-year old girls' experiences of learning to play football (soccer) positive by drawing on PPed with a focus on a strength-based approach in Sydney, Australia. She conducted two sessions using a PPed approach over the 2019 season, which focused on supporting players to feel empowered to learn by building on what they could do and supporting them in identifying and celebrating their own, and others, strengths and capabilities.

In the next chapter (Chapter 8), Nick Hill shares his experience of teaching PPed during a one-off striking and fielding session conducted at the Ohio University Global Coaching Symposium in 2019. He chose to use cricket because of the US graduate students' lack of familiarity with it. He wanted to show how, despite the students' lack of knowledge and experience in cricket, they could develop game appreciation and understanding through his use of PPed. After explaining what he did in the session, how he felt the group responded to it and why, he reflects on his experience and outlines changes that he has made to the session since then for any further opportunities he might have to teach cricket to similar participant groups using PPed.

Part 2: Individual sports

Chapter 9 is a little different to the others yet provides valuable insight into young coaches' application of PPed to a number of team sports. In it, Mohammad Shah Razak and I draw on an empirical study that inquired into the influence of a university course on PPed on the coaching practice of six young New Zealand coaches. The study looked at the effectiveness of the student–centred, experiential learning pedagogy we used but, in this chapter, we focus on how it influenced their coaching outside university and how they dealt with the challenges that faced them. It provides useful insight into how they adapted PPed to their particular sports and contexts. The course focused on individual sport but three of the six coaches worked in team sports, which is why Stephen and I locate it here as a transitioning chapter from team sport to individual sport.

In Chapter 10 I reflect on a postgraduate workshop on swimming I conducted in Leeds, England. In it I suggest that learning to swim efficiently involves a process of interpretation and adaptation on an individual basis that can benefit from PPed coaching, that moves beyond the limitations of direct instruction and eschew an objective view of it as a process of replication. At the seminar I presented on Positive Pedagogy for sport coaching I taught a handful of adolescent swimmers, with a focus on developing the second kick in butterfly, to demonstrate my ideas in action for coaching a very technical aspect of swimming.

Like Chapter 9, Chapter 11 draws on an empirical study. In it, Julie Paterson and Kass Gibson draw on a study Julie conducted on the implementation of a PPed approach for coaching youth triathlon in the UK. The findings suggest that PPed provided a comprehensive coaching approach that enabled significant improvements in technical and tactical performance and provided positive learning experiences. Reflecting on the coach's dedication to understanding, persistence in planning, critical self–reflection and continuous adaption during implementation of PPed the authors suggest this chapter can offer guidance for coaches aiming to prioritize the holistic development and early positive experiences of young triathletes in their care.

Chapter 12 focuses on my experience of teaching junior secondary students in Singapore as part of a four-day seminar on *Positive Pedagogy for sport coaching* I delivered to physical education teachers in mid-2019. To demonstrate to the teachers how PPed can be applied in physical education classes in Singapore, I taught three classes with this chapter considering them all but focused on the javelin session with a 'difficult' class. In it I reflect upon the challenges involved in teaching PPed to classes of 40, 14-year old students with whom I had no relationship and no knowledge of their skills and dispositions. In what I would describe as a challenging, yet satisfying, teaching experience I recount how I had to adjust the progression of activities I had planned, my questioning strategy and my expectations of their learning. This chapter identifies how, despite significant challenges for me, there were sections of sustained, engagement, enthusiasm, joy and moments approaching flow.

In Chapter 13, Bianca Aguiar explains how PPed has encouraged her to challenge the domination of direct instruction and total coach control in gymnastics. She has previously written a chapter on using PPed to inform gymnastics in the first edition of Positive Pedagogy for sport coaching (Light, 2017) but this chapter focuses on a different aspect of gymnastics coaching, with two more years of coach development 'under her belt'. Like swimming, the complexity, demand and danger involved when executing some gymnastics skills has pushed coaches to be very strict but, Bianca's experiences over the last ten years have led her to believe that generating lasting effects requires more than merely telling gymnasts how to perfectly execute a skill. Creating awareness through experience, feel and dialogue are some of the features of Positive Pedagogy that became key elements of her coaching over the past four years in New Zealand. In this chapter, she reflects on how her coaching has increasingly been guided by the features of Positive Pedagogy and how this has influenced her gymnasts' experiences. In it she reflects on how she had to adapt different elements of Positive Pedagogy for different age groups, according to their needs and levels of understanding.

Tactics, awareness and decision-making are very important in boxing when sparring or competing, but the focus of the session I reflect on in Chapter 14 was purely technical and aimed at learners with no, or little, knowledge or experience of this sport. It focuses on teaching the jab and cross as two basic punches in boxing to undergraduate Sport Coaching students in a New Zealand university as a way of showing them how to use PPed for coaching technique as an alternative to direct instruction. In this chapter, I trace how I have gradually developed my teaching of this class over the past three years by critically reflecting on student experience in New Zealand and in the US and how in my teaching I must consider the influence of context.

Chapter 15 outlines Letitia Price's experiences of working as a strength and conditioning (S&C) coach for a historically pivotal semi-professional women's football (soccer) team in the United Kingdom. In it she outlines how she drew on PPed to design creative and meaningful learning experiences in the delivery of S&C sessions to overcome the normative culture of traditional S&C. This helped her empower the athletes by helping them understand, not only how to train, but also why they trained like this and to realize her aim of helping them develop into autonomous learners who did not always have to rely on the coach to tell them what to do. This propelled the team to becoming the country's first ever regional team promoted to the national Women's Super League and stands as testimony to the effectiveness of PPed. Chapter 16 is in a different country, in a different sport and with much younger athletes but its aims are similar to those of Letitia in the previous chapter. It recounts a session I ran when coaching 'nippers' (junior lifesaving program, 5–13 years) as an age group manager in a Sydney surf lifesaving club in Australia. It recounts my coaching of a group of eight to ten-year old nippers in start technique for the beach sprint during the early development of Positive Pedagogy for sport coaching through an emphasis on establishing a dialectic between theory and practice. The learning activities I used placed a constraint on the use of the arms in running to create awareness of the role they play in sprinting and starts by the young nippers with a pedagogical emphasis placed on reflection, dialogue and collective inquiry. These activities focused on developing the children's awareness and understanding of the role that the arms play in sprinting and the important role they play in starts.

The final chapter (Chapter 17) provides an example of using PPed as an alternative to direct instruction for technical aspects of a sport by focusing on teaching rock climbing as a highly technical sport that has been included in the 2020 Tokyo Olympics. In this chapter, Shah recounts his experiences of coaching a group of primary school rock climbers aged 10 to 12 years in a Co-Curricular Activity (CCA) in a Singapore school. One of the foci of the CCA is to provide climbers with exposure to participation in competition at a national level while also developing fitness and good health that Shah focused on by using the principles and philosophy of *Positive Pedagogy for sport coaching*. In the session he reflects on in this chapter his aim was to help the young rock climbers improve their balance and climbing techniques through the development of an awareness and use of their centre of balance and to understand the central importance it plays in climbing.

The book closes with Stephen Harvey providing concluding thoughts and reflections that identify major themes running through the seventeen coach reflection chapters. To do this, he draws on the concepts of reflective practice and critical reflection as a way of thinking about changing behavior and practice to address the four aspects of pedagogical change suggested by Casey (2010), which are: a) betweenness; b) becoming; c) unlearning; and, d) pedagogical fluency. He uses these as a way of bringing together his thoughts and reflections on the practitioners' stories in this volume.

References

Antonovsky, A. (1996) 'The salutogenic model as a theory to guide health promotion', *Health Promotion International*, 11(1): 11–17.

Armour, K. (ed.) (2014) *Pedagogical case studies in physical education and youth sport* (1st edn), London and New York: Routledge.

Baghurst, T. M. and Parish, A. S. (2017) *Case studies in coaching: Dilemmas and ethics in competitive school sports*, London and New York: Routledge.

Casey, A. (2010) *Practitioner research in physical education: Teacher transformation through pedagogical and curricular change*. Unpublished PhD thesis, Leeds Metropolitan University.

Light, R. L. (2013) *Game Sense: Pedagogy for performance, participation and enjoyment*, London and New York: Routledge.

Light, R. L. (2014) 'Learner-centred pedagogy for swim coaching: A complex learning theory informed approach', *Asia-Pacific Journal of Health, Sport and Physical Education*, 5(2), 167–180. doi:10.1080/18377122.2014.906056

Light, R. L. and Harvey, S. (2017a) 'Positive Pedagogy for sport coaching', *Sport, Education and Society*, 22(2): 271–287.

Light, R. and Harvey, S. (2017b) *Positive Pedagogy for sport coaching: Athlete-centred coaching for individual sports*, London and New York: Routledge.

Light, R. and Harvey, S. (2019) *Positive Pedagogy for sport coaching: Athlete-centred coaching for individual sports* (2nd edn). London and New York: Routledge.

Pill, S. (2018) (ed.) *Perspectives on athlete-centred coaching*, London and New York: Routledge.

Seligman, M. E. P. (2012) *Flourish: A visionary new understanding of happiness and wellbeing*, Sydney: Random House.

POSITIVE PEDAGOGY FOR COACHING TEAM AND INDIVIDUAL SPORTS

An overview

Richard Light and Stephen Harvey

In this chapter we provide an overview of Positive Pedagogy for sport coaching for all sports. It begins with its development from the features of game-based approaches (GBA) to then move on to the appropriation of Antonovsky's sense of coherence (SoC) model and the use of Positive Psychology to enhance its inherently positive nature.

Game-Based Approaches

GBAs such as Game Sense, TGfU (Teaching Games for Understanding), Play Practice and the Tactical Games Approach improve team performance by developing tactical knowledge, decision-making, awareness and the ability to adapt at non-conscious and conscious levels of cognition in match conditions across a range of team sports (see Chappell and Light, 2015; Jones, 2015; Light, Harvey and Mouchet, 2014). They generate positive experiences of practice sessions for athletes and enable the transfer of learning from practice to competition instead of training to train (Jones, 2015). This occurs across a range of cultural and institutional settings from primary school physical education in Australia (Chen and Light, 2006) and secondary school physical education in Hong Kong (Wang and Ha, 2009) to interscholastic sport in the USA (Harvey, 2009) and professional sport played at the most elite levels in New Zealand, Australia and Japan (Evans, 2012; Jones, 2015). GBAs can also foster positive personal, social and moral development as important outcomes of participation in sport and of particular importance for youth sport (De Martelaer, De Bouw and Struyven, 2013).

The potential for GBAs to improve performance make practice enjoyable, develop the ability and inclination to learn, and the 'value added' personal, social and moral learning it can encourage, arises from their athlete-centred, inquiry-based pedagogy that emphasizes reflection, collaboration, dialogue and collective inquiry. TGfU can be seen as the father of GBA in the English-speaking world with an increasing range of variations of it. These variations have been influenced by their different foci and the cultural contexts from which they have emerged but, share a reasonably common focus on the game as a whole, locating learning in modified games and emphasising questioning over instruction (Light, 2015; Stolz and Pill, 2016). *Positive Pedagogy for Sports Coaching* reduces the four pedagogical features of Game Sense (Light, 2013a) to three by combining features 3 and 4 to emphasise the importance of the inquiry-based approach to learning in individual sports.

GBAs focus on developing better performance but can also generate positive experiences that are enjoyable, satisfying and which facilitate learning how to learn (see, Light, 2003). This is due to their athlete centred pedagogy with the positive learning experiences they provide as a key strength of this approach (Kinnerk, Harvey, MacDonncha and Lyons, 2018) that contributes to positive affective, personal, and social-moral development (see, Dyson, 2005; Kinnerk et al., 2018; Sheppard and Mandigo, 2005). It is, however, not an automatic out-come of GBA that 'caught', but instead, must be 'taught' (Harvey, Kirk and O'Donovan, 2014). This positive learning needs to be facilitated by coaches building positive affective and social-moral environments where players are motivated to learn by having the freedom and autonomy to test out new ideas and to speak up in group discussions without fear of failure (Kinnerk et al., 2018). The same applies to coaching individual sports using PPed.

Team sports (and invasion games in particular) coached using GBA provide ideal contexts for improving performance while also promoting positive learning experiences and positive social, moral and personal development at any level but the undeniable importance of technique and skill in most individual sports, and the hegemony of the technical, command approach have discouraged any significant consideration of its possible application to individual sports (Light and Wallian, 2008). Indeed, efficacy for the development of decision-making and tactical awareness is one of the prevalent findings from a recent systematic review of the GBA literature in competitive team sports (Kinnerk et al., 2018). This review fur-ther noted that there was no evidence that developing players technical skills using traditional methods of coaching was any more efficacious in the development of these technical skills than when a coach employs a GBA (Kinnerk et al., 2018).

The notion of PPed presented in this book draws on the Game Sense framework (Light, 2013a) and the positive approach to wellbeing proposed by Antonovsky (1987) and Seligman's (2012) Positive Psychology, with a focus on the PERMA model for wellbeing (Seligman, 2012).

Positive Coaching

A number of teaching/coaching approaches specifically focus on promoting posi-tive development for young people through sport and other physical activity that include Positive Youth Development (see Holt, Sehn, Spence, Newton and Ball, 2012), Sport Education (Siedentop, 1994) and Teaching Personal and Social

Responsibility (Hellison, 2003). Although not specifically aimed at promoting personal development, GBAs also foster its development due to the nature of their athlete-centred, inquiry-based pedagogy. These essentially holistic and humanistic approaches challenge traditional approaches informed by behaviourist perspectives on learning that objectify athletes and reduce participation in sport to a number of discrete and quantifiable components in traditional coaching.

Traditional approaches to coaching tend to feature direct instruction, feedback, and demonstrations based upon the assumption that the more the coach intervenes the more the athletes will improve (Williams and Hodges, 2005). Even for confident and experienced athletes who have the necessary skills to meet expectations of performance with this approach the learning involved is not necessarily positive because it can promote a fear of failure that limits their capacity to learn from mistakes (Kinnerk et al., 2018; Partington et al., 2014) and an inclination to take risks. It can also promote selfishness, egotism and a lack of empathy or compassion for others, which is counterproductive for building a team, squad or club identity and culture, cohesion and sense of common purpose.

Technical approaches to coaching sport assume that learning to play team games requires a level of technical competence *before* playing it and focuses on reducing errors and moving the athlete closer to *the* 'correct' performance of the technique. This negative view of learning as a process of correcting mistakes highlights what athletes *cannot* do and is exacerbated when less confident young athletes attempt to perform these skills under the gaze of their peers and their coach. Conversely, the PPed coach in both individual and team sports sees mistakes as providing opportunities for learning rather than being something used to control and pressure athletes (Renshaw, Oldham and Bawden, 2012). From this perspective mistakes are constructive errors that play an important role in learning (Kinnerk et al., 2018; Light et al., 2015).

Making Learning Positive

The pedagogical features of Game Sense proposed by Light (2013a) encourage positive learning experiences with PPed focusing on maximising this positive learning through the appropriation of Antonvosky's salutogenic theory and sense of coherence (SoC) model (1979, 1987) and the application of Positive Psychology (Seligman and Csikszentmihalyi, 2000) to bolster positive experiences of learning by athletes of any age and at any level.

Antonovsky's Salutogenic Theory and Sense of Coherence (SoC) Model

Antonovsky's (1979, 1987) salutogenic theory and SoC model take a positive approach by focusing on the socially constructed resources that allow people to achieve and maintain good health. To facilitate positive experiences of learning in sport PPed adapts and applies Antonvosky's SoC as a framework for considering what is needed to make learning positive.

The concept of 'salutogenesis' refers to *the origins of health* to emphasizes what supports health and wellbeing rather than focusing on what causes disease or the 'lifestyle' approach that focuses on identifying risk factors (Antonovsky, 1996). His holistic approach is concerned more with the affective and social dimensions of life and a focus on experience than with its cognitive aspects. His SoC model comprises three conditions that most encourage good health which are when life has: a) comprehensibility, b) manageability and, c) meaningfulness. Here we briefly explain these elements and suggest how they can be used to coach in ways that contribute toward positive learning experiences.

Comprehensibility

Developed through experience, comprehensibility refers to the extent to which things make sense for the individual and to which events and situations appear ordered and consistent for him/her. For learning to be comprehensible in sport it should help athletes know, not only how to do something, but also when, where and why to do it. It should foster deep learning that involves understanding the concepts or 'big ideas' (Fosnot, 1996) that constructivist perspectives on learning suggest underpin learning by doing. This is because comprehensive understanding involves not only rational, conscious and articulated knowing, but also a practical understanding, or a practical sense of things (Bourdieu, 1986) developed through experience and engagement in a process of learning as the unfolding of knowledge that includes learning how to learn. This would be evident in the athletes' understanding of the fundamental concepts of manipulating space and time in team sports. Harvey (2018) further documents how the use of a GBA by two high performance field hockey coaches enabled their players to develop a holistic conception (technical, tactical, physical, and social) of the game of field hockey. When applied to individual sports such as swimming or throwing events in athletics (see, Light, 2014; Light and Kentel, 2013) it would be evident in the development of 'feel' as a practical understanding and relating technique to the core concepts of the activity or sport. For example, in swimming the core concepts are the maximization of propulsion (or thrust) and the minimization of resistance, whether swimming, diving or turning and streamlining off the wall (Light and Wallian, 2008).

Manageability

Manageability is the extent to which an individual feels that s/he has the resources at hand to manage stress and challenge. Resources can be objects such as tools and equipment, skills, intellectual ability, social and cultural capital and so on. In PPed this includes the resources available from interaction within groups and teams and/ or the whole team as the 'debate of ideas' (Gréhaigne et al., 2005). In PPed learning is seen to be manageable when the challenges set extend the athlete but with him/her feeling that s/he can manage the task. The concept of manageability is of central importance in establishing and maintaining an optimal level of challenge and learning in PPed by engaging the athlete(s) and providing experiences of flow (Csikszentmihalyi, 1997). One of the Olympic field hockey coaches in a study by Harvey (2018) noted how using a GBA helped the US Women's National Team (USWNT) that finished fifth at the Rio Olympic Games manage chaos, handle pressure and anxiety. Both coaches in the study scaffolded the players' learning within and between sessions using strongly guided instruction, which links cognitive and behavioural skills needed to learn and be successful (Harvey, 2018; Mayer, 2004).

Challenges are manageable when they can be met by drawing on individual resources such as skill, physical capacity and/or the social resources available from social interaction with peers and the coach. The provision of a supportive socio-moral environment assists in making challenges manageable and rewarding. For a task to seem manageable the athlete should feel that s/he has the skill and understanding, and can draw on the resources of teammates and the coach to meet them. The collective, social element is of prime importance here in both team sport and individual sport because both are essentially social. In a study on high performance sport regular off-field meetings further helped two Olympic field hockey coaches develop an athlete-centered team culture that was further developed through the use of questioning and peer feedback. Moreover, the coach of the USWNT's use of GBA further enabled his players to develop a sense of curiosity, creativity, engagement and individuality in their learning journey across a full Olympic Cycle.

Meaningfulness

Meaningfulness refers to how much the individual feels that life makes sense and that its challenges are worthy of commitment. According to Antonovsky, meaningfulness promotes a positive expectation of life and the future and encourages people to see challenges as being interesting, relevant and worthy of their emotional commitment. In sport coaching athletes are highly unlikely to commit to meeting a challenge if it lacks meaning and relevance for them. When activities engage learners affectively and socially as well as physically and intellectually they are likely to be meaningful. For example, the Game Sense approach in team sport makes learning/practice meaningful because it is situated within the game or game conditions to make it and what the athletes feel they have learned relevant. Both Olympic coaches in Harvey's (2018) study noted how situating learning in game-based contexts made learning fun and enjoyable so they could also connect affectively and socially as well as physically and intellectually. Games were developed by the USWNT that focused specifically on the team's style of play.

Engagement gives meaning to tasks and experiences because the athletes understand what they are trying to achieve and why. Learning is meaningful in all sports when its comprehensibility gives meaning to the tasks and activities because they make sense within the 'big picture'. Coaching should make learning meaningful by making the links clear between detailed foci on particular aspects of the sport, its most fundamental concepts and to the end aims of the activity. Having the coach explain what each session involves and why the team, group or individual are/is doing it would add to making it engaging and meaningful with having athletes well informed central to empowering them. The Olympic field hockey coaches in Harvey's (2018) study made sure there was alignment between the off-and on-field aspects of team development in how they worked with players using questions, and offered open feedback loop systems such as the development of a leadership group, which acted as an open feedback loop between the coaching staff and the players.

Positive Psychology

Positive Psychology sets out to redress a preoccupation of psychology with pathologies and repairing the 'worst aspects' of life by promoting its positive qualities (Seligman and Csikszentmihalyi, 2000). It focuses on wellbeing and satisfaction in the past, on happiness and the experience of flow in the present and on hope and optimism in the future (Jackson and Csikszentmihalyi, 1999). It aims to build 'thriving individuals, finding and nurturing talent and making, normal life more fulfilling' and draws on the concepts of *flow* and *mindfulness* as positive states that generate learning (Seligman and Csikszentmihalyi, p. 5). Flow has also been proposed as a way of explaining the experiences possible when learning through sport and practice/modified games that provide appropriate levels of challenge and engagement (Harvey, Kirk and O'Donovan, 2014; Jackson and Csikszentmihalyi, 1999; Kretchmar, 2005). It refers to a state of being absorbed in the experience of action through intense concentration, as the athlete is 'lost' in the flow of experience to provide optimal (non-conscious) learning. A well-designed and managed coaching session with good transitions that maintains an appropriate level of challenge is able to provide flow experiences for the athlete(s) (Harvey, 2018).

The PERMA Model

Positive Pedagogy does not specifically focus on developing wellbeing or happiness but all five elements of Seligman's (2012) PERMA (positive emotions, engagement, relations, meaning and achievement) model are evident in it. Applied to team and individual sports, PPed can generate positive emotions such as enjoyment or delight (Kretchmar, 2005), engagement in learning, the building of meaningful relationships, a sense of belonging (Light, 2008), meaning and opportunities for achievement, both individually and collectively (Harvey, 2018). It emphasizes what the learner *can* do and how s/he can draw on existing individual and social resources to meet learning challenges through reflection and dialogue. It is forward focused. Players in both squads in Harvey's (2018) Olympic field hockey coaches study saw problems as obstacles they drew on resources to solve, even if this meant they needed additional time or practice to build these resources.

The Pedagogical Features of Positive Pedagogy

This section briefly outlines the core pedagogical features of PPed, which are discussed in more detail in following chapters, while noting some of the challenges facing coaches in taking it up. The pedagogical features of PPed are that: 1) it emphasizes engagement with the physical learning environment or experience, 2) the coach asks questions that generate dialogue and thinking in preference to telling player/athletes what to do, 3) it adopts an inquiry-based approach to provide opportunities for athletes to collectively formulate, test and evaluate solutions to problems that is supported by a socio-moral environment in which making mistakes is accepted as an essential part of learning.

Designing and Managing Learning Experiences

When coaching team sports using PPed the game is seen as a complex phenomenon within which learning to play well involves the emergence of tactical knowledge, skill execution and decision-making as knowledge-in-action (Light 2013a). Learning is located within modified games or game-like activities based on the assumption that it occurs through engagement with the learning environment (Dewey 1916). This is also initially learning that largely takes place through a process of adaptation at a non-conscious level over time and which forms the basis of ensuing learning experiences as attempts are made to bring it to consciousness through language. This means that the ability of the coach to manage the activity or a game to establish and sustain the appropriate level of challenge is of pivotal importance. Designing practice activities and managing them through the analysis of performance and initiating appropriate changes is possibly the biggest challenge facing coaches in implementing a Positive Pedagogy approach, an aspect noted in several or the studies a recent review of the GBA literature in competitive team sport settings (Kinnerk et al. 2018). Time spent planning is one key factor affecting the designing of games within sessions (Pill, 2015) that is dealt with in more detail in Chapter 6. Pedagogical principles such as modification representation and modification exaggeration also seem crucial to good game design when planning (Kinnerk et al., 2018). Planning for good transitions between activities and for moving from simple to more complex, while maintaining appropriate levels of challenge, also contributes to achieving and maintaining flow in a coaching session.

PPed for individual sports such as running and swimming, adopts a similar approach to team games but typically involves providing learning experiences that place constraints on the athlete as a challenge that they have to meet and learn from. These constraints are usually used to create problems to be solved and processes of non-conscious thinking and conscious thinking but can also be used just to develop awareness of a technique or aspect of a technique. They typically involve structuring learning in a way that restricts possible solutions compared to coaching in team sports and which could be seen as being a guided discovery teaching style rather than a problem solving one (Mosston and Ashworth, 1986).

When a coach introduces a new group or an individual athlete to a PPed approach s/he should begin with a more structured approach that the athletes are used to and move gradually toward empowering them which is something suggested by New Zealand rugby coaches in a recently published study (Hassanin, Light and Macfarlane, 2018). As athletes adapt to the approach and embrace it they can take on more autonomy, ownership and responsibility to participate in the design, modification and evaluation of learning games or activities (Almond, 1983) as well as the formulation, testing and evaluation of tactical solutions. This leads to increasing empowerment achieved through a growing understanding of games and of how to learn. As player/athletes adapt and become more prepared to engage in purposeful social interaction they rely less upon the coach and begin to take more responsibility for their own learning which is an important and positive learning experience. This typically involves a coach-athlete relationship that is more equitable in the repositioning of the coach and the empowerment of the athlete.

Learning by doing occurs at a non-conscious level as a process of adaptation that is emphasized by in psychological constructivism (Piaget), enactivism (Varela, Thompson and Rosch, 1991) and complex learning theory (CLT – Davis and Sumara, 2003). The use of practice games designed to achieve particular outcomes suggests that they improve player motivation in a range of team sports (see, for example, Light, 2004; Kinnerk et al., 2018; Evans and Light, 2008; Harvey, 2009). While some practice activities can be designed to focus on a particular skill they should always include developing awareness and some degree of decision-making (see, Tan, Chow and Turner, 2011 for an overview of learning game design using GBAs).

Ask Questions to Generate Dialogue and Thinking

Questioning is a central mechanism employed for promoting player/athlete-centred learning in Game Sense and one that typically presents challenges for coaches (Harvey and Light, 2015; Forrest, 2014; Roberts, 2011; Wright and Forrest, 2007). In PPed questions are employed to promote thinking and dialogue but it takes time for coaches to become skilful enough with questioning to achieve these aims. Questions should create a range of possible answers or solutions rather than lead to predetermined answers that are deemed to be either correct or incorrect but this can vary when coaching a skill or skill intensive sport. The commonly used Initiation, Response, Evaluation (IRE) questioning shuts down interaction between the coach and athletes and between athletes (Forrest, 2014; Harvey and Light, 2015).

Positive Pedagogy requires the coach avoiding, or at least minimising, being critical or telling learners they are wrong to promoting divergent thinking, creativity and a positive approach to learning. When a solution developed by an athlete or athletes does not work the coach should asked them why it did not work and to consider how it could be modified to work or decide it cannot work and seek a different solution. This is a 'solution-focused' approach that focuses the athlete's attention on the goals of the activity and what they can do to achieve these goals (Clarke and Dembowski, 2006; Grant, 2011). Here the athletes solve problems by drawing on the resources they have available and within the constraints of the rules or limits of the task that shape the solution and the learning that takes place (Harvey, 2018). This approach ensures that discussions are future-paced and focused directly on solutions to help prevent the athletes disengaging from the task (Grant, 2011). In terms of Antonvosky's SoC, it promotes *manageability*.

Within athlete discussions there will be often be some disagreement because this is the nature of debate but as the athletes develop their ability to debate and interact to achieve a common purpose this interaction will be more effective (Gréhaigne et al. 2005; Harvey and Light, 2015; Light, 2014). In their recent review of the GBA literature in competitive teams sport settings, Kinnerk et al. (2018) noted inadequate pedagogical content knowledge, ineffective feedback sessions due to the lack of pre-planned questions, and the negative emotions this created among the athletes as a major barrier to the coach's effective use of questioning in GBAs. It was further noted that the coaches felt uneasy moving from being the font of all knowledge (den Duyn, 1997) to a facilitator of learning, which was exacerbated by the lack of efficient role models. Athletes unused to being empowered and taking responsibility for actions and learning may also take some time to realize the opportunities on offer (see Roberts, 2011 and Harvey, 2018). It can also be demanding for the coach because it requires skill in shaping and facilitating productive the interaction that can foster players'/athletes' abilities to negotiate, compromise and arrive at outcomes without making any participants feel 'wrong' or excluded and disengaged (Harvey, 2018; Kinnerk et al., 2018).

Developing effective questioning is not an easy task for coaches used to telling athletes what to do. The coach's contribution here is to promote a positive experience of inquiry and ask questions about what options or strategies might be appropriate to guide inquiry or to guide discovery when working on skill. This approach should help athletes learn to learn independently of the coach and that making mistakes is an essential part of learning when approached in this positive way. Such learning experiences can also promote resiliency, creativity, social learning, collective effort and an enjoyment of inquiry and discovery (Forrest, 2014).

Inquiry-Based Coaching

In the modified practice games used in Game Sense the teams are given opportunities to have 'team talks' at appropriate times (Light, 2013a) to collectively formulate strategies that they test and evaluate as an inquiry-based approach with the same approach adopted for individual sports. For example, two relay runners may generate and test ideas for improving their baton changeover after which they gather again to critically reflect upon how the strategy worked. If it didn't work the coach would ask them why it didn't work and formulate a new strategy or plan and test it. If they are experienced in this approach the coach would not need to ask them.

While more confident and experienced players/athletes may initially dominate discussion the less experienced can make valuable contributions when encouraged by the coach (Harvey, 2018). This way, athletes improve in their sport while developing confidence in their ability to become independent learners and problem solvers and so remain motivated to participate in the activity for the longer term (Renshaw et al., 2012). This social interaction can also develop improved athlete relationships and understanding of each other. It can encourage empathy, compassion, meaningful relationships, a sense of connection and care for each other as well, both on and off the field.

To get athletes to speak up, take risks and be creative coaches have to build an environment in which they feel secure. This must involve coaches making it clear how mistakes are essential for learning and how they provide opportunities for learning (Kinnerk et al., 2018; Renshaw et al., 2012). Mistakes should be seen as constructive errors that are made into positive learning experiences with the provision of opportunities for adequate reflection and analysis. This can be facilitated though a focus on the longer term of the season or the development trajectories of teams or athletes so that they do not feel immediate pressure to succeed (Harvey, 2018; Renshaw et al., 2010). The idea that 'mistakes are often the best teachers' (Rach, Ufer and Heinze, 2013, p. 22) helps develop an awareness of the process of learning and can develop the meaningfulness required to make it worthy of emotional commitment (Antonovsky, 1979).

Discussion

Here we discuss what the challenges are for coaches in its implementation and the opportunities it offers.

The Challenges

PPed is not a model but more a framework for thinking about high quality coaching and with no intention of being prescriptive. We are not proposing a step-by-step model for coaching but, instead, making broader suggestions about a pedagogical approach that coaches could draw on to think about making their coaching more positive and effective.

The challenges involved in taking up what would be a significant change for many coaches can be uncomfortable or even confronting. Designing and managing learning experiences and managing them to maintain optimum levels of engagement and learning require significant ability to analyze performance in practice, tune in to how athletes are feeling and adjust the activity to get the best results. The effective use of questioning to stimulate thinking and interaction, as part of its inquiry-based approach, is also a substantial challenge and particularly for coaches who have previously relied upon direct instruction (see Roberts, 2011; Kinnerk et al., 2018).

Research on Game Sense over the past decade or so identifies how even experienced athlete-centred coaches can struggle with the relationships between coach and athletes that it requires (Evans, 2012). This is typically compounded by the perceptions of others who see a good coach being explicitly in charge, transmitting knowledge, and of his/her practice session looking ordered and running smoothly typically contrast with the sometimes chaotic appearance of a Game Sense session (Kinnerk et al., 2018; Light, 2004). The problems that this presents for coaches who are taking up PPed is tied into issues of power relationships in coaching (see for example, Taylor and Garrett, 2010).

The possibilities

Despite the challenges involved in taking up Positive Pedagogy and the need to account for them, the Positive Pedagogy framework can provide a means of making learning more positive across a wide range of sports settings. It emphasizes learning through the social interaction that has been strongly linked to joyful experiences (see for example, Kinnerk et al., 2018; Kretchmar, 2005; Harvey, 2018; 2009; Renshaw et al., 2012) with large-scale research in psychology also suggests strong links between happiness, social interaction and social networks within which people respect others and are respected by them (see Fowler and Christakis, 2008). The social nature of learning emphasized in PPed and its inclusive nature can also facilitate a sense of belonging and self-esteem (see for example, Light, 2002) with Deci and Ryan (2000) arguing that this *relatedness* is a psychological requirement for human growth and the promotion of wellbeing (Renshaw et al., 2012).

PPed focuses on the improvement of performance but also helps athletes learn how to learn and develop both the motivation and confidence to learn and can facilitate social, moral and personal development (Kinnerk et al., 2018). It can also encourage the development of compassion, resilience, self-confidence, creativity, or the competence, coping ability, health, resilience, and the wellbeing that Positive Youth Development through Sport aims at promoting.

Positive Pedagogy emphasizes the holistic, social nature of learning, and the role of experience, the body and its senses in it. It encourages the development of the social skills involved in engaging in purposeful dialogue, a willingness and ability to negotiate and compromise and the understanding of democratic processes involved in making and enacting collective decision-making while making learning enjoyable (Harvey, 2018). Learning to learn and the positive inclinations toward learning it can generate, and some of the social learning that can accompany it, are more likely to transfer into life off the court, pool, track or field than improved sport technique and fitness are. The way in which PPed can develop a positive inclination toward learning, and the contribution it can make toward wellbeing would clearly be beneficial for children and young people participating in sport. It would also assist in improving performance at any level and could make a contribution toward helping elite-level, professional athletes meet the challenges of developing post-playing careers and enhance their wellbeing during this often-difficult transition.

References

Almond, L. (1983) 'Games making', *Bulletin of Physical Education*, 19(1): 32–35.

Antonovsky, A. (1979) *Health, stress and coping*, San Francisco: Jossey-Bass.

Antonovsky, A. (1987) *Unraveling the mystery of health*, San Francisco: Jossey-Bass.

Antonovsky, A. (1996) 'The salutogenic model as a theory to guide health promotion', *Health Promotion International*, 11(1): 11–17.

Bourdieu, P. (1986) *Distinction*, London: Routledge and Kegan Paul.

Bruner, J. (1999) 'Folk pedagogies', in B. Leach and B. Moon, eds, *Learners and pedagogy*, London: Open University Press, 4–20.

Bunker, D. and Thorpe, R. (1982) 'A model for teaching games in secondary school', *Bulletin of Physical Education*, 10, 9–16.

Chappell, G. and Light, R. L. (2015) 'Back to the future: Developing batting talent through Game Sense', Special issue of *Active +Healthy Magazine*, 23(2/3), 31–34.

Charlesworth, R. (2002) *Staying at the top*, Sydney: Pan MacMillan.

Chen, Q. and Light, R. (2006) 'I thought I'd hate cricket but I love it!': Year six students' responses to Game Sense pedagogy', *Change: Transformations in Education*, 9(2): 7–15.

Csikszentmihalyi, M. (1997) *Finding flow: The psychology of engagement with everyday life*, New York: Basic Books.

Clarke, J. and Dembowski, S. (2006) 'The art of asking great questions', *The International Journal of Mentoring and Coaching*, 4 (2): 1–6. Retrieved from www.solutionsurfers.com/pdf/TheArtOfAskingGreatQs.pdf

Davis, B. and Sumara, D. (2003) 'Why aren't they getting this? Working through the regressive myths of constructivist pedagogy', *Teaching Education*, 14(2): 123–140.

Deci, E. L. and Ryan, R. M. (2000) 'The "what" and "why" of goal pursuits: Human needs and the self-determination of behavior', *Psychological Enquiry*, 11: 227–268.

den Duyn, N. (1997) *Game Sense: Developing thinking players workbook*, Canberra: Australian Sports Commission.

De Martelaer, K., De Bouw, J. and Struyven, K. (2012) 'Youth sport ethics: Teaching pro-social behaviour', in S. Harvey and R. Light, eds, *Ethics in Youth Sport: Policy and Pedagogical Applications*, London and New York: Routledge, 55–73.

Dewey, J. (1916) *Democracy and education*, New York: Free Press.

Douge, B. and Hastie, P. (1993) 'Coach effectiveness', *Sport Science Review*, 2(2), 14–29.

Dyson, B. (2005) 'Integrating cooperative learning and tactical games models: Focusing on social interactions and decision-making', in L. L. Griffin and J. I. Butler, eds, *Teaching Games for Understanding: Theory, research, and practice*, Champaign, IL: Human Kinetics, 149–168.

Evans, J. and Light, R. (2008) 'Coach development through Collaborative Action Research: A rugby coach's implementation of Game Sense pedagogy', *Asian Journal of Exercise and Sport Science*, 5(1): 31–37.

Evans, J. R. (2012) 'Elite rugby union coaches' interpretation and use of Game Sense in New Zealand', *Asian Journal of Exercise and Sport Science*, 9(1): 85–97.

Foucault, M. (1977) *Discipline and punish: The birth of the prison*, New York: Vintage Books.

Foucault, M. (1979) *The history of sexuality*, Volume I, Harmondsworth: Penguin.

Forrest, G. (2014) 'Questions and answers: Understanding the connection between questioning and knowledge in game-centred approaches', in R. Light, J. Quay, S. Harvey and A. Mooney, eds, *Contemporary developments in games teaching*, London: Routledge, 167–177.

Fosnot, C. T. (ed.) (1996) *Constructivism: Theory, perspectives and practice*, New York and London: Teachers College, Columbia University.

Fowler, J. H. and Christakis, N. A. (2008) 'Dynamic spread of happiness in a large social network: longitudinal analysis over 20 years in the Framingham heart study', *British Medical Journal*, 337(768): a2338. doi:10.1136/bmj.a2338

Friere, P. (1993) *Pedagogy of the oppressed*, New York: Continuum Books.

Grant, A. M. (2011) 'The solution-focused inventory: A tripartite taxonomy for teaching, measuring and conceptualising solution focused approaches to coaching', *The Coach Psychologist*, 7(2), 98–105.

Gréhaigne, J.-F., Richard J.-F. and Griffin, L. L. (2005) *Teaching and learning team sports and games*, London and New York: Routledge.

Harvey, S. (2009) 'A study of interscholastic soccer players' perceptions of learning with Game Sense,' *Asian Journal of Sport and Exercise Science*, 6(1): 29–38.

Harvey, S. (2018) 'Developing athlete-centred coaching in high performance field hockey', in S. Pill ed., *Perspectives on athlete-centred coaching*, London and New York: Routledge, 79–92.

Harvey, S. and Jarrett, K. (2014) 'Recent trends in research literature on game-based approaches to teaching and coaching games', in R. L. Light, J. Quay, S. Harvey and A. Mooney, eds, *Contemporary developments in games teaching*, London and New York: Routledge, 87–102.

Harvey, S. and Light, R. L. (2015) 'Questioning for learning in games-based approaches to teaching and coaching', *Asia Pacific Journal of Health, Sport and Physical Education*, 6(2): 175–190.

Harvey, S., Cushion, C. and Massa-Gonzalez, A. (2010) 'Learning a new method: Teaching Games for Understanding in the coaches' eyes', *Physical Education and Sport Pedagogy*, 15 (4): 361–382.

Harvey, S., Kirk, D. and O'Donovan, T. M. (2014) 'Sport Education as a pedagogical application for ethical development in physical education and youth sport', *Sport, Education and Society*, 19(1): 41–62.

Hassanin, R., Light, R. and Macfarlane, A. (2018) 'Developing "good buggers": The influence of culture on New Zealand club rugby coaches' beliefs and practice', *Sport in Society*, 21(8), 1223–1235. doi:10.1080/17430437.2018.1443598

Hellison, D. R. (2003) *Teaching responsibility through physical activity* (2nd edn), Champaign, IL: Human Kinetics.

Holt, N. L., Sehn, Z. L., Spence, J. C., Newton, A. S. and Ball, G. D. C. (2012) 'Physical education and sport programs at an inner city school: exploring possibilities for positive youth development', *Physical Education and Sport Pedagogy*, 17(1), 97–113.

Jackson, S. A. and Csikszentmihalyi, M. (1999) *Flow in sports*, Champaign, IL: Human Kinetics.

Jones, E. (2015) 'Transferring skill from practice to the match in rugby through Game Sense', *Healthy + Active Magazine*, 22(2/3): 56–58.

Kinnerk, P., Harvey, S., McDonncha, C. and Lyons, M. (2018) 'A review of the game based approaches to coaching literature in competitive team sport settings', *Quest*, 70(4): 401–418.

Kirk, D. and MacPhail, A. (2002) 'Teaching games for understanding and situated learning: Rethinking the Bunker-Thorpe model', *Journal of Teaching in Physical Education*, 21: 177–192.

Kitson, R. (2005, July 2) 'How All Blacks went back to their roots', *The Guardian*, 8–9. Retrieved from www.guardian.co.uk/sport/2005/jul/02/lions2005.rugbyunion2

Kretchmar, S. (2005) 'Understanding and the delights of human activity', in L. Griffin and J. Butler, eds, *Teaching Games for Understanding: Theory research and practice*, Champaign, IL: Human Kinetics, 199–212.

Launder, A. G. (2001) *Play Practice: The games approach to teaching and coaching sports*, Champaign, IL: Human Kinetics.

Light, R. (2002) 'The social nature of games: Pre-service primary teachers' first experiences of TGfU', *European Physical Education Review*, 8(3): 291–310.

Light, R. (2003) 'The joy of learning: Emotion, cognition and learning in games through TGfU', *New Zealand Journal of Physical Education*, 36(1): 94–108.

Light, R. (2004) 'Australian coaches' experiences of Game Sense: Opportunities and challenges', *Physical Education and Sport Pedagogy*, 9(2): 115–132.

Light, R. (2008) *Sport in the lives of young Australians*, Sydney: Sydney University Press.

Light, R. L. (2013a) *Game Sense: Pedagogy for performance, participation and enjoyment*, London and New York: Routledge.

Light, R. L. (2013b) 'Game Sense pedagogy in youth sport: An applied ethics perspective', in S. Harvey and R. L. Light, eds, *Ethics in youth sport: Policy and pedagogical applications*, London and New York: Routledge, 92–106.

Light, R. L. (2014) 'Learner-centred pedagogy for swim coaching: A complex learning theory informed approach', *Asia-Pacific Journal of Health, Sport and Physical Education*, 5(2): 167–180.

Light, R. L. (2015) 'Managing practice activities and games in Game Sense coaching: Reflections upon teaching in Asia', *Proceedings for 2015 ACHPER International Conference*, 246–254. Available at: www.achper.org.au/professionallearning/past-international-con ference-proceedings/2015-international-conference-proceedings

Light, R. L. and Evans, J. R. (2010) 'The impact of Game Sense pedagogy on elite level Australian rugby coaches' practice: A question of pedagogy', *Physical Education and Sport Pedagogy*, 15(2): 103–115.

Light, R. L. and Kentel, J. A. (2013) 'Mushin: Learning in technique-intensive sport as uniting mind and body through complex learning theory', *Physical Education and Sport Pedagogy*. doi:10.1080/17408989.2013.868873

Light, R. L. and Lémonie, Y. (2012) 'Constructivisme et pédagogie dans l'enseignement de la natation [Constructivism and pedagogy for coaching in swimming]' *eJRIEPS*, 26: 34–52.

Light, R. L. and Wallian, N. (2008) 'A constructivist approach to teaching swimming', *Quest*, 60(3): 387–404.

Light, R. L., Curry, C. and Mooney, A. (2014) 'Game Sense as a model for delivering quality teaching in physical education', *Asia-pacific Journal of Health, Sport & Physical Education*, 5(1): 67–81.

Light, R. L., Harvey, S. and Mouchet, A. (2014) 'Improving "at-action" decision-making in team sports through a holistic coaching approach', *Sport, Education and Society*, 19(3), 258–275.

Light, R. L., Evans, J. R., Harvey, S. and Hassanin, R. (2015) *Advances in rugby coaching: An holistic approach*, London and New York: Routledge.

Mayer, R. E. (2004) 'Should there be a three strikes law against pre discovery?' *American Psychologist*, 59(1): 14–19.

Metzler, M. W. (2005) 'Implications of models-based instruction for research on teaching: A focus on Teaching Games for Understanding', in L. L. Griffin and J. Butler, eds, *Teaching Games for Understanding: Theory, research & practice*, Champaign, IL: Human Kinetics, 193–198.

Mitchell, S. A., Oslin, J. L. and Griffin, L. L. (1995) 'The effects of two instructional approaches on game performance', *Pedagogy in Practice – Teaching and Coaching in Physical Education and Sports*, 1: 36–48.

Mosston, M. and Ashworth, S. (1986) *Teaching physical education* (3rd edn), Columbus: Merrill.

Partington, M., Cushion, C. J. and Harvey, S. (2014) 'An investigation of the effect of athletes' age on the coaching behaviours of professional top-level youth soccer coaches', *Journal of Sport Sciences*, 35(2): 403–414.

Pill, S. (2015) 'Using appreciative inquiry to explore Australian rules football coaches' experience with Game Sense coaching', *Sport, Education and Society*, 20(6): 799–818.

Poerksen, B. (2005) 'Learning how to learn', *Kybernetes*, 34(3/4): 471–484.

Rach, S., Ufer, S. and Heinze, A. (2013) 'Learning from errors: Effects of teachers' training on students' attitudes towards and their individual use of errors', *PNA*, 8(1): 21–30.

Renshaw, I., Oldham, A. R. and Bawden, M. (2012) 'Non-linear pedagogy underpins intrinsic motivation in sports coaching', *The Open Sports Sciences Journal*, 5: 1–12.

Roberts, S. J. (2011) 'Teaching Games for Understanding: The difficulties and challenges experienced by participation cricket coaches', *Physical Education and Sport Pedagogy*, 16(1): 33–48.

Seligman, M. E. P. (2012) *Flourish: A visionary new understanding of happiness and wellbeing*, Sydney: Random House.

Seligman, M. E. P. and Csikszentmihalyi, M. (2000) 'Positive Psychology: An introduction', *American Psychologist*, 55(1): 5–14.

Sheppard, J. and Mandigo, J. (2009) 'PlaySport: Teaching life skills for understanding through games', in T. Hopper, J. L. Butler, and B. Storey, eds, *TGfU … Simply good pedagogy: Understanding a complex challenge*, Toronto, HPE Canada, 73–86.

Siedentop, D. (1994) *Sport Education: Quality PE through positive sport experiences*, Champaign, IL: Human Kinetics.

Stolz, S. and Pill, S. (2015) 'A narrative approach to exploring TGfU – GS', *Sport, Education and Society*, 21(2): 239–261.

Tan, C. W. K., Chow, J. Y. and Davids, K. (2011) 'How does TGfU work?': Examining the relationship between learning design in TGfU and a nonlinear pedagogy', *Physical Education and Sport Pedagogy*, 17(4): 331–348.

Taylor, B. and Garrett, D. (2010) 'The professionalization of sport coaching: relations of power, resistance and compliance', *Sport, Education and Society*, 15(1): 121–139.

Thorpe, R. and Bunker, D. (2008) 'Teaching Games for Understanding – Do current developments reflect original intentions?' Paper presented at the Fourth Teaching Games for Understanding Conference, Vancouver, BC, Canada, May 14–17.

Turner, A. (2014) 'Learning games concepts by design', in R. L. Light, J. Quay, S. Harvey and A. Mooney, eds, *Contemporary developments in games teaching*, London and New York: Routledge, 193–206.

Varela, F. J., Thompson, E. and Rosch, E. (1991) *The embodied mind: Cognitive science and human experience*, Cambridge, MA: MIT Press.

Vickers, J. N., Livingston, L. F., Umeris-Bohnert, S. and Holden, D. (1999) 'Decision training: The effects of complex instruction, variable practice and reduced delayed feedback on the acquisition and transfer of a motor skill', *Journal of Sport Sciences*, 17(5): 357–367.

Wallian, N. and Chang, C. W. (2007) Language, thinking and action: Towards a semio-constructivist approach in physical education, *Physical Education and Sport Pedagogy*, 12(3): 289–311.

Wang, C. L. and Ha, A. (2009) 'Pre-service teachers' perception of Teaching Games for Understanding: A Hong Kong perspective', *European Physical Education Review* 15(3): 407–429.

Weimer, M. (2002) *Learner-centered teaching*, San Francisco: Jossey-Bass.

Williams, A. M., and Hodges, N. J. (2005) 'Practice, instruction and skill acquisition in soccer: Challenging tradition', *Journal of Sports Sciences*, 23: 637–650.

Wright, J. and Forrest, G. (2007) 'A social semiotic analysis of knowledge construction and games centred approaches to teaching', *Physical Education and Sport Pedagogy*, 12(3): 273–287.

PART I

Team Sports

1

PROVIDING A POSITIVE EXPERIENCE OF LEARNING

An Australian Football (AFL) Experience

Shane Pill

My profile of experience is typical of the 'sporty' profile of those entering PETE courses (Dewar and Lawson, 1984; Sikes, 1988; Valtonen, Kuusela and Ruismaki, 2011) and of a custodial orientation that favours the teaching styles and programs experienced and which they were successful with (Morgan and Hansen, 2008). Lortie (1975) called this experience the 'apprenticeship of observation', which has a distinct and traceable influence on a practitioner's perspective as it informs the value orientation of the individual. On reflection, my experience of PETE in the mid-1980s confirmed my apprenticeship of observation of sport coaching and the primacy of what Kirk (2010) has called sport as sport techniques. That is, sport taught in physical education and sport teams coached through a sequence of drills leading to a game or 'scratch match' at the end, with the coach commanding and controlling practice, frequently demanding replication and conformity to a technique which they had demonstrated.

After completing my degree, in 1988 I moved from Adelaide to Perth to begin my teaching and sport coaching career. It was here that I was exposed to game-based ideas about sport teaching and coaching in a meaningful way. I worked with a head of department who had been trained in England. After a warm-up, I observed how his physical education classes went straight into game play. He would walk around taking to individual students during the lesson, occasionally stopping the whole group for a conversation, which most often took the form of a question and answer with the students and not direct instruction. This contradicted my apprenticeship of observation of good physical education teaching and sport coaching, which led me to engage my head of department in many conversations to understand why he taught this way. I began to question the concept of the ideal lesson as a 'notion of progression as an additive process' (Kirk, 2010, p. 85) as I observed the enthusiasm the head of department's students had for his lessons. Progressively, I shed a technique oriented 'skill and drill' approach in both my physical education teaching and sport coaching.

In 1994, I commenced a Level 2 Australian football (AFL) coaching course during which, the concept of coaching game sense was introduced to me in a meaningful way through the work of Rick Charlesworth, and his concept of 'designer games' (Charlesworth, 1974). This was a 'light bulb' moment for my teaching and coaching.[1] I began to play with the idea of designer games initially in my sport coaching, and then in my teaching. Not long after this, the Game Sense coaching approach was introduced in Australia as the preferred pedagogy (Australian Sports Commission, 1996). The Game Sense coaching approach matched with the beliefs that I had developed about sport coaching and teaching sport in physical education (Pill, 2015a). Upon reflection, I had developed from a transmission-focussed coach to one attempting to be the sport coach as educator (Jones, 2006), with an athlete-centred focus (Pill, 2018a) on positive pedagogy (Light and Harvey, 2017). In particular, the move to asking questions to generate dialogue and learning in a Game Sense approach (Light, 2017) to effect the development of thinking players (den Duyn, 1997) became a focus of my continuing coach education.

Light and Harvey (2019) explained how positive pedagogy enhances the inherently positive experience of learning that game-based approaches promote and that the notion of *positive pedagogy for sport coaching* draws on the Game Sense framework. The session I recall in this chapter came after 20 years of 'playing with' the idea of Game Sense coaching and coming to understand the Game Sense approach as a *positive pedagogy for sport coaching*.

The Session

The session I reflect on here occurred during a semi-professional State League season. I was an assistant coach but, for this training session, I had responsibility for session design and implementation. It was the main session of the week and lasted for nearly 120 minutes. It occurred late in the pre-season during which trial games were being played and the playing system (Grehaigne, Richard and Griffin, 2005; Pill, 2015b) was being consolidated. The purpose of the session was to further develop players' understanding of the midfield-forward connection and was part of a training block focussed on the midfield-forward connection. Pre-season had begun with players initially training to develop understanding of strategies for defending opposition forward entries, and then progressed to developing strategies associated with the defense-midfield connection. In this way, the teaching of the teams' system of play and players' tactical decision making had been 'periodised' (Pill, 2015b). Table 1.1 outlines the structure of the session.

I started the session in the briefing room with an overview of the session conducted as a question and answer with the players. Traditional coaching approaches are often referred to as 'directive' as the coach largely commands and directs training. The coach appears to do most of the talking and most of the thinking, and players comply with the coach directions. Game Sense coaching as a positive pedagogy places a greater emphasis on players responsibility for thinking and understanding. This occurs by the coach use of pre-planned and in the moment well considered questions. I focussed the

TABLE 1.1 Game Sense training plan for Australian football

Players meeting	*Session Focus* *- Midfield-forward connection* *Focus questions* *What are we trying to do? (isolate a forward who can mark the ball or free a space for a running shot at goal)* *How do we achieve this? (fast ball movement, forwards shifting the defense with their running patterns, forwards working for each other with blocks and screens)* *How does it connect to our game plan? (creating marking opportunities inside 50)*	*10 minutes*

Warm-Up	(with strength and conditioning staff)
	1. Dynamic mobility and running
	2. Off the line ball handling drills
	   *groups of three
	   begin with handball/finish with kicking
	3. 7 v 4 Keeping off – kicking (possession overload with the +3 out-number)
		30 minutes

Midfield-Forward game	Aim
	Offensive team (12 players) wins by scoring a goal
	Defensive team (8 players) wins by either: gaining possession at the stoppage; gaining the ball in defense and clearing the ball to the assistant coach positioned in the midfield.
	Conditions
	   *12 v 8 game
	   (6 forwards v 4 defenders)
	   (6 offensive mids v 4 defensive mids)
	   *Forwards play 1–3–2 structure at stoppage
	   *Game starts at midfield stoppage. Assistant coach decides if stoppage is a ball-up, throw-in, or fee kick situation
	   *If a point is scored defensive team brings the ball back into play attempting to get the ball to the midfield coach. The offensive team attempts to keep the ball in the forward area and win back possession to score a goal.
	   *When a goal is scored, players return to starting points and assistant coach starts the game with a midfield stoppage.
	Inquiry strategy: Assistant coach in charge will use 'freeze moments' if appropriate, and allow 'tactical time-outs' after goals to permit the player leaders of each team to discuss with their playing group – 'What's working?' 'What's not?' 'What do we change?'
		60 minutes

Warm-Down	Practice stations (players work with assistant coaches on the players identified focus) Group 1 'One step' kicking Group 2 Ground ball pick ups Group 3 Tackling Group 4 Strong hands in a marking contest	20 minutes

session outline (see Table 1.1) through use of the pre-planned questions. The questions I planned were purposefully convergent, targeted at engaging knowledge that should be known by the players, therefore engaging recall and not the development of new understanding. They are not the only questions I used, as this means potentially only three players voices are heard. Rather, I engaged in a 'debate of ideas' (Grehaigne et al., 2005). In a debate of ideas, player knowledge is elaborated, not left at the first answer provided, in response to a question posed by the coach. A debate of ideas requires in the moment questioning by the coach to fully draw-out the knowledge expected of the playing group. Individual past experiences should be encouraged to enrich the meaning of the information (Zerai and Mekni, 2017). Traditional approaches to player coaching have been found to feature direct instruction and feedback. Positive pedagogy requires inquiry-based athlete-centred pedagogy (Light and Harvey, 2019; Pill, 2018a), such as the debate of ideas.

The warm-up phase moved from closed 'unopposed' to an open drill progressively increasing physical and cognitive demands on players to prepare for the game development phase. The warm-up phase is an opportunity to focus on technical movement models – kicking, marking, handball, and athletics (such as running mechanics); and running patterns as the players are able to focus more on the internal coordinative dynamics of their movements, as the activities do not have the time, space, and decision-making complexities of the game (Farrow, Pyne and Gabbett, 2008).

When using a Game Sense coaching approach, the game or a game form becomes the focus of training following the warm-up (Australian Sports Commission, 1996). In traditional coaching scenarios, game play and/or match simulation often comes at the end of training or with juniors, as a form of reward for trying hard and getting things 'right' during the practice drills. However, adopting a positive pedagogy positions the game-centred practice component as where skill development occurs because tactical and technical aspects of movement are complimentary pairs in creating skilled behaviour (Pill, 2014). Skill is a concept only having meaning in context to the 'real' performance, which is the game (den Duyn, 1997). Game Sense coaching is not a 'kick out the ball and play' approach. It is also not game-only and rather game-centred (Light and Harvey, 2017a; Pill, 2018b). In the session in focus, the game-centred practice is an example of phase practice. Phase practice is that which reinforces a phase of play through repetition by repeated restarts (Worthington, 1974).

The session did not finish with players running a few laps and then doing some stretches, common in a traditional coaching session structure. The warm-down consisted of what is colloquially referred to in Australian football caching as 'craft work'. It is where the playing group divides into groups to work on specific areas of performance that need improvement. This deliberate practice is undertaking by players with awareness of what technique they are trying to improve. The term for this type of practice is 'related practice', as what is practiced is related to the game, however, the practice is not 'game like' (Worthington, 1974). Players were allocated to a related practice with very specific perception-action coupling and unambiguous success criteria based on a narrow set of affordances for action by the specific development need of the player (Renshaw, Davids, Newcombe and Roberts, 2019).

Reflection and Evaluation

I can identify the four pedagogical principles of a positive pedagogy for sport coaching developed from Light's work on Game Sense in this coaching session, which are:

1.   deliberate design of the game as a learning environment;
2.   an emphasis on questioning to promote inquiry and interaction;
3.   promoting inquiry through problem solving; and,
4.   providing a supportive environment. *(Light, 2013)*

The session I detailed in this chapter demonstrates each of the four pedagogical principles. I initiated game play as the focus of the practice session with a clear learning intention communicated to players before training commenced, during the players meeting in the rooms before players went out for the warm-up. I conditioned the game play with specific focus. For example, I deliberately, numerically overloaded the team trying to score by reducing the number of players in defensive roles to give more chance of successful execution of the team offensive strategy and to provide offensive players tactical in-the-moment decision making to be more successful (Pill, 2014). Light and Harvey (2019) describe this as beginning with a high rate of success but increasing the level of challenge and pressure on the players as the session progresses. It is also an example of game modification consistent with Game Sense coaching pedagogy (Australian Sports Commission, 1996).

I placed an emphasis on questioning in preference to coach instructing. Initially, I focussed the session learning intention by using questions that facilitated a debate of ideas. Before the player meeting, I met with the coaches assisting training to ask that during training they facilitate an ongoing 'conversation' with players by initiating their interaction with players with the question 'what happened there?', to open up a dialogue with players that assists player development as 'thinking players'. This dialogical direction creates a moment of reflection on action while the memory of the event is likely clearer to the player than in would be later in a break in play. Approaching coach-player interactions this way in a Game Sense approach is part of the process of developing 'thinking players', which is the focus of Game Sense coaching (den Duyn, 1997). In a Game Sense coaching approach, questioning is used create dialogue to stimulate thinking and reflection from which learning in and about games emerges (Light, 2013).

Problem solving through inquiry processes was also evident in the session. For example, I asked the coaching group to use 'freeze moments' (Worthington, 1974) whereby play was stopped (frozen) and player behaviour at the moment analysed with the question 'what happened there?' Players had also been instructed during the player session briefing that player-led 'tactical time-outs' were available after a goal had been scored and the ball was transitioning back to the midfield restart. Tactical timeouts are an opportunity for the players to discuss what is working and what needs to change. In a game of Australian football, players have time to meet in their player groups (forwards, midfielders, and defenders) for reflection and strategising. Typically, the 'captain' of the group will facilitate the conversation. Incorporating this opportunity into the practice design enables the players to practice this behaviour. I also argue that it is also an example of athlete centred coaching (Light and Harvey, 2017; Pill, 2018a) as initiative and responsibility for player learning is shared with the players at training, and players are assisted to develop as independent decision-makers during the game. Athlete-centred coaching requires an emphasis like this example of placing the playing group at the centre of their own learning and reflection as it is directed at providing a supportive environment.

When reviewing the training plan (Table 1.1) and the description of how the session was implemented, it is pertinent for me to highlight the difference between recall and guided discovery of new knowledge and capability for action. I have often found that coaches using questioning with players struggle to differentiate between questioning for recall and questioning for discovery and knowledge formation. A structured series of questions leading to revelation of understanding may be a reminder of expected understanding. A structured series of questions may also lead to the development of new understanding. One of the areas of *positive pedagogy for sport coaching* that took me a long time to fully understand and appreciate is the need for good knowledge of players to be able to distinguish which cognitive process (recall or new understanding) is displayed in answer to a question. It also took many years of reading and reflection on my coaching to know when to use questioning for recall and consolidation of knowledge and understanding, and when to stimulate 'new thinking'. For example, a player answers a question in front of the playing group that leads to new understanding for the group of players. Later in the session, I ask a similar question in front of the playing group but direct the question to a different player in the group, who comes up with an answer similar to the previous player. The answer is unlikely to be 'discovery'. This is because the player now answering the question heard the previous players answer. Therefore, in the later instance it is likely recall of understanding.

Reflecting on my Journey to that Point of Understanding

I found understanding how to modify, condition, or constrain games purposefully towards a tactical concept the 'easy' part of Game Sense coaching. Understanding the nature of a question that can guide discovery of understanding of a targeted concept, converge on an answer, or create the opportunity for divergent and creative thinking took longer to understand, and was more difficult to habituate into my coaching practice. I now appreciate that coaches need to know what cognitive behaviour they are attempting to encourage through their use of questions. For example, if I ask, 'What do we do in this instance?' player responses will converge on an expected answer. If I ask, 'What were three things you had to consider in the moment, and what options were available to deal with them?' I open the dialogue to exploration and the potential for divergent and/or creativity thinking. I now appreciate that a player's thinking will only be encouraged if the coach allows time for players to 'process' questions, and so coaches need to avoid the temptation to answer their own questions if answers are not immediately forthcoming from the playing group. It may be the coach has to let a question or two stay with the players and return to a period of play to allow time for further experience of the problem or concept to occur.

When I first began to engage with the Game Sense approach, it was explained in coaching literature as small-sided game play, with an emphasis on modification to condition the game purposefully to give the play a focus on a learning intention. The Game Sense Cards showing games to develop fundamental sport skills was indicative of this focus in the literature (Australian Sports Commission, 1999). The Game Sense coaching approach was not explained as to how it was differentiated across coaching from entry level through to elite sport to meet the different learning needs of players at these different stages of development. Sports like Australian football adopted the concept of 'game sense games' for the purpose of training players 'how to think' (Australian Football League, 2012, p. 26). I find this 'conditioned' or 'constrained' game form a concept very similar to Rick Charlesworth's (1974) concept of a 'designer game'.

In this chapter, I have written about a lived experience of implementing a Game Sense approach as positive pedagogy in a state league semi-professional Australian football setting. As adults, the players had fifteen years or more experience with the game. Some of the players came to the club program via progression through the club's junior talent development pathway, recruited to the club from another state league club, or via delisting from the professional elite competition, the Australian Football League (AFL), and recruitment to the state league club I was working with. Game Sense coaching with less experienced players would necessarily 'look different' to the example I provide in this chapter. The experience I recall demonstrates the distinct features of *Positive Pedagogy for Sport Coaching* (Light and Harvey, 2019):

- I emphasised engagement with the physical learning environment using phase practice (Worthington, 1974);
- I and the other coaches asked questions to generate dialogue to engage player thinking in preference to instructing them what to do;
- an inquiry orientated environment was fostered to test and evaluate solutions collectively using 'tactical time outs' and 'freeze moments' (Worthington, 1974); and
- mistakes in decision-making and movement execution were learning opportunities.

Note

1 Rick Charlesworth is arguably Australia's 'best ever' national sport team coach, with eight world coach of the year awards (Charlesworth, 2016).

References

Australian Football League (2012) *The coach: The official level 1 coaching manual*, Melbourne, Vic: Australian Football League.

Australian Sports Commission (1996) *Game sense: Perceptions and actions research report*, Canberra, ACT: Australian Sports Commission.

Australian Sports Commission (1996) *Game Sense cards: 30 games to develop thinking players*, Belconnen, ACT: Australian Sports Commission.

Charlesworth, R. (1974) 'Designer games', *Sport Coach*, 17(4): 30–33.

Charlesworth, R. (2016) *World's best: Coaching with the Kookaburras and the Hockeyroos*, Nedlands, Western Australia: RC Sports.

den Duyn, N. (1997) *Game sense: Developing thinking players. A presenter's guide and workbook*, Belconnen, ACT: Australian Sports Commission.

Dewar, A. and Lawson, H. (1984). 'The subjective warrant and recruitment into physical education', *Quest*, 36, 15–25.

Farrow, D., Pyne, D. and Gabbett, T. (2008) 'Skill and physiological demands of open and closed training drills in Australian football', *International Journal of Sports Science & Coaching*, 3(4), 489–499.

Grehaigne, J-F., Richard, J-F. and Griffin, L. L. (2005) *Teaching and learning team sports and games*, London and New York: Routledge.

Jones, R. (ed.). (2006) *The sport coach as educator: Re-conceptualising sports coaching*, London, UK: Routledge.

Kirk, D. (2010) *Physical education futures*, London, UK: Routledge.

Light, R. (2013) *Game Sense: Pedagogy for performance, participation and enjoyment*, London and New York: Routledge.

Light, R. (2017) *Positive Pedagogy for sport coaching: Athlete-centred coaching for individual sports*, London and New York: Routledge.

Light, R. and Harvey, S. (2017) 'Positive Pedagogy for sport coaching', *Sport, Education and Society*, 22(2): 271–287.

Light, R. and Harvey, S. (2019) *Positive Pedagogy for sport coaching: Athlete-centred coaching for individual sports* (2nd edn). London and New York: Routledge.

Lortie, D. (1975) *Schoolteacher: A sociological study*, London: University of Chicago Press.

Morgan, P. and Hansen, V. (2008) 'The relationship between PE biographies and PE teaching practices of classroom teachers', *Sport, Education and Society*, 13: 373–391.

Pill, S. (2014) 'Informing Game Sense pedagogy with constraints led theory for coaching in Australian football', *Sport Coaching Review*, 3(1): 46–62.

Pill, S. (2015a) 'Valuing learning in, through and about sport–physical education and the development of sport literacy', in H. Askell–Williams (ed.) *Transforming the Future of Learning with Educational Research*, Hershey, PA: IGI Global, 20–35.

Pill, S. (2015b). *The game sense approach for Australian football (AFL)*, Hindmarsh, SA: ACHPER Publications.

Pill, S. (ed.) (2018a) *Perspectives on athlete centred coaching*, London, UK: Routledge.

Pill, S. (2018b) 'The game sense approach: Developing thinking players', *Runner: The Journal of the Health & Physical Education Council of the Alberta Teachers' Association*, 49(1), 32–39.

Renshaw, I., Davids, K., Newcombe, D. and Roberts, W. (2019) *The constraints-led approach: Principles for sports coaching and practice design*, New York and London: Routledge.

Sikes, P. (1988) 'Growing old gracefully? Age, identity and physical education', in J. Evans (ed.) *Teachers, teaching and control in physical education*, London, UK: Falmer Press, 21–40.

Valtonen, J., Kuusela, J. and Ruismäki, H. (2011) 'The leisure time physical activity background of pre-service class teachers', in H. Ruismäki and I. Ruokonen (eds.)*Design learning and well-being: 4th International Journal of Intercultural Arts Education: Post-Conference Book*, Helsinki: Unigragia, 61–74.

Worthington, E. (1974) *Learning and teaching soccer skills*, UK: Lepus Books.

Zerai, Z. and Mekni, R. (2017) 'How to evaluate interactions during a debate of ideas', *Creative Education*, 8: 539–548.

2

POSITIVE PEDAGOGY IN CRICKET COACHING

A Season of Reflections

Kendall Jarrett and Elliot Wilson with Andy Siddall

Engagement in ongoing professional development is a hallmark practice of a sport coach keen to develop their craft. As experienced coaches we recognise the value of such investment and consistently seek to expose ourselves to new coach development opportunities. Thus, when approached by Richard to write about our experiences as cricket coaches of using positive pedagogy (PPed) we reflected on what we knew about the concept to then inform how we might go about responding. With our stated interest in engaging in continuous professional development (CPD) we decided that of greatest benefit to our coaching practice would be to engage in a season-long conversation that required us to reflect upon the many different aspects and principles of PPed that influenced our coaching practice.

When developing this collaborative approach to exploring our own personal understanding and experiences of PPed, we were conscious of the need to consider the many factors that make up a successful CPD investment. Research into CPD for sport coaches over the past decade has led to widespread acceptance of the following key elements for CPD success; that CPD should be interactive, collaborative, located in practice, self-regulated and informal (Griffiths, Armour and Cushion, 2018; Nash, Sproule and Horton, 2017). For us our decision to engage in a season-long conversation held within it all of the above stated key elements for CPD success, whilst at the same time being a timely and affordable investment in our coaching development.

In addition to our desire to engage in what we saw as a unique CPD opportunity, this collaborative endeavour also meant we could invest our time in a burgeoning area of coaching research that resonated with aspects of our current coaching practice. As coaches we both strive to be athlete-centred, to develop thinking players through their empowerment as athletes (Pill, 2018). Thus, in our view there already existed a synergy between what informs what we currently try to do as coaches and what PPed offers us as a coaching resource. And despite coaching in vastly different cricket environments (see coaching context section below), our desire to explore our use and understanding of PPed in our own coaching contexts supports comments by Nash, Sproule and Horton (2017) that it is equally as necessary for coaches to advance their practice 'whether they work at participation level … or at the performance or elite level' (p. 1905).

Our Coaching Contexts

As with any reflection on coaching practice it is important to share the contexts within which we coach. Our season-long conversation took place from May to September with each of us coaching in quite different cricket environments:

> Kendall: I am coach/captain of a village league cricket team in rural England. The season consists of 18 weekly matches and each week there are typically three to four team line-up changes. Player ages range between 14- and 71-years-old with approximately 30 players playing for the team in any given season. We have non-compulsory preseason training sessions, thus, the majority of coaching occurs on match day preceding and during play. I have 15 years' experience coaching a number of junior and senior cricket teams in both Australia and England as well as 12 years of experience as a tertiary lecturer delivering sport pedagogy modules on a variety of education and sport focused courses.
>
> My knowledge of PPed as a concept to inform my coaching practice has developed considerably since 2017. As one of the first contributors to Richard's blog on his PPed website well before this publication, I have been at 'close quarters' to its development as a guiding framework for sport coaching practice. With a research background in game-based approaches (GBA) and the range of instructional pedagogies this umbrella term covers (e.g. TGfU, Game Sense), the team and game focused nature of such approaches meant the teaching of certain individual sports and recreational activities that were clearly not team or game focused was always problematic. Thus, with PPed recognised as a concept intended to extend interrogation of pedagogical practice 'beyond games and team sports' (Light and Harvey, 2017, p. 271), my awareness and use of PPed as an overarching pedagogical concept when coaching and lecturing has developed considerably.
>
> Elliott: For the last seven years I have acted as the talent pathway manager at Worcestershire CCC. This role has a focus on player development and effective player transition from academy to professional. From a player perspective, I am responsible for establishing a supportive learning and development environment that places significant emphasis on equipping players with life skills to survive and thrive. From a club perspective, a key focus of my role is to support a culture of individual and team growth that provides those within and outside the Academy with a positive impression of the club and the game itself. I have 20 years' experience coaching within County academy, university and secondary school programmes along with running my own cricket

coaching business. In 2009 I completed my Level 4 Cricket Coaching certificate with the ECB.

My knowledge of PPed was limited until my involvement in the CPD commitment outlined in this chapter. I belief all of the key elements associated with PPed can be found within my coaching practice, thus I was keen to learn more about the concept from the outset as a means to enhance aspects of my cricket coaching.

The Season

Our Season-Long Conversation

Questions derived from Light and Harvey's (2017) *Positive Pedagogy for sport coaching* article were used to drive our coaching correspondence and provide a framework for a season-long reflective conversation on personal coaching practice. Our use of written email exchange as the primary method for correspondence also meant our conversation could be shared with a coaching peer at season end to invite him to comment on aspects of our PPed-related CPD. This was done at season end to maintain the reflective momentum generated by conversation involvement and to also help us to consider future opportunities to enhance our understanding of PPed.

Using key statements about PPed contained in Light and Harvey (2017) – e.g. PPed is a framework for meeting coaching challenges through a focus away from 'fixing mistakes'; PPed focuses on promotion of dialogue, reflection and purposeful social interaction to build intellectual self-sufficiency; PPed is used to inform current coaching practice, not redevelop it – we developed a list of questions to ask each other periodically throughout the season to stimulate reflection on our understanding of PPed and our coaching practice in general (see Table 2.1). For us the selection and posing of a question (typically every two or three weeks) acted as a prompt to exchange emails and reflect on a specific aspect of PPed apparent within our practice.

TABLE 2.1 List of prompt questions used to stimulate conversation and reflection on coaching practice throughout the season

Question 1	What is your understanding of positive pedagogy and how it could be used to inform your players' development?
Question 2	How do you go about framing 'mistake making' in a positive light?
Question 3	How do you go about enhancing a player's capacity to learn from mistakes and to not 'fear failure'?
Question 4	What importance do you place on getting the socio-cultural environment 'right' and how do you go about this?
Question 5	When do your players typically take on more autonomy and ownership of engagement?
Question 6	When does collaborative problem solving become the central focus of a session?

What we found when we reviewed our season-long conversation was less a 'back and forth conversation' about our use of PPed, but more a 'reflective account' of where aspects of PPed were reflected in each of our current cricket coaching practices. Thus, instead of a conversation, we present below a compilation of reflections relating to four prominent characteristics of PPed: 1) fixing mistakes; 2) viewing the game as a whole; 3) promoting social interactions, and 4) player self-sufficiency.

1 Fixing mistakes

> Kendall: Today I shared with the team my key foci for the season ahead. I prioritised 'fun' and 'mateship' as two key values underpinning my coaching and on-field leadership along with 'whatever each of you prioritise'. My reasoning here being the desire to support ownership of their playing experience and for each player to take on more autonomy when contributing to the team. Specific to PPed, I did this as a means to articulate to the team my desire to be seen as a coach who is less about 'fixing mistakes' and more about supporting a self-sufficiency model of engagement and development.

> Elliot: What you have said [in your email] reflects my views also. One of the key responsibilities for me as a cricket coach is getting players to problem solve for themselves and not being reliant on coach direction. Being brave to let players make mistakes and allowing them to fail, especially when parents are involved and they believe that mistakes are avoidable, is a challenge. The feeling a mistake leaves for a player is far more permanent than them seeing the problem solved FOR them. Ultimately, we want creative, aware, resilient, decision making, skillful players. But if we do it all for them, we will not get them further any faster. PPed acts a reminder to both myself and my players that making mistakes and fixing them yourself are GOOD THINGS for cricketers to experience.

2 Viewing the game as a whole instead of its component parts

> Elliot: We always look to see if we can make practice and training look and feel like the game as opposed to practice. In essence we are trying to view the game as a whole instead of its component parts which is a key message in the PPed literature with holism being one of its two philosophical foundations (Light and Harvey, 2019). Running alongside this is a focus on developing tactical awareness through problem solving which in my opinion is easier to achieve if players are approaching training (and thus developing behaviours) the same way as they would a match.

> Kendall: This is less challenging for me as having no in-season training sessions scheduled means that viewing the game as a whole, instead of its component parts, is the norm for players. For me as coach this situation means that players seem to quickly become accustomed to viewing the game as a challenge in its entirety because there is limited opportunity to break down their development into component parts. I believe what this also inadvertently does is promote a sense of reliance on the resources present – that being themselves and their teammates.

3 Purposeful social interaction

Kendall: Three key pillars of PPed are: 1) the facilitation of dialogue; 2) reflection; and 3) purposeful social interaction. After a number of losses leading into the mid-season stretch of matches, I was keen to alleviate the pressures of match day performance that had taken hold of the team. Team discussions prior, during and post-match are commonplace in cricket yet the tone and focus of these deliberations can be negative and unconstructive. So, last week I trialled a more purposeful and positive approach to social interaction encouragement. Prior to fielding, at the fall of a wicket, and after drinks breaks, I tried to facilitate more purposeful and humour-laden 'team chats' designed to get players to remind themselves of overall game strategy and to outwardly discuss and reflect on positive aspects of their match performance. I have also spoken about the importance of partnerships (e.g. working together in a bowling partnership) and have encouraged some of the younger players to ask questions of their older teammates post team chat to help strategize and implement game plans. This seems to be working well with comments back from younger players acknowledging the performance-related benefits of these chats.

4 Promoting player self-sufficiency

Elliot: Your mention of experience ownership resonates with me and what we do here. Right from my first interaction with new Academy members I place considerable importance on the player experience. So, I am constantly looking at player interaction, engagement and feedback. We want everything we do in the Academy to be fun, competitive and challenging. Throughout the summer we have regular touch points, usually via the sharing of short video messages. The flavor of these is to encourage reflection on performance. We ask players to label how their performance made them feel with the aim to look at how to re-create that feeling or how to change it. We found this a creative way to encourage reflective practice.

Kendall: Engaging players in reflective practice is a key for me too, although limiting myself to the asking of questions instead of offering specific verbal directions has been challenging - especially when working with younger players e.g. 14–16 yrs. For the younger players articulation of feelings and how to action tactics and strategy is rare when asked in group settings, as typically the older players are more confident and au fait with required responses. Knowing when to ask questions (i.e. when in 1-on-1 conversation or within a group) and what questions to ask (i.e. whether it relates to a team strategy or an individual bowling/fielding tactic) continues to be a focus of mine during matches.

Reflections and Evaluations

Our Understanding and Use of PPed

Each reflection above holds within it discussion of a key aspect of PPed and in doing so reaffirms how closely our current coaching practices are aligned to the practices of PPed. Only a few reflections ended up outlining an intentional change in practice to better reflect principles of PPed e.g. the introduction of more purposeful team chats on match days and the encouragement of one-on-one conversations between younger and older players. It is important for our own coaching development around future use of PPed, though, to detail; 1) what went well and what didn't go so well; 2) what we learnt about ourselves as coaches (specifically cricket coaches); and 3) what we could do more of to inform our use of PPed in our respective coaching contexts.

What Went Well and What Didn't

Our facilitation of key elements of PPed, such as the promotion of opportunities for peer dialogue and purposeful social interaction, created few challenges for us both as the facilitation social learning opportunities reflects existing coaching practices. However, recognising when and how to assist players build their intellectual self-sufficiency was a challenge, especially during the latter part of the season. We believe this to be a result of the pressures of competition involvement and players' expectations about the role of the coach in helping to 'fix mistakes'. Furthermore, when responding to a player's technical weakness our emphasising of what they CAN do often manifested into a somewhat challenging coaching episode, particularly when working with junior players. It was often the case then that each of us would resort to offering specific verbal directions/instructions which in its purest sense overrides the PPed principle of dialogue engagement and question asking. For us as coaches working with modern adolescent players there is an inherent challenge in designing and supporting a development environment that modern adolescent players can relate to and stay committed. We feel, however, that the concept of PPed when used as a framework to coach adolescent cricketers supports our existing commitment to humanistic coaching endeavours (for more on this see the first and second editions of *Positive Pedagogy for sport coaching*).

It is an obvious thing then to say that the key principles that underpin our current coaching practice are neatly aligned to the principles of PPed – but not all. At times finding the right balance between player autonomy and coach encroachment necessitated a not-so-positive learning experience which conflicted with stated principles of PPed (e.g. when determining team selections based on match day coaching strategy). We believe the coveting of such situations (specifically in elite level sport coaching contexts) can be an effective tool for coach/player/organisation development if managed appropriately.

What We Learned about Ourselves as Coaches

Engaging in a season-long conversation framed around the concept of PPed meant an opportunity for serial commitment to coaching practice reflection. We feel our use of PPed to frame our season-long conversation served to heighten our already existing interest in our own pedagogical practice whilst also reinforcing our personal coaching philosophies. With regards to our respective use of PPed:

Kendall: I learnt that the process of introducing more purposeful social interaction opportunities was generally well received by players no matter what their age or length of time playing for the club. When I asked players why they thought I was trialling a new coaching approach the common response received was that I was a coach 'wanting to help us all improve' (Player quote). I also learnt that the most challenging aspect of using PPed over the season related to my often perceived need to effect change swiftly through my 'telling' of players rather than encouraging them to affect their own change through my asking of questions.

Elliot: Throughout the season I became more accustomed to 'catching myself out' when slipping into 'tell' mode. For me this highlighted the occasions when I was not being strong in my commitment to my coaching principles e.g. to be fun, competitive and challenging. In the eyes of many the role of the coach is to plan training sessions, establish behaviours, and set game plans. I see me role as a coach as much more than just these transactional moments. My point here being that as a product of being involved in this season-long conversation I now understand the concept of PPed to mean 'coaching that is transformative' which through its application asks me to be 'braver' in letting players make mistakes to ultimately inform their development.

A Peer Coach Perspective

Nelson et al. (2013) discuss the coaching practice benefits gained from active learning interactions with coaching mentors and fellow coach collaborations. Thus, to offer further insight on our understanding and use of PPed as cricket coaches we shared our conversation with a coaching mentor (Andy) to seek additional perspective on our season-long reflections.

Andy: I have 20 years' experience coaching in a number of cricketing and educational environments. This includes working as a development coach at Yorkshire County Cricket Club and as Academy Director at Leicestershire County Cricket Club. I have also acted as a coach educator on the ECB Level 2 award.

During my 20 years of coaching it has been common practice for cricket coaches to engage with CPD through attendance at the odd course or visiting another sporting organisation. We expect players to improve year by year, week by week, game by game but rarely have I witnessed coaches being prepared to shine the light on themselves in such a serial manner and to reflect, analyse and share their experiences with a colleague in order to be better tomorrow than they were today. To that end I felt that the journey Kendall and Elliot embarked on with regards to their season-long exploration of PPed to enhance their coaching practice has considerable upside.

Challenges I offer both coaches moving forward:

1   How will you both best deliver PPed principles in the aspects of the game which are very technical and individualised, where there is very little scope to view the game as a whole?
2   How might an academy coach in a professional cricket club (often judged on player throughput into the professional game) justify use of PPed to develop players' self-sufficiency capacities within the limited time scales available to them?
3   How are you both going to influence other coaches in your club to embrace principles of PPed to inform their own coaching practices?

What Can We Do in the Future?

From our perspective as cricket coaches, what resonated with us was the potential of PPed to be used to offer broader suggestions about pedagogical offering that coaches could reflect upon e.g. how to view the game-as-a-whole and how not to focus coaching efforts on the fixing of mistakes (Light and Harvey, 2017). As a coaching concept we see potential benefit in fellow cricket coaches reviewing and taking note of what PPed can offer them as coaches just as we have done. It is important to note, however, that this season-long focus on our use of PPed lacked a degree of practice verification. As a result we agree that, despite having access to a coaching peer who offered us an end-of season perspective on our understanding and use of PPed, an on-site coaching peer or mentor able to view and feedback on how we were actioning the concept of PPed 'in real time' would have been beneficial. Furthermore, we learnt that better management of players' expectations about what PPed means and what it can offer them as athletes prior to season start is advisable. Our failure to adequately do this, particularly when liaising with younger players' parents (in an elite programme) and older players (in a village team) meant the occasional stalling of PPed as a coaching concept and time lost through having to reset player expectations.

A full response to the challenges Andy presented to us via his role as our peer coaching mentor is beyond the scope of this chapter, however, we feel compelled to respond to his first challenge in order to showcase how we might coach the technical requirements of cricket through use of PPed. With elements of batting, bowling and fielding in cricket being highly technical we have and will continue to use the following activities to develop players' skills with a game-as-a-whole emphasis:

1.   Setting of scoring zone restrictions for batters during net sessions (e.g. can only score behind square) requiring them to focus on and make constant adjustments to specific shots.
2.   The removal of the off-side netting of the end net to allow fielders to practice aspects of fielding technique and positioning as well as encourage captain-bowler communication with regards to delivery choice and field settings for different game situations.

3.   Getting bowlers to bowl with their front arm pinned to their body as a starting point to help them explore the influence of technique on pace generation. Such activities are accompanied by questions such as 'How did that feel?', 'What effect did this have on your pace?', 'When might a change of pace in a match be effectively utilised?'

Summary

We believe our engagement in a season-long coaching conversation driven by reflection on the key principles of PPed included a range of CPD success elements; namely that the experience was interactive, collaborative, located in practice, self-regulated and informal (Griffiths, Armour and Cushion, 2018; Nash, Sproule and Horton, 2017). Our use of the principles of PPed to inform our development as cricket coaches provided us with an engaging framework to guide our reflection on coaching practice and stimulate engagement with our coach mentor. With existing personal coaching principles already closely aligned to the principles of PPed, our reflections (in addition to comments made by our coach mentor) reveal a growing understanding of PPed and appreciation of its value to coaches in both professional and village cricket contexts.

References

Griffiths, M., Armour, K. and Cushion, C. (2018) 'Trying to get our message across: successes and challenges in an evidence-based professional development programme for sport coaches', *Sport, Education and Society*, 23(3): 283–295.

Light, R. (2017) *Positive Pedagogy for sport coaching: Athlete-centred coaching for individual sports*, London and New York: Routledge.

Light, R. and Harvey, S. (2017) 'Positive Pedagogy for sport coaching', *Sport, Education and Society*, 22(2): 271–287.

Light, R. and Harvey, S. (2019) *Positive Pedagogy for coaching team and individual sports*. London and New York: Routledge.

Nash, C., Sproule, J. and Horton, P. (2017) 'Continuing professional development for sports coaches: A road less travelled', *Sport in Society*, 20(12): 1902–1916.

Nelson, L., Cushion, C. and Potrac, P. (2013) 'Enhancing the provision of coach education: The recommendations of UK coaching practitioners', *Physical Education and Sport Pedagogy*, 18(2): 204–218.

Pill, S. (2018) 'Developing thinking players: A coach's experience with game sense coaching', in S. Pill, ed. *Perspectives on athlete-centred coaching*, London and New York: Routledge, 93–103.

3

APPLYING POSITIVE PEDAGOGY TO A SEASON OF BASKETBALL

Ricardo Pimenta

Without realizing it at the time, my approach to coaching basketball was significantly shaped by one coach in Portugal whose approach had a lot in common with what I now recognise as Positive Pedagogy for sport coaching (PPed). However, my other coaches all had very traditional approaches to the game. Typically, this involved learning the core skills through repetitive drill and then applying them in a practice game. It was always a case of learn the skills first so you can play the game later, which seems to be common theme in traditional coaching (Wormhoudt, Savelsbergh, Teunissen and Davids, 2017). As Light and Harvey (2019: p. 15) suggest, 'traditional approaches tend to feature direct instruction, feedback and demonstrations based upon the assumption that the more the coach intervenes, the more the athletes will improve' and this was my experience in Portugal until I was 16 years of age. This was when I was coached by a Brazilian named Xexeu and whose approach was very different to all my previous coaches. He was always interacting with us, engaging our minds to help us understand the game, creating challenges that we had to work together as a team to overcome and working on our skills. I enjoyed this very much and it made me start to think about becoming a coach so I enrolled in a degree in Sports Sciences.

I began my coaching with an U14 boys B team in Coimbra, the city where I was going to University and, as many starting coaches do, I was coaching the same way that I had been coached by most of my coaches. I was very focused on drilling skills but through my interaction with other coaches, and my exposure to different coaching approaches in my university classes I began to remember how Xexeu coached me when I was a teenager. I started to read more and more about how I could apply game-like situations in my practice and still make my athletes learn valuable skills. I found two major approaches Teaching Games for Understanding (TGfU – see Thorpe, 1990) and Game Sense (GS – see Light, 2013). These two approaches allowed me to experiment with ways that I could give my athletes the experiences Xexeu had given me. That was the year I learned the most about coaching and had the most fun playing basketball. After finishing my undergraduate studies in Sports Sciences, I started a Masters' degree in Youth Sport Coaching that gave me a career-changing opportunity to participate in a two-week intensive program on coaching with three other European Universities, one from France, one from England and one from Bulgaria. And it was here that I first met Richard Light who presented on Game Sense and player-centred coaching in team sports. I had read his GS book and it was a great opportunity to develop even more as a coach.

A few years later I decided to do a PhD with Richard in New Zealand which presented a great chance for me to coach in a foreign country. I studied in New Zealand for four years and coached several different girl's and women's age groups. I coached six school teams, Senior teams, A and B, Intermediate teams and a Year 9 team, Canterbury Representational teams, U17s, the University of Canterbury women's team, 5v5 and 3v3, and even participated in a New Zealand U14 Girls National Talent Camp. Over this time, I worked as a tutor teaching sport pedagogy and was exposed to Richard's work in Positive Pedagogy for sport coaching (see Light and Harvey, 2019), which shaped my thinking about coaching and linked with my early positive experiences of being coached by Xexeu.

This chapter focuses on my most recent season of coaching that was significantly shaped by PPed. Here, I reflect on my experience of coaching my girl's Intermediate private school team and use three activities where I describe how I used features of Positive Pedagogy and how I adapted my approach to the different challenges that my athletes presented to me. I provide examples of how I tackled each drill, and how I helped the learning process of my athletes. Moreover, I will also describe what I believe my athletes response was in terms of their learning, motivation, and feelings (engagement, happiness, frustration, etc.) in the Reflection and Evaluation section.

Context

Through my years interacting with, and working for Richard, I have become much more aware of how I coach, with my coaching style moving progressively toward a complete athlete-centred approach. I'm now much more aware during my practice about the features of Positive Pedagogy, and what I love about this approach is that there is so much more to understand and learn, with the best part being how it encourages me to reflect on my own practice every training session and game.

In the school where I coached, I noticed that coaches across the more important sports such as rowing and netball for girls, in the school were always trying to poach basketball players to play their sport. Although basketball participation rose over the four years I spent at that school, this made it difficult to have a consistent team through the seasons and to have a long-term development plan. Another struggle that I'm sure many other coaches go through either in clubs or schools, is court availability. We were only allowed to train once a week with one game on Friday nights. My team in the year I am focusing on in this chapter was comprised mainly of netball players. I met five of my players in the previous year, but at that time they were being coached by my assistant coach, and our styles were completely different. She would focus a lot on single skill drills without transitioning to a game situation where they could apply those skills, so my approach was different to what my players had been used to and none of my 12 players had any experience of being taught using an athlete-centred and/or inquiry-based approach.

The Season

My usual training session always started with a review of the previous training session or the previous game, if we had one. As most coaches do, I would go around the group asking what they thought about the previous session/game, asking them to provide one positive and something to improve on, without repeating, for the next session/game. I believe this allows players to reflect on their experiences and helps them recognize the areas they need to improve. This approach was difficult for them because it was so different to how they were coached in other sports. They told me their coaches tell them what to do and what to improve in, then they just do what they are told. This was a challenge for the first couple of months in trying to get them to think. It was very frustrating because I felt I wasn't going anywhere, and my questioning wasn't developing their thought process. But in the end, they were actively engaging with each other and accurately analysing their session/game, which encouraged me to keep at it.

I used the activities I describe below to address one of the major problems my team had through the year, which was full court defence and traps. The activities are one of the few I constantly ran throughout the year to develop their court awareness and communication and were influenced by PPed.

Activity 1: 1-on-1 Full Court Defence

I believe that a basketball player has to be able to withstand pressure while carrying the ball up the court. Instead of the usual spread the cones on the floor and making the girls switch direction with a different dribble every time, I put a defender on them straight away to replicate game conditions and ensure they were engaged in awareness and decision-making (Light and Harvey, 2019). I tried to pair them with partners who had the same skill level to do zig-zags full court and finish with a layup. The defence here is just passive and I believe it's a valuable time to teach the defence how to position themselves to make the offensive player switch direction.

Initially I let them do the drill, with not much direction coming from me but would then reduce the space, to about half size of the court, just to create pressure on the ball carrier and make the defenders protect the middle of the court. My goal here was just to get them used to the pressure of having somebody there and to make learning transferrable to the competition game (Jones, 2015). To increase the intensity in the drill, I would ask the defence to play passive up until half-court and from the halfway line 'it's live and we make it a competition to score a lay-up under pressure'. I would always tell the defenders that if they can make the offensive player lose the ball by themselves, just by making them switch directions and using different dribbles all the time, they have done their job. Most of the girls I coached couldn't handle the simple pressure of having a player in front of them in practice at the beginning of the season.

If I have players that can dribble, I usually tell the defence to try to steal the ball when the opportunity presents itself. One of the main issues with using passive defence is the offensive player knows that there is no risk, so they usually stick to the same dribble, usually a crossover, and when it's live they have to use all of their arsenal to beat the defender. Providing the chance to the defender to steal the ball makes the offensive player aware that she has to protect the ball. Here is where I start questioning the offensive player about how to protect the ball, and the defensive player where they want to take the offensive player, to the side line, where they have little space or give them the middle where she has the most space and can see the whole court.

Activity 2: 2-on-2 Full Court Defence with Trap

Transitioning from the previous drill, I kept the space as half side of the court, but I would introduce two extra players, one for offence one for defence, so the pairs stay together. I usually did it with one of the players as the inbounder, (the player who stands outside the court to throw the ball in), either sideline or baseline. The goal here is to try to inbound the ball and score on the other end of the court. The players only have 5 seconds to inbound the ball, and if the ball is inbounded, offence has 8 second to go over half-court. If the defence can stop them, they get a point; if offence scores, they get a point.

The defence here has to communicate and create an opportunity for a trap, which happens when you put a player in a small space where she can't move, and you have two defenders pressuring the ball. But the offensive players also have to create strategies to be able to inbound the ball and quickly progress up the court. Here the same principles that I talked about in the previous activity apply. The defenders have to figure out how to lead the offensive player to the space where she has no room to dribble or pass the ball. In turn, offence has to figure out how to create the space. This is a great opportunity to stop the drill after your players have done it a few times and ask questions or have a break and let them talk about how to overcome the obstacle. Obviously, most of the times this activity is direc-ted towards creating communication between defenders and create an easy still. With more skilled players they are able to break the trap before it sets up, hence the defenders have to work together to be as fast as possible to set up their trap.

If my team was struggling to go past half court, I would use a few techniques to help them understand what is going on. For example, I would widen the space they have to play in or stop the players in action just to ask them or show them physically where they have space or ask them where do they think they can go to create that space. Most of the times the inbounder is completely forgotten and, in my team's case, she would stand outside of the court looking at her teammate forgetting that she is still part of the drill.

Activity 3: 5-on-5 Full Court Defence with or without Traps

Moving on to more of a real game situation, I would tell the defenders that the idea we applied in the previous two exercises are the same. That is, always take the offensive player to a space where she can't move, doesn't have a lot of options and can't see the whole court. They rapidly find that the spots are the corners of the court, the corners between sideline and baseline, and the corner between the sideline and the half-court line. You can create a trap anywhere near a sideline but has stated before the least space the offensive player has to move and make decisions the better it is for the defence.

How to break this full court press with traps is where my team struggled the most throughout the year and is something I had to work on. Defensively, they could understand where to position themselves and how to put the offensive players in a tough position, in part I believe because of their netball training. The issue was when they were on offense. They always tried to break the press by dribbling through the two defenders time and time again. So again, I stopped and took the time to ask questions like 'When does the defence moves to trap you? When you hold the ball or when you dribble?' The answer they usually gave me is when they dribble, which in my view is correct, because that's what usually happens in our games. A few years ago, I probably would have just told them what to do but now know the power of questioning to develop thinking players. The defence pushes the ball carrier to the sideline and the trap happens. Then I would give a follow up question such as, 'So what do we want to do?' and the principles and ideas we talked before would come back into their heads, which is, 'We dribble where we have space, or somebody moves to an open space'. The latter is what I was looking for.

Although they would be able to explain to me how to beat the trap, they couldn't put what they said into practice. This is common when using athlete centred approaches like TGfU and Game Sense where players can typically articulate knowledge before they are able to enact it in games (Light, 2017). They would make the same mistakes over and over again in practice and competition games. For a few weeks I tried to calmly remind them of the principles we were working with, but usually to no avail. Once, we went to a school exchange, where different sports play against the teams of another school, and I got the opportunity to watch one of their netball games. If you don't know what netball is, simply put, it is a game where you have a hoop, with no backboard, that you have to shoot in order to score and you can't dribble the ball at all with all the work done off the ball. In order to score, players need to move around to open spaces to create opportunities and work off the ball. As I expected, their defensive understanding was 'on point' (they knew how to reduce the space for the ball carrier and knew how to cover each other's areas because of their netball training), but offensively there was flow in their movement, that caught me by surprise. On my way home it clicked for me. What if I used the netball movement to make them understand how to beat a trap in basketball? Next training, I implemented that small idea by saying to them, 'Imagine if we are playing netball, the principles are the same on offence, move to open spaces and pass the ball to the open player'. A light seemed to switch on in each of their heads and their movement completely changed. From that week's game on, we started to beat the opposing team's trap to a point where they completely stopped doing it.

The moment they started switching into the mindset that in order to beat full court pressure with traps would be to play as they would in netball, my job became a lot easier. My questioning turned into, 'What would you they do if they were playing netball', and every time my team or the opposition would adjust during the Friday, I would intervene and ask them, what the difference was between netball and basketball. They would remember that they could dribble the ball and from that point onward it opened up more options to explore with them directing their teammates to positions that sometimes I wouldn't even see that it was open. I believe that by understanding to their main sport I was able to apply their invasion game knowledge to basketball. I did this by allowing them to make mistakes and try different options during practice and even games.

Reflection

When I was first introduced to the concept of Positive Pedagogy for sport coaching, I thought I understood it, because of my past experience applying Game Sense and TGfU approaches and how they seemed very similar, but there is a difference. PPed made me realize how much I needed to be able to be flexible with my coaching style and my approach to basketball. My players were mostly netball players, and in New Zealand, it seems that if you are a girl you play netball first and then you can do other sports. In retrospect my biggest mistake was not taking into account their sport experience in general and using it to my advantage. I was sure that it was my coaching that was helping them being good defensively, which in some situations like the 1-on-1 and 2-on-2 was correct. However, with the overall game of 5-on-5, it was their netball experiences that helped them play the game, I think that emphasising the basic concepts common to both sports and linking my coaching and questioning to them mad a big contribution to their learning. Research supports the idea of young people playing different sports, and by doing this it will help them improve their own game (DiFiori et al., 2017). The common tactical problems faced across all invasion games and how this is used in TGfU lends strong support to this (Almond, 1983).

Although all of the girls knew each other, and played netball together, initially I struggled with my questioning of the team. It felt like they were embarrassed to give the wrong answer. Most of the times I would ask the question to the entire group and nobody would give me an answer, which was frustrating. One way I found that worked really well, was having them work in small pairs, I would pull them aside after and ask question and they didn't seem to be afraid to answer. I slowly started to build their confidence. With every good answer, and not necessarily the one I was looking for, I would give them a high-five. As they started to work with more teammates, they began to answer me more and more. By the end of the season we had our Junior South Island Tournament, where we played against teams from all over the South Island, and they were taking over my time-outs. They were calling each other out, helping each other on the court and asking me to give them time on the court to figure what was going on before I ask for a timeout. I felt I had empowered them

Basketball is a game of adjustments (Pimenta, 2019) and you have to coach in a way that prepares the players to be able to adjust in games. Looking back on it now, I believe being able to adjust relates to everything about coaching basketball. It took me a long while to be able to understand that my impact on my basketball players' learning and development of basketball was minimal until I started to relate to their main sport of netball and have them relate to the fundamental tactical concepts that the two sports share. As a coach, my goal is to always make my players better than they were in the beginning of the season so I watched netball games and asked my athletes about terminology that I thought would be relevant and helpful to use when explaining basketball movements to them. The moment I started to do this, our season took a $180°$ turn. There was a lot more interaction between the girls and me, because they started to understand what I meant when explaining basketball movements using netball terms. In my case, with just one training a week and one game, I had to adjust my way of talking to my team, and this boosted their commitment and engagement. I had a few of my athletes come and ask me to correct their shooting form and asking for what to look for when they are training by themselves.

According to Guerreiro and Nordengren (2018), engagement increases when young people have fun doing any type of activity, and also their interest about sport increases with the more fun they have. Drawing on Seligman's PERMA model, Light and Harvey (2019) suggest in sport engagement occurs when people see an activity worthy of emotional, physical and intellectual commitment. My players' engagement made me realise that the time I spent learning about their main sport seemed to be well worth it. I believe that in the end they were more interested in continuing to play basketball than they were at the beginning of the season, with some of them telling me they were going to make a team and play basketball in the summer and possibly play club basketball the following year.

Despite of many ups and downs during this last season for me at the school, overall, I believe that the humanistic side of Positive Pedagogy helped me tremendously this season to develop better relationships with my athletes and to be able to better understand their learning and experiences of practice. I saw my 'athletes as thinking, feeling humans with a life outside of their sport that has an influence on how they practise and perform in competition' (Light and Harvey, 2019, p.4). I took the time to understand their thought process, by talking and questioning them individually and as a group, but also trying to understand how I could help them incorporate their understanding of invasion games from their main sport netball to basketball. It took some time and it was hard to learn a terminology for a new sport all together and use effectively in training and games, but in the end, it was well worth it because it made them that more engaged and waiting to learn more which I believe to be one of the core principles for Positive Pedagogy.

References

Almond, L. (1983) 'Games making', *Bulletin of Physical Education*, 19(1), 32–35.

DiFiori, J. P., Brenner, J. S., Comstock, D., Côté, J., Güllich, A., Hainline, B. and Malina, R. (2017) 'Debunking early single sport specialisation and reshaping the youth sport experience: An NBA perspective', *British Journal of Sports Medicine*, 51(3), 142–143. doi:10.1136/bjsports-2016-097170

Guerreiro, M. and Nordengren, C. (2018) '"No fun games": Engagement effects of two gameful assessment prototypes', *Journal of Research on Technology in Education*, 50(2), 134–148.

Jones, E. (2015) 'Transferring skill from practice to the match in rugby through Game Sense', *Healthy + Active magazine*, 22(2/3), 56–58.

Light, R. L. (2013) *Game Sense: Pedagogy for performance, participation and enjoyment*, London and New York: Routledge.

Light, R. L. (2017) 'Positive Pedagogy for sports coaching: The influence of positive psychology', in *Positive psychology in sport and physical activity*, London and New York: Routledge, 193–203.

Light, R. and Harvey, S. (2019) *Positive Pedagogy for sport coaching* (2nd edn), London and New York: Routledge.

Pimenta, R. (2019) 'High school girls' basketball', in R. Light and S. Harvey, *Positive Pedagogy for sport coaching* (2nd edn), London and New York: Routledge, 107–111.

Thorpe, R. (1990) 'New directions in games teaching', in N. Armstrong (ed.) *New directions in physical education*, Leeds, UK: Human Kinetics, 79–100.

Wormhoudt, R., Savelsbergh, G. J., Teunissen, J. W. and Davids, K. (2017) *The athletic skills model: Optimizing talent development through movement education*, London and New York: Routledge.

4

COACHING BASEBALL WITH POSITIVE PEDAGOGY

Clayton Kuklick

My interests with teaching and learning as they relate to coaching are derived from my parents being physical education teachers and coaches. Their careers in physical education and coaching began in the early 1970s, where they taught physical education at the K-12 and collegiate level for more than 30 years and was supplemented with youth, interscholastic, and collegiate level coaching. I was brought up in an environment where my parents used a variety of pedagogical approaches that promoted learning through games and by doing, while empowering creativity, decision making, reflection, and critical thinking abilities in respect to developing sport skills and engaging physical activity. Such games included, wall ball, 3-way run the bases, tag games, half ball, 3 v 2 stick ball, and other games that we made up on our own and which would take too long to describe. Needless to say, they have had a big influence on my approach to coaching

After playing interscholastic football, baseball, and basketball, I went on to play collegiate baseball with a brief stint at the professional level and from there, really focused on coaching baseball. Because of my passion for sport and previous experiences that encouraged me to think about teaching and learning, I enrolled in and acquired a bachelor's degree in elementary education with a minor in sport pedagogy, a master's degree of education in kinesiology, and then a PhD in pedagogy. This formal education has afforded me a breadth of knowledge pertaining to teaching, coaching, and learning that has also helped me as a coach.

The Context

During my higher education, I was actively coaching at the collegiate level, during which I had noticed that many of the pedagogical research that were being presented in courses regarding best practices for facilitating skill development, creativity, problem solving abilities, decision making and empowerment in athletes, did not necessarily 'jive' with the traditionally used college baseball coaching practices that I was involved in. Typically, the flow of practice sessions would involve five sets of five or eight swings for batting practice, while pitchers were doing their drill work and bull pens. Then, off to a defensive individual period, which would encompass a series of daily rotating drill sets for all players depending on their position. This was usually followed up by team defense, which also involved a set of revolving team drills that presented different tactical scenarios practiced in a drill like fashion. Finally, practice was concluded with some sort of conditioning that involved baserunning technique and tactics.

Regardless of the team I was coaching at the time, through my observations, I kept seeing similar coaching problems. Specifically, I saw athletes struggling to be motivated, learn different hitting, fielding, and pitching techniques and tactics needed for competition, transfer confidence at practice onto the field, and make decisions in various scenarios. Watching their on-field play I also noticed how they operated like a group of individuals instead of as a team and had problems with decision-making. These were all issues that were identified as potentially being solved with game-based approaches (GBA) I was exposed to in class and through my readings of Game Sense and Positive Pedagogy for sport coaching.

As part of my education, I had been introduced to GBA like Game Sense that teach techniques and tactics in and through games and emphasize questioning to produce thinking players (den Duyn, 1997). The literature I read suggested that they could yield more positive outcomes for athletes in comparison to traditional approaches to coaching baseball I had been involved with as an assistant coach. My introduction to Positive Pedagogy for sport coaching (PPed) extended these ideas beyond team games to individual sports and to coaching technique, and skill (Light and Harvey, 2017). PPed also seemed to encourage other positive effects beyond improving technical and tactical skills and paid attention to how to make learning positive. PPed and GBA seemed to be able to enhance athletes' creativity, empowerment, motivation, problem solving capacities, and reflective abilities (Cassidy and Kidman, 2010; Light, Harvey and Mouchet, 2014; Mitchell, Oslin and Griffin, 1995). As I reflected on my early experiences of playing sport, I came to feel that the environments these approaches created seemed very similar to my early enjoyment of sport.

Learning by playing creative games that changed time and space and required problem solving, free of coach surveillance and over-controlling 'helicopter coaching' when it came to physical activity and sports, appealed to me. It reminded me of the pleasure I had playing sport and games when younger and motivated me to try to use it in my baseball coaching. However, the challenge for implementing a game sense approach was that baseball is a start and stop type sport. It does not have the flow of other team sports like soccer, lacrosse, and basketball, but I was determined to see how it would work in baseball and took on the challenge of moving away from 'helicopter coaching', towards a PPed approach. In the remainder of this chapter, I describe how I attempted to implement a PPed approach to coaching baseball.

The Season

Prior to the season, I had been exploring the concepts of PPed to help construct games to be used in practice sessions for a baseball team I was an assistant coach for. Fundamental to Positive Pedagogy and Game Sense are manipulations of time and space, using constraints or rules to create challenges, and using questioning to facilitate collaboration and problem solving to overcome barriers faced out in the field of competition (Grant, 2011; Light, 2014; Light and Harvey, 2017). I was not sure how to apply games in the context of practicing and teaching baseball skills but, my knowledge of effective teaching and coaching practices told me to start with some objectives. So, I started with one main offensive objective and one main defensive objective, and then developed the game around them. The main focus was to ensure the objectives were accomplished by engaging my athletes in challenges and providing opportunities for them to collaborate in problem solving, while keeping them on task in order to create deep and meaningful learning experiences. I was aware of how PPed encourages the coach to design and develop challenges the players must meet individually and as a team, and how the coach should adjust the level of challenge to produce flow. I soon came to realize, after the implementation of the first game, that I could change the rules daily or regularly to meet new objectives and therefore create new challenges for athletes to collaboratively solve. I looked to create a foundational game from which multiple objectives could be accomplished depending on athletes' needs, while keeping positive pedagogy and a learner-centered approach in mind. The game was called 'Racing for Runs and Outs', which utilized many Positive Pedagogy features. The offensive objective for the first game that we implemented in practice sessions was to facilitate the hitter's successful instances and abilities to hit with teammates in scoring position, while the defensive objective was to enhance the effectiveness of ball exchanges amongst players as it would relate to double plays and relays.

The foundational components of the game were that it comprised of playing with whiffle balls and regular bats, in a 5 v 5 timed game set up, which allowed for multiple games to be played at once. It was played on an open-ended triangle, where the foul lines from home plate made-up the boundaries that extended out to about 85 feet. The pitching area was about 40 feet from home plate and pitchers threw to a square box that indicated a strike. The game was 16 minutes in duration, where each side received 8 minutes to score (i.e., offensive team) or acquire outs (i.e., defensive team) before switching roles. At the four-minute mark of each eight-minute half, I offered questions on note cards to prompt tactical thinking and collaboration on problems faced by each team. The team with the most totaled amount of runs and outs, which were dependent on the offensive and defensive objectives in the 16 minutes, won the contest. As another fundamental rule to the game, the defenders were allowed to be stationed out in the field in any set up they chose as long as it was behind the pitcher, and they always needed to have a ball in their throwing hand. The purpose of this was for defensive players to engage tasks that were counted as outs depending on the defensive objective. In contrast, the hitters scored by accomplishing tasks that depended on the offensive objective.

As I have mentioned, the offensive and defensive objectives dictated how to score runs and get outs. The defensive team acquired outs by fielding a struck whiffle ball and then making 4 successful throws to other defensive players regardless of where they were positioned as if in a relay or double play. To accomplish this, remember from the foundational rules I discussed in the previous paragraph, that all defensive players had a regular ball in their throwing hand, while keeping their glove hand free to field or catch balls. In this process, the athletes strategized with pitchers on where to throw pitches in locations to accomplish ground balls, while the defense worked to set up accordingly. I facilitated these collaborations with the questions I had created for the four-minute intermissions but, the athletes soon realized that they were able to strategize and work together on the fly, unprompted by me as the coach. For hitters, line drives and grounded balls past the pitcher were the only ways to score runs, which would be the case in a true baseball game with teammates on second and third base. In some cases, if a ball went through the infield, but was fielded cleanly by an outfielder and was accompanied by 4 additional throws to teammates as in a relay or double play, it resulted in an out for the defensive team and a run for the offensive team. The defensive rules prompted athletes to exchange balls with teammates from various angles, distances, arm angles, and speeds, which I found to engage quite a bit of creativity while also improving throwing accuracy, reaction time, and decision making. Fly balls counted as neither a run or an out, which helped ensure that pitchers were pitching to get ground balls to acquire outs in collaboration with how their defense was set up, while offensive players were using bat control and coordination to hit ground balls and line drives to spaces where defenders were vacant. The fly ball rule of neither counting as a run or out also kept the game moving because athletes wanted to get the ball back to the pitcher promptly in order to have more chances of acquiring outs.

In order to increase time on task, I added a few other rules to keep the multiple games of 5 v 5 rolling. The time constraints on the game kept the pace moving, while unlike the actual rules of baseball, this changed the game from a race to scoring more runs in unlimited time until 27 outs are accomplished, to a race against time with an unlimited number of ways to accomplish outs or score runs. The thought was, the more runs and outs, the better. So, the longer it took athletes to get whiffle balls back to the pitcher, the less time they had to accomplish outs. Also, to keep the game moving, each at bat for offensive players were two pitches, where walks were considered a run if the pitcher threw two back to back misses to the square net target that acted as the strike zone. For offensive players, swings and misses or taking a strike yielded an out. The pitchers were allowed to pitch in any sequence they wanted, which dictated some of the different strategies they sought to use as a defensive team to get outs as the offensive players strategized to acquire runs.

Evaluation and Reflection

I started with this initial game which soon evolved into addressing other offensive and defensive objectives beyond the one's described in this chapter. Some of those objectives which focused on how to score runs included: two strike hitting, opposite way hitting, pull side hitting, hitting with runners on first base, 2–0 count hitting, or off-speed hitting. Some of the defensive objectives which focused on how to get outs required communicating amongst teammates, catching and fielding backhands or forehands, setting up double relays, or charging balls vs. moving backward to track down balls.

One challenge I faced was that it took a bit of time for the athletes to learn new rules when there were such drastic rule changes, and therefore would get caught up in the rules rather than experiencing the game. So, I tried to keep some of the basic rules as consistent as possible so that athletes were familiar with them. Those rules being, using whiffle balls and ensuring all defensive players had a ball in their throwing hand. Other consistent rules included two pitch at bats, a run for two back to back misses by the pitcher, and outs acquired for swings and misses, and taken strikes. In this way, some of the components of the game stayed consistent so that the athletes were able to focus on problem solving and strategizing. For example, when the defensive objective was for athletes to work on backhands, the rule for getting outs was for defensive players to cleanly field a backhand. I was amazed at how the players were able to be creative with their bodies to get into positions for backhanding balls even if normally it would have been easier to field a ball as a forehand. While some of the foundational rules stayed consistent, I would change the duration of the games from 16 minutes to 10 or eight minutes on occasion depending on what the objectives were, and other times, changed the shape of the field by making it more narrow or wide to create other challenges for athletes to solve. This is obviously a case of not only using the PPed coach's toolbox to modify game to create particular challenges as problems to be solved but also of tuning into athlete progress and learning (Light and Harvey, 2017). The challenge for me was thinking about how these games would work during my pre-practice planning to ensure they would go smoothly out on the field.

I found that pre-planning these games to create changes in the ways of scoring runs and outs quite invigorating due to being challenged to think creatively and the problem solving that I needed to engage in as a coach. I enjoyed meeting the challenge of creating novel and innovative strategies that I had never seen before in baseball coaching practices. As much as I enjoyed these thinking processes needed to create the games, I found that at times, there was conflict between my inner traditional baseball coaching voice saying, 'You can't have athletes do that' and my Positive Pedagogy voice saying, 'Why can't athletes explore these things? Why not?' At first, the athletes seemed to be bewildered by the bit of novelty as well. However, after more consistent engagement in the games, they seemed to come to life with energy, creativity, and teamwork. As Light and Harvey (2019) warn, it takes time for coaches and players to adapt to PPed.

One last reflection on implementing Positive Pedagogy would be that, although I mentioned the invigorating feeling from creating new ways of thinking about and coaching baseball, it was quite a challenge once the game was implemented, in some practice sessions, to just let the athletes play the game and try out new things.

A part of me kept wanting to tell them what to do and when to do it when the games were being played, rather than letting them explore, make mistakes, and do things that normally wouldn't be done in any of our traditional drills. This also involved setting up and maintaining an environment that supported taking risks and accepting that making mistakes is part of learning. For example, in some of the games, athletes might have explored throwing from different arm angles or underhand from throw to throw, which traditionally in baseball coaching, would probably be a big no-no. So, this took quite a bit of effort at first to not jump in to tell them to use the same throwing motion or correct them on keeping their arm up, rather than thinking there is quite a bit of value in practicing multiple arm actions as it would occur in different competition scenarios. From my under-standing, this is when good questioning is so important in PPed from which I really focused on constructing solid questions to prompt athletes to think about their movements and experimentation with different ways of moving in order to overcome subtle problems out in the field. I used these questions to prompt indi-vidual athletes as the games were going on, and also for their own collaboration during the four-minute intermissions where athletes strategized with their team-mates on adjustments to be made during the game.

In my own experiments with questioning athletes, I have found that, almost equally as important as asking good questions, is allowing time for athletes to think about them and work through problems to come up with responses. I found in my early experiences with questioning, I would often answer for the athletes if they didn't know, rather than having them experiment or try to figure out a response on their own. In other cases, I would ask more questions before other questions were even responded to or realized. In some of the first games I had implemented, I had spent so much time thinking about the rules to 'Racing Runs and Outs', that I almost forgot about engaging athletes with high quality questions that prompted them to go explore and find out, rather than me telling. In hindsight, with the Positive Pedagogy approach I was using, I felt I was spending a majority of my time planning and less coaching on the field because I wasn't constantly telling what and how to do. However, this planning to create challenges, explorations, and problem solving through collaboration in practice activities, goes hand in hand with PPed and athlete-centered approaches to coaching. It is an approach where athletes learn by doing and trying on their own. I am glad that, in this chapter, I was able to share my experience of implementing a PPed approach in coaching baseball with all the challenges I faced and the satisfaction of seeing such positive results.

References

Cassidy, T. and Kidman, L. (2010) 'Initiating a national coaching curriculum – A paradig-matic shift?' *Physical Education and Sport Pedagogy*, 15(1), 307–322.

den Duyn, N. (1997) *Game Sense: Developing thinking players.* Canberra: Australian Sports Commission.

Grant, A. M. (2011) 'The solution-focused inventory: A tripartite taxonomy for teaching, measuring and conceptualizing solution focused approaches to coaching', *The Coach Psychologist*, 7(2), 98–105.

Light, R. L. (2014) 'Learner-centered pedagogy for swim coaching: A complex learning theory informed approach', *Asia-Pacific Journal of Health, Sport and Physical Education*, 5(2), 167–180.

Light, R. L. and Harvey, S. (2017) 'Positive Pedagogy for sport coaching', *Sport, Education, and Society*, 22(2), 271–287.

Light, R. L. and Harvey, S. (2019) *Positive Pedagogy for sport coaching* (2nd edn), London and New York: Routledge.

Light, R. L., Harvey, S. and Mouchet, A. (2014) 'Improving "at-action" decision-making in team sports through a holistic coaching approach', *Sport, Education and Society*, 19, 258–275.

Mitchell, S. A., Oslin, J. L. and Griffin, L. L. (1995) 'The effects of two instructional approaches on game performance', *Pedagogy in Practice – Teaching and Coaching in Physical Education and Sports*, 1(1), 36–48.

5

FOOTBALL IN A JAPANESE WOMEN'S UNIVERSITY

Richard Light

In this chapter I reflect on a coaching session I conducted in a Japanese women's university, late in 2019. While in Tokyo at Waseda University, I was invited by Sonoda Women's University in Amagasaki (near Kobe in the Kansai region) to run a seminar on Positive Pedagogy for sport coaching as an example of an athlete centred approach to coaching. I did a workshop on football for a little over an hour that I followed with a ninety-minute lecture on athlete-centred coaching, focused on PPed. Two years prior to this visit I did a workshop on basketball at the same university but none of the girls who participated in that basketball session were at the session I did on football this time.

The Context

I conducted the one-hour football (soccer) workshop I reflect on here with female university students and followed it with a 90-minute lecture to about 80 students and staff. As I have noted in other chapters where I reflect on one-off PPed workshops, the context is very different to coaching a regular team. In these workshops I do not know the participants and they do not know me. With no significant knowledge of what the team or group is like, their experience in, and knowledge of, the sport, their dispositions to the sport, or to student or athlete centred teaching/coaching. I am usually 'going in cold'.

Having coached rugby in Japan, I am familiar with coaching in Japan but working in a culture that is different to your own always requires sensitivity and being prepared, and able, to adapt. Even working with New Zealand under-graduate students at The University of Canterbury is different for me when compared to working with Australian undergraduate students and required a little adjustment. Sport coaching and physical education teaching in Japan tends to follow a traditional focus on skill and technique with a strong emphasis on repetition and using direct instruction. Two years prior to this session I write on here, I ran a workshop on basketball at the same university and it went very well. It had flow, high energy and was so enjoyable for the girls that a few young female teachers who were watching tapped a couple of the girls on the shoulder so that they (the teachers) could participate. According to a staff member I communicated with later, the girls loved it, but some senior teachers felt it was poor teaching and not what the students should be exposed to. This was disappointing, but not surprising for me and gives an indication of the school context and of some of the culture of sport in Japanese schools. For more insight into this issue and others please see an article I wrote with a Japanese colleague on girls' basketball in a Japanese high school (Light and Yasaki, 2016).

Twenty-six female university students from first year to third year volunteered to participate in the football workshop I write about in this chapter. None of them were in the school soccer club with most of them from the university basketball club. As I noted, I did not know any of the participants and had no real idea of their skills and other abilities in football until beginning the session, but they were all very enthusiastic and a pleasure to work with.

The Session

For this workshop I drew on four activities from my Game Sense book (Light, 2013, pp. 118–133) that I organised to provide a progression from simple to complex and from a high success rate to more challenging tasks and games. I conducted the entire session on a basketball court and in two of these activities I manipulated the space available to increase pressure and raise the level of challenge that is encouraged in PPed (see, Light and Harvey, 2019). The activities used were: 1) Dribbling in traffic, 2) multi-goal passing; 3) pass and run and 4) four goal football.

1 Dribbling in Traffic

I often use the activity, 'dribbling in traffic' for demonstrating how to use PPed when coaching football and basketball to develop dribbling technique in contexts that replicate elements of game conditions to assists in the transfer of technique and skill at practice to the real game. To begin, I had the girls pick up a ball each and dribble within half the basketball court while exploring as much space as possible. I asked them to cover as much ground as possible while avoiding making contact with anyone else and having their ball touch anyone else's ball while staying within the half court.

Understandably, all the girls started slowly with limited engagement and movement because of their lack of familiarity with the activity. I verbally encouraged them to cover as much ground as they could and to pick up the pace and after about two to three minutes there was much more energy and movement. I also stopped them to ask what technique they could use to improve control of the ball such as which side of their feet and how far away from their feet should the ball should be? After about five minutes I asked them (shouted out) to 'freeze' and then asked them what they were looking for and what they were thinking about when doing this activity. There was a little hesitancy, but one girl said she was looking out for other people to avoid bumping into them. I then asked them, 'When you saw, or sensed, someone who you might bump into, where did you move to?' 'What were you looking for?' With a little prodding I got the answer I was after, which is, 'into space'. I would have focused a little on dribbling technique here if I had the time but wanted to get through four activities in around an hour. For this reason, I kept my focus on them being aware of space opening and closing in a dynamic environment and dribbling the ball into it.

Next, I stepped up the complexity by putting them in pairs with one ball per pair. I had one dribbling, as they had been doing, with the other acting as a shadow trailing them about a metre behind. They did this for a couple of minutes and then swapped roles. I then asked the shadow to follow as they had before, but to sometimes move up the right or left shoulder of the dribbler who, as soon as they picked up the shadow being on their shoulder in their peripheral vision, had to move the ball away from the 'defender'. This introduced more for the player with the ball to be aware of and react to while practising dibbling. It also makes the physical environment more complex and dynamic. Once I felt they were all handling this activity well I reduced the space available to them down to about ¾ of the half court they had been working in. I waited until I thought they had adjusted to this reduction in space then reduced it further to about ¼ of the court. It was messy to start with, but I could see and feel the lift in concentration among them all as they responded to the extra pressure and began to re-establish flow and movement but reducing the space any more would have seen the activity break down. I then called them all in ('shugo') to ask them how they felt when I reduced the space and prodded by asking them what changed. One girl said that she had to concentrate more as it became more challenging to which I then asked them all, 'do you remember what you were thinking about?' There was no reply, but quite a few looked like they were trying to remember. A few suggested it increased their concentration and immersion in the activity.

2 Multi-goal

For activity 2 I had the class form new pairs but still with a ball between them. With 13 pairs I set out 11 goals using large cones, using the full basketball court. The aim of this game is to score goals by having the partner in possession push the ball between the two cones with his/her partner taking control of the ball on the other side of the goal. I set up two goals fewer (11) than pairs of players because I wanted there to be competition for available goals that would demand awareness and effective decision-making. The player who just passed then runs to another goal to receive the ball while the one who just received the ball now has possession and must go to the same goal to push the ball though. This activity is designed to improve passing and controlling the ball but while also improving awareness, decision-making and communication. I let the girls play this game for a minute or two to get a feel for it then told them I would be giving them three seconds in which to score as many goals as possible. After each round I would ask what scores they had by asking for hand up for whatever score I called out. They did two rounds after which I gave them time for a quick team talk (in pairs) to refine their technique and tactics and to do three more rounds. They then changed partners and I suggested they could draw on good ideas from the previous pairing. They then did another three rounds to finish the activity, after which I called them all in to form a circle in which they share their learning and what tactics and/or techniques worked for them.

3 Pass and Run Five

For activity three, the girls changed partners to continue working in pairs and using the full court to build on the previous passing activity. This activity develops passing, receiving and controlling the ball as well as awareness, anticipation and communication with its main focus on the need for players to think and move immediately after passing the ball in all invasion games. They had to pass ball at least five metres to their partner and then run at least five metres away from where they had been to receive the pass from their partner. As they adjusted to the game the pace of play picked up and after a few minutes I called 'freeze'. I asked them what they were looking for when running after passing the ball and was happy to get quite a few girls shout out, 'space!' Reminding them about how crowded it was and how much movement there was, I asked how the receiver could help their partner see when they have found space to which one answered, 'call out'. I then encouraged the receivers to shout out loudly when they have found space and are open for a pass. This brief intervention made a big difference with the energy level going up and with a lot of enthusiastic and positive shouting.

Next, I introduced timing them for 30 seconds during which they had to complete as many passes as they could to increase intensity, concentration and motivation. After three rounds I had them change partners and, as performance and understanding increased, I asked questions about how they could improve their scores such as by one-touch passing if they could, putting the ball in front of the partner and to where s/he is running instead of where s/he is, and even leading the receiver into space. I then reduced the area they were operating in down to ¾ of the court like I had in activity 1 with the same response of an initial loss of flow but with adjustment after a couple of minutes and what looked and felt like increased concentration and engagement. This was a very lively activity with a lot of movement shouting, excitement and enthusiasm.

4 Four Goal Football

For the final activity we moved to playing a modified practice game. I divided the players into three teams that I rotated every five minutes with the team off the pitch, watching their next opponent, discussing tactics and developing a plan. We played 'four goal football' on a full basketball court using a goal made with large cones on each side of the court and no goalies. When a goal is scored there is no stopping and the game continues with whoever has possession, but s/he cannot score in the same goal. The conceptual challenge of not having fixed direction meant there was a slow start to the game, but the pace and engagement increased as the game progressed, and the girls adjusted to it. I gave the two teams for the first game a minute or two to get a feel for the game and then two minutes to discuss the game and develop some tactics before starting the first five-minute game.

The team waiting on the sideline to play knew which team they would be facing in the second game so, at the completion of the first game I gave the team staying on the court and the team that had been watching time for a two-minute team talk and started the second game. I did not have to interfere in these discussions as there was plenty of lively discussion with all involved with a high energy game following. I was running out of time but squeezed in one last game. I didn't have time for more team talks but, although they would have been useful, they did not really need them. I only had a little over an hour and wanted to squeeze in four activities which did not really give me enough time with each activity, but I was really surprised at how well the girls adapted to the game and the PPed approach. They really seemed to enjoy this game and to be able to transfer and apply learning from the previous activities.

Reflections and Evaluation

This chapter is one of three in this book conducted in Asian settings, with all of them inviting attention to the influence of culture on learning and coaching or teaching, but particularly when the coach or teacher is from outside that culture. I wrote this chapter and Chapter 12 as reflections on my experience of using PPed in Asian settings and as a non-Asian. Chapter 17 was written on the experiences of teaching rock climbing teaching in Singapore but, by a native Singaporean. In Chapter 13, I identify a range of problems I faced teaching javelin to secondary school students in a Singapore school, which usefully highlights how culture and institutional context can influence learning and require adaptation but my experience of coaching female university students in Japan did not present any of these problems. Indeed, it was one of the most enjoyable coaching sessions I have done for some time.

There was a little bit of hesitancy when answering my questions during the all-group sessions when transitioning from activity to activity, but it did not present a problem for me and discussions during the 'team talks' were very active, positive and productive. This was particularly the case when we moved from working in pairs to working in teams of seven. Had I provided myself with the time to have more team meetings during the four-goal football game I am confident that discussion and interaction would have been even more vibrant and productive.

Like my last visit to this school two years prior to this workshop, I was struck by how quickly the girls adapted to being empowered and how they embraced and ran with this freedom of movement and empowerment. As I have suggested before, girls seem to adapt to and embrace the social interaction and collaboration involved in GBA such as Game Sense (Light and Kentel, 2010), with this workshop lending support to this for me. I should however, recognize how these girls were undergraduate university students who enjoyed sport and volunteered to take part in the workshop, which would have made a significant contribution to their positive attitude and enjoyment. Once the girls adapted to the pedagogy I was using and the session gained momentum the girls' enjoyment develop at the same pace as a sign of good engagement and the positive emotions PPed seeks to encourage.

As a final reflection, I comment on my attention to technique and skill in this session. The relationship between coaching technique or skill (technique in context) and tactics is often a problem for coaches who can sometimes feel it is a case of tactics versus technique when in fact, they are interrelated. As has been noted many times in the coaching and PE teaching literature, knowing *how* to perform a technique is of little use without knowing *when* and *why* to execute it. Likewise, knowing *when* to execute a technique and *why* is of little help in game if the player does not know *how*. As the girls were not basketball players and I had limited time available, I did not pay much attention to technique, apart from asking a few questions aimed at having them think about aspects of technique. With more time available I would have paid more attention to technique for each of the first three activities in particular and my lack of specific attention to technique should not be misinterpreted as de-emphasising the importance of technique. One of the advantages PPed has over the range of GBA such as TGfU is how it can be used to focus on technique without abandoning an athlete-centred approach as is so clear in the reflections on coaching individual sports in Part II. In PPed, when a coach wants to work on a specific technique s/he does not have to leave the game or game-like contexts and revert to decontextualized 'skill drill'. Instead, s/he narrows the focus while retaining enough of the game context to retain the need for, and development of, awareness and some decision-making (see Light, 2017).

I really enjoyed this session and was very happy with how it progressed, the positive emotions of the girls and how quickly they learned. However, if I did it again, I would change the number of activities to give me more time for each activity than I had. I would probably omit the dribbling activity to focus on passing leading into the four goal football game. This would mean beginning with 'multi-goals' as an activity that allows for a low pressure, high success rate activity. I would then take it up a step by moving onto 'pass and run five' and give myself time to experiment with reducing space to raise the level of challenge before shifting up to the modified game that I would have more time to develop.

References

Light, R. L. (2013) *Game Sense: Pedagogy for performance, participation and enjoyment*, London and New York: Routledge.

Light, R. L. (2017) *Positive Pedagogy for sport coaching: Athlete centred coaching for individual sports*, London and New York: Routledge.

Light, R. and Harvey, S. (2019) *Positive Pedagogy for coaching team and individual sports*, London and New York: Routledge.

Light, R. and Kentel, J. A. (2010) 'Soft pedagogy for a hard sport: Disrupting hegemonic masculinity in high school rugby through feminist-informed pedagogy', in M. Kehler, and M. Atkinson (eds) *Boys' bodies*, New York: Peter Lang Publishers, 133–154.

Light, R. L. and Yasaki, W. (2016) 'The nature of experience and learning for Japanese girls in a high school basketball club', in O. Vors, and D. Kirk (eds) Special Issue on *L'écologie de la classe: approches contextualisées en éducation physique et en sport* [The ecology of the class: Contextualised approaches in physical education and sport], *Recherches & Educations*, 15, June, 51–68.

6

ENHANCING ENJOYMENT THROUGH POSITIVE PEDAGOGY, WEARABLE TECHNOLOGY AND FLOW

Michael Sup

High school sports are an integral part of the youth sporting experience in the United States and serve as a platform with many benefits such as improved academic achievement and self-esteem, and enhanced physical and mental health (Brant, Johnson and Brou, 2019). While the benefits of youth sport participation are positive, there are also negative aspects that are seldom discussed in a similar regard (Coakley, 2011; Eley and Kirk, 2002). Some research shows that high school sports can prove to be a problematic space in youth development, such as with an over-emphasis on competition, high rates of overuse and overtraining injuries, and negative relationships between players and coaches (Côté, Lidor and Hackfort, 2009) but PPed has the potential to redress many of these problems (Light and Harvey, 2019). In this chapter I reflect on how, as an assistant soccer coach at a US high school, I drew on PPed to make learning positive but in combination with the use of wearable technology. What probably sounds like an odd combination, contributed to a shift from the traditional ways in which team had been coached toward a more game-based and athlete-centered approach that provided positive experiences for the young athletes, and in which the use of wearable technology was central to its success.

Context

As a young soccer player in the UK, my experiences as an athlete were subdued by coach-centered playing environments. Given the authoritarian style of coaching I was regularly exposed to, I suffered immensely from a fear of failure that ultimately pushed me to quit sports participation altogether by the age of 18. Determined to maintain my involvement in soccer, I embarked on my coaching journey. In the beginning, I was determined to not be like my coaches, but I seemed to carry forth some aspects of their coaching style into my own, without being aware of it at the time. For example, I believed that for my sessions to be successful, I needed to be in control of every element of the practice. The session content usually centered around technical drills that isolated skill development in a structured and disciplined manner. This is how I was formally taught to play soccer, and I was replicating what and how I had previously been taught, which seems to be a common phenomenon for new coaches (Harvey, Cushion and Massa-Gonzalez, 2010).

As a young soccer coach in the UK, I was fortunate enough to experience (and survive) some key learning opportunities that highlighted the differences between coach–centered and player–centered environments. These experiences exposed me to multiple elements of PPed that focused my attention on developing the skills to create a 'learner-centered environment'. This included the ability to facilitate active learning and deep understanding among athletes, as well as creating environments that made learning authentic and meaningful (Light and Harvey, 2017). I was fortunate to have held roles in prestigious soccer environments such as Manchester United FC and Luton Town FC alongside my full-time studies in sports management at the University of Bedfordshire. These formative years sharpened my awareness and ability to deliver an athlete-centred, game-based coaching approach like PPed through this combination of both applied and theoretical settings.

After completion of my bachelor's degree in the UK, I was a awarded a graduate assistant position at Ohio University while completing a master's degree in Coaching Education where I was exposed to PPed in a more rigorous academic setting. This qualification led to a full-time coaching role at a youth soccer club in New York City before returning to graduate school to complete a Ph. D in Ohio University's College of Education in 2019. Today my coaching and teaching is wholeheartedly committed to embracing multiple elements of PPed and this chapter will focus on my application of what I had learned about PPed, to coaching a small high school youth soccer team in Southeastern Ohio.

At the beginning of my Ph.D. studies in 2015, I accepted a role as a volunteer assistant coach of this third division high school soccer team. The team had limited expectations for their season, and I was given a certain amount of freedom and flexibility from the head coach to 'do as I please' when coaching the team. My vision for how to train them was to provide an experience the players had not had before in their high school sporting careers by embracing components of PPed. I was determined to give them ownership of their practices, encourage them to make decisions in forms of play that both developed their tactical understanding of the sport and their overall fun and engagement.

The Season

During pre-season with this team we had the opportunity to try out some heart rate monitoring technology and decided to have the players wear the belts when completing a running fitness test. The test we had the team complete was the 'Vameval Run Test'. This test takes place on a 400-meter athletics track and is designed to push the athletes to achieve their maximal aerobic speed and VO2

Max. Without the support of a sport scientist on site, we simply took note of the maximum heart rate the players achieved having completed the test and how much time the players spent working above 80 percent of their max heart rate.

Two days later, we returned and ran a full practice on the field, which gave us another opportunity to use the heart rate monitors we had previously used for the Vameval Run Test. In one of the practice segments we played a 2 vs. 2 game for approximately 20 minutes in a 20 x 30-meter square. The players worked in a 1–3 work/rest ratio and when it was their turn, the game was continuous for 45 seconds. This meant that if the ball went out of play then another ball was served in immediately to maintain the flow of the game for the full 45 seconds. Additionally, before starting their turn, the players responded to stimuli and completed a short agility and speed run before then engaging in the 2 vs. 2 opposed game.

Post practice, we had a look at the heart rate data for the team and were stunned to see how high the players' heart rates were during the 2 vs. 2 activity. At this time, we did not plan to make any direct comparisons between the players heart rate responses for the Vameval Run Test and the 2 vs. 2 game but the data were significantly different, and it struck a chord with me instantly. Again, without the qualification of a sport scientist, it was simply noticeable that more players reached closer to their maximum heart rate and also spent more time working above eighty percent of their maximums during the 2 vs. 2 game. This was in comparison to the more traditional fitness test we previously completed with some studies showing how certain types of small sided games have a greater possibility of players achieving their VO_2 max than more traditional forms of fitness tests (Ford, Yates and Williams, 2010).

The purpose of this chapter is not to join the debate about whether or not fitness testing should be based upon traditional testing and/or small sided games. Instead, it is to highlight how wearable technology helped to shine a light on some significant differences in physiological responses, and how this one example opened up the coaching to a PPed approach. This experience connected with the idea that you can use the game itself to authentically reproduce or exceed the fitness demands of competition but this was only scratching the surface of how a slightly different perspective on how the use of data could shine light on the coaching process in such a powerful way. This experience triggered additional ideas for me about how this data was strikingly revealing about the type of practices and activities we as coaches were planning and delivering.

As the season continued, we started to pay more attention to the data we were collecting, not necessarily because we were interested in individual player's performances, but because of the connections we could make to our own performance as coaches. There were some major ways in which the data collected through the technology opened up some key areas of focus with coaching which were then related to key outcomes for the players. I have summarized these areas into the three key considerations for us as coaches which were session planning, coach delivery and coach reflection and how they positively affected our perceptions of player engagement, enjoyment and commitment to the team.

Session Planning

By starting to monitor the team's average heart rate information, it became clear and obvious to me when there was significant downtime in the practices. This was simple to observe because in times of activity the team's heart rates visibly climbed. Naturally this contrasted with the times in the session when the team's heart rate zones dropped as it represented times of inactivity. The low heart rates were typically aligned with moments in practices when players were having drinks breaks and when coaches were transitioning from one activity to the next. These transitions usually involved wrapping up and debriefing one activity, sending players for a drink, the coaches then setting up the next part of the practice and summoning the players again to explain the next activity, before finally setting the players up to play. It suddenly became very clear these transitions accounted for a significant amount of the practice.

By identifying the long gaps in between the practice activities, this heightened awareness around the importance of planning the practice properly. Planning that needed to go beyond simply having the activities in mind while driving to the field. Instead, all elements of the session needed serious consideration in making sure that time spent transitioning from one activity to the next was drastically limited. Specifically, this required careful planning of the practice logistics. For example, considering using all available space on the practice field to run the session. Rather than using the same area of the field and relaying the equipment each time, it was important to have as much of the session already set up in different areas of the field so that less time was spent on reorganizing cones and moving the goals. As soon as one activity had finished, this allowed a fast transition into the next area that was already organized. This immediately contributed to the flow of sessions that is encouraged in PPed.

Additionally, being mindful of how much time it took to set up activities where lots of equipment was required forced us to reconsider doing these activities at all. Instead, planning activities where limited equipment was needed not only saved valuable playing time, but ultimately led to the design and management of more game-based activities that did not require arduous set-up. Together these slight adjustments in using the full field and limiting the amount of equipment being used help to streamline the transition times between activities for the players and facilitated the smooth movement from simple to complex activities and from high success to more challenging activities that is typical of a PPed session (Light and Harvey, 2019). However, this shift required more planning before the session to ensure that the logistics of practice were optimized when it was time to deliver the session.

Coach Delivery

Another key coaching element that received heightened attention from us through the observation of the team's heart rate responses was in the delivery of the session. This related to how, as coaches, we actually ran the practice. Once more, it was clearly noticeable in the heart rate data when activities were constantly stopping and starting which often represented frequent interventions from the coaching staff. These interventions were preventing any type of flow in the activities where players were able to play continuously and that has received attention in the latest edition of PPed. Not only were the number of stoppages highlighted, but also the length of those stoppages. It also became clear when a stoppage was made it sometimes lasted minutes at a time before playing resumed. It was a combination of seeing how many times we intervened as coaches and the length of these interventions that also highlighted the importance of our coaching delivery.

In response to the observations, we felt it was crucial to try and limit the number of interventions in the practice. This happened in three different ways. First, understanding that as coaches, it was not necessary to step in and correct every mistake the players were making. Second, trying to engage in different intervention methods, such as pulling individual players out from an activity to speak with them rather than stopping the entire group. Not only did this allow for more specific and individualized feedback, but it also meant that overall activity flow could be maintained. Lastly, this focused our attention during the activity on observation and identifying more crucial moments to intervene and interact with the entire group. When these interventions occurred, it became much more important to be clear and concise with the instructions being shared since the length of the stoppage was also key. We also used the 'natural' stoppages where players paused for a drink as times to encourage them to engage in dialogue and discuss any tactical components of the practice among themselves. This allowed us to maximize the times in the session when players were actively learning.

Coach Reflection

The major learnings for me from observing the team's heart rate response data during practice included heightened awareness around the importance of session planning and session delivery. Checking the data after each session became almost an obsession to see how efficiently and effectively a practice was delivered. This ultimately encouraged reflection among the coaches after every practice – something that, from my experience, is seldom achieved at the youth sports level. Too often for coaches, the emphasis seems to be simply placed on planning the session and delivering the session with little attention paid to reflecting on how the session went and what the athletes learnt. This is something the data organically inspired the coaches to do immediately after each practice.

In this reflective period, our conversations were centered around the types of activities that were selected. Were they appropriate? Did they allow for flow? Did we engage the players? Did they understand the goals of activity? Were they afforded enough time to purposefully practice and achieve success in those goals? Oftentimes this boiled down to a reflection of how the activities were delivered by us as coaches. The focus of the session's success became more about coaching performance instead of simply player performance. Together, these combined learnings and heightened attention towards session planning, session delivery and our own reflections as coaches led to noticeable improvements among the team and the players.

Player Engagement

When we took the time to plan for an efficient practice session, the players were more engaged in the practice and the content being delivered. Limiting the down time in between activities led to the players seeming more focused on the practice with limited distractions and contributed toward deeper immersion in the activities, while seeming to move them towards a flow experience. The players needed breaks in between activities to offer a physical and mental rest and refocus them again for the next activity but the shorter breaks helped in maintaining a high tempo of concentrated activity throughout the session.

Use of the wearable technology also engaged the players in learning more about their own health, fitness and performance. The players bought into the idea of wanting to see their heart rate data after the practice thus triggering an opportunity to self-reflect on the session. After an initial learning curve in understanding what the data showed, this opened up opportunities for the coaches to have conversations with the players about their training preparation, execution and how they were taking care of themselves off the field and thus improving relationships between the players and coaches.

Player Enjoyment

As the season progressed, it became clear to me that with an increased level of session flow and engagement, the players were starting to enjoy themselves more in the practices. PPed draws on Positive Psychology to enhance positive and happy experiences of practice and on the PERMA model in particular (Light and Harvey, 2019; Seligman, 2012). Not only did engagement contribute to positive experiences but also positive emotions, relationships in the team and a sense of achievement through better data. Making fewer stoppages and interventions in the practice activities and keeping intervention times at a minimum allowed the players to simply play more and maintain a higher level of activity that they ultimately enjoyed more than having their engagement in the activities constantly interrupted.

This enjoyment was visibly noticeable in the players expressions and the mood of the sessions and they commented on how the practices were more fun, without being asked. It is important to note here that the players are referencing fun as a by-product of practices that was both engaging and challenging. They felt connected throughout the full practice and this in turn made sessions more enjoyable. This was crucial in keeping the players fresh and motivated throughout the course of the season.

Player Commitment

The players became more engaged in practice sessions through the increased activity time and enjoyed the sessions more because they were now being afforded more time and opportunity to play. Reflecting on their own performances by checking their data at the end of practice, also stimulated intrinsic motivation that led to increased levels of player commitment. This was quantitatively evident in high and sustained practice attendance numbers and the punctuality in showing up at practices early and not simply on time. They also stayed behind after the session to see and discuss their data.

Given the small size of the school, many of the athletes played in multiple teams and multiple sports. One of the most telling factors in the success of the transformation of practice sessions was that players were favoring soccer above other sports. This was recognized when players started talking more openly about how they enjoyed their soccer practices more in comparison to other sports, where the players were simply getting 'drilled' and suffering from a lack of engagement. This was the biggest compliment for us as a program. It also highlighted the contrast between athlete experiences generated by combining PPed and wearable technology and what seemed to be coaching ineffectiveness across multiple other sports at the school.

Reflection and Evaluation

This experience taught me something valuable as a coach. Initially I was suspicious of how any type of wearable technology could really support the realities of being a youth soccer coach, whether in high school or club soccer. However, the chance experience of combining a traditional fitness test and small sided games activity in relation to heart rate responses, stimulated my interest as a coach. This initial insight suited my positioning on how we could use the game itself for fitness gains but ultimately led to a far greater connection with the coaching process. By looking at the heart rate responses for players, little attention was placed on the physical fitness of the players, contrary to how wearable technology has been applied in the past. Instead this opened up a whole new perspective on coaching behaviors during practices.

The data opened up my understanding of the importance of session planning, session delivery and reflection in becoming better coaches. What is most striking for me is that these messages of how to plan and deliver better practices and the necessity of reflecting on them is not necessarily a new concept in the realm of coaching education and best practices in youth sport. Recognizing an opportunity provided by the use of wearable technology opened up opportunities to apply elements of PPed to enhance this and to ultimately provide highly efficient coaching sessions and almost an organic development. Probably the most influential aspect of the changes created by using the wearable technology was the flow of each session that we enhanced with PPed. More time on task, more engagement and even immersion in the activities lead to better performance, motivation and enjoyment. The numbers visible to us before, during and after each session presented an inviting opportunity to engage in ways to improve how we plan, deliver and reflect on our role as coaches and in which we drew on PPed. By doing so, we noticed an immediate response from our players in their own engagement, enjoyment and commitment to the program in a way that was previously invisible to us.

This experience presented a way to improve the learning environment at the high school team in which I was coaching, but also suggested how the application of simplified technology could spread across the entire youth sporting spectrum and significantly improve the experience for young people in sport. If I fast forward a few years to where I am now, I am a co-founder of a wearable technology company – Beyond Pulse – that is wholeheartedly committed to the mission of empowering youth sports coaching with objective data. This is primarily achieved through one metric that is used to capture the activity time versus time standing still in each session – labelled 'Active Participation' – a metric that we believe can transform the way in which we highlight best practices in coaching education and youth sport development.

References

Brant, J. A., Johnson, B. and Brou, L. (2019) 'Rates and patterns of lower extremity injuries in all gender-comparable US high school sports', *Orthopaedic Journal of Sports Medicine*, 7(10): 1–7.

Coakley, J. (2011) 'Youth sports: What counts as "positive development?"' *Journal of Sport and Social Issues*, 35(3): 306–324. https://doi.org/10.1177/0193723511417311

Côté, J., Lidor, R. and Hackfort, D. (2009) 'ISSP position stand: To sample or to specialize? Seven postulates about youth sport activities that lead to continued participation and elite performance', *International Journal of Sport and Exercise Psychology*, 7(1), 7–17. https://doi.org/10.1080/1612197X.2009.9671889

Eley, D. and Kirk, D. (2002) 'Developing citizenship through sport: the impact of a sport-based volunteer programme on young sport leaders', *Sport, Education and Society*, 7(2), 151–166. https://doi.org/10.1080/1357332022000018841

Ford, P. R., Yates, I. and Williams, M. A. (2010) 'An analysis of practice activities and instructional behaviours used by youth soccer coaches during practice: Exploring the link between science and application', *Journal of Sports Sciences*, 28(5), 483–495. https://doi.org/10.1080/02640410903582750.

Harvey, S., Cushion, C. and Massa-Gonzalez, A. (2010) 'Learning a new method: Teaching Games for Understanding in the coaches' eyes', *Physical Education and Sport Pedagogy*, 15(4), 361–382. https://doi.org/10.1080/17408980903535818

Light, R. L. and Harvey, S. (2017) 'Positive Pedagogy for sport coaching', *Sport, Education and Society*, 22(2): 271–287.

Light, R. L. and Harvey, S. (2019) *Positive Pedagogy for sport coaching* (2nd edn), London and New York: Routledge.

Seligman, M. E. P. (2012) *Flourish: A visionary new understanding of happiness and wellbeing*, Sydney: Random House.

7

PROVIDING POSITIVE EXPERIENCES OF LEARNING IN GIRLS' SOCCER (FOOTBALL)

Christina Curry

There is range of health and wellbeing benefits for young people playing sport and associated physical activities. These include assisting with weight management, reducing the risk of chronic diseases such as cardiovascular disease and type 2 diabetes, improving mental health and reducing depression and anxiety (Rebar et al., 2015) but keeping them involved in sport can be a challenge. Throughout my teaching and coaching experiences, my natural inclination has always been to use a strength-based approach because I always had a sense that positive exposure to sporting or physical education experiences would provide a platform for encouraging participation and feelings of success. The foundations of my reflections come from my own exposure to coaching and physical education from a young age, and across various sports and activities. It is the positive experiences as a young athlete that I remember such as those of being supported by coaches and peers in an environment that made me feel good feel that I belonged. These feelings of acceptance and belonging are vital as a motivating factor in young people wanting to continue to play and remain engaged in sport. As a coach, I believe I have a responsibility to provide an environment that is positive, and which develops both the soft skills and tactical awareness skills of the young people that we work with.

My experiences have predominantly been in coaching team sports, which require a coach to consider all players as individuals, yet part of a whole group that is ultimately focused on performance. Performance is determined by a range of factors and varies from team to team. Performance for some teams is getting out there each week, having fun, feeling a sense of achievement with the hope of improving along the way. For other teams, performance is led by expectations of external factors, such as the club, the coach, or parents who are more focused on the success of the team through winning games and ultimately the competition. This conundrum plagues sport for young people and can be both an impediment and an incentive.

The Context

Over the years I have had a close association with a local football club in Sydney, Australia through their engagement with the broader community. Getting to know the executive over the years meant we often engaged in conversations about participation, community coaching and the role of sport in young people's lives. The club has a membership of 1,600 players starting from age five through to adult teams and was started by European migrants in the early 60s, who wanted to continue to play football, but also provide an opportunity for the local kids to learn the skills of football and create a local competition. The club grew significantly over the years, with an ongoing, dedicated volunteer executive and coaches and epitomises a true local community club. It supports local charities, a competition for people with disabilities and in recent years, has commenced a play-based football experience for under 4s which was established because they wanted to play instead of just watch their older siblings play. Community sport is an important setting in Australia for providing access to physical activity for children and young people and where they can taste the social and mental health benefits of participation (Robertson, Eime and Westerbeek, 2018).

The club has had a strong focus on female players, with a particular emphasis on encouraging girls to play throughout their teenage year and was successful in lobbying the local council to build a new amenity to accommodate change rooms for the girls due to the high participation and providing appropriate facilities. The club found that the participation of girls in sport declined in their teenage years around 15 years of age and this had become an ongoing concern that they have been trying to redress.

I was having a conversation with the secretary, Jess (pseudonym), just before the season was due to commence during which she expressed her concern with the fact that a number of girls had stopped playing but there was a group that still wanted to play and she did not want to lose them. This meant recruiting some additional girls to create a full team which is always challenging due to the lack experience playing together.

Jess is a big advocate for girls in sport and did not want to see any who wanted to play not be able to, so she offered to coach the girls and help create a full team. She had been a state representative footballer and had a very traditional coaching background but after some discussion she asked me to give her a hand as she felt a games-based approach would be effective for this particular group of girls and I agreed with no hesitation.

The Session/Season

I took the opportunity to go and watch the team's first couple of games to get a feel for the girls playing abilities, teamwork and interactions with each other, and Jess. The team was very mixed in ability, with some strong attacking players, other players who knew their role on the field well, and some players who were there purely for the social connections. I noticed that many of the parents of the girls would come to watch, and it appeared that some of the fathers in particular, had a big interest in football and being part of this club and its culture.

In discussion with Jess, we determined that I would lead a couple of training sessions using a game-based approach with a focus on developing their tactical awareness and decision making. My first session with the girls focused on building rapport through fun, modified games while I determined their individual skills and motivation. The resource used for designing the sessions was *Game Sense, Pedagogy for performance, participation and enjoyment* (Light, 2013: 118–133).

Session 1

I commenced with a simple game in which I put the girls into pairs with one player dribbling a ball within a designated area, while their partner tried to take control of a ball. The girls found this activity fun, with lots of laughter, not really aware that my focus here was to develop their dribbling skills while under pressure from a defender. I stopped the game to ask some simple questions about where to focus their vision for control of the ball, and about their awareness of space within their peripheral vision. This challenged the girls thinking as I felt like they were anticipating coach direction and monologue. As is common in all my coaching and teaching experience, it takes a while for players to recognise the value of questioning and dialogue and to adapt to it. Following suggestions from some of the girls, we played the game again but reduced the size of the space, which intensified their need for ball control, perception, decision-making and concentration. Some girls were agile and enjoyed the activities, while others took longer to respond which I believe was also associated with their level of fitness. I asked how they could stay in control of the ball to be able to change direction quickly. It always amazes me how young people come up with concepts when they are challenged within a supportive learning environment and this time it was no different.

I then distinguished the two teams from each other with braids and developed the game by incorporating a pass. This challenged the girls to focus on their dribbling with defenders at play, while trying to determine when to pass and the type of pass that would be most effective in that situation. After a few minutes of playing the game, I stopped the girls and asked them to reflect on their positioning in both their role as an attacker and a defender, and in what ways did they work together. I took the opportunity to review the different types of passes and used a highly skilled player to demonstrate effective passing. They then tried this in pairs for a couple of minutes to increase their kicking skills. They were then able to incorporate these skills into another game. I stopped the game and asked the attackers what type of pass is best to ensure it goes to your teammate and how they can find space.

We then moved to the next game 'multi-goal', where a number of goals are set up with large cones, in a playing area of twenty by twenty metres, varying the size of the goal mouth to allow more tactical complexity. Players were put in pairs, changing partners regularly, with eight pairs playing at once. The aim was for each pair of players to score as many goals as possible. Part of a strength-based approach involves player participation in game design to promote engagement through ownership of the game. I gave the girls the opportunity to determine the size of the goal mouth, the number of goals, and together we determined the playing rules. The girls showed great enthusiasm and I used a simple technique of putting them in pairs avoiding any process where a player would feel left out. The process I find most effective is asking for two even lines, asking one line to face the other line with the person each is facing being their partner in the first round.

I believe that, as coaches, we have a responsibility to ensure that all players feel included and are not put in a position where they could be exposed to ridicule based on their skill, ability or coordination. For me it is important that game design encompasses all players engaged in a way where they are all active but also focused on their role in the game. This allows players with developing skills to feel less exposed and more able to focus on developing their skills within a safe learning environment. The multi-goal game allowed for that while at the same time, I could see the girls engaged in decision-making and communing in their pairs. As the game progressed, I could see a number of players extending their manipulation of the ball, along with greater perception of the gameplay. In order to extend the girls further, the next activity I used was four passes. The aim of this game is to score as many points as possible with one point being scored when one team makes four consecutive passes. This was a good progression because it built on the skills from the previous game to develop their ability to maintain possession and their passing under pressure. Once the girls developed an understanding of the game I asked them the following questions; 'If the defence is tight, what can the player with the ball do to help find open spaces?' followed by; 'What did you learn from the previous game that you could apply here about passing to a moving receiver?' The girls indicated that they wanted to reduce the size of the game playing field to increase the challenge.

The girls continued to play for a few minutes, and I noticed they were more conscious of keeping control of the ball and passing only when they'd felt they could get it to the receiver successfully. I noticed that when in defence, players were putting pressure on attackers in a one-on-one approach which I had not observed in their earlier matches. We stopped the game again to consider modifications to the game and decided to change the ratio of players with five defenders and three attackers. They challenged themselves for a few minutes and then decided they were tired and ready to finish. From my experience, this is the challenge with community sport in that often players are there for the social interaction and to spend time with their friends more than to learn to play better. This is important to be aware of as a coach and to strike a balance between improving and learning as players and providing the type of social interaction they are after and to have them leave the session feeling good and looking forward to the next one. We took some time at the end to talk about their weekend game and then moved on to things happening in their lives outside sport because young people often see coaches as their role models and we have a responsibility to nurture and guide them, and not just in sport.

This session took place a month after the first session but, in the meantime, Jess continued to apply the coaching principles informed by positive pedagogy using a GBA approach. During the month, Jess and I continued to have conversations about the coaching sessions, to continue to improve not only their game performance, but also their enthusiasm for attending training and applying themselves to the session. A frustration Jess found was that the girls were very distracted by their own conversations. They wanted to share what was going on in their lives during training so were only able to concentrate for short periods of time. Being a strong performer and competitor herself, Jess was challenged by the mixed ability and the lack of real desire to be strong competitors in the local competition. Interestingly, my role morphed more into supporting Jess, with structuring her coaching sessions in a way that kept the girls interested while developing their skills and tactical awareness in a subtle way.

It was important for Jess to consider the factors that brought the girls to the team environment and be cognisant of the group dynamics at play. I was not able to attend additional training sessions due to a clash with another commitment I had, but supported Jess and the team remotely. I was able to attend two of their match games during that month, and I did notice there was a slight improvement in their tactical game play and greater encouragement of each other on the field. Following this observation, I focused my second session on developing their tactical awareness further, through greater awareness of each other, and the different strengths they each brought to the team. Teenagers can be very sensitive and ongoing reassurance and praise is vital. It is also important to choose your battles wisely, don't push players if you can see they are not in the right frame of mind. Having a high level of emotional intelligence is vital for anyone working with young people.

Session 2

This session commenced with a reflection on how they felt the season was going for them, where they'd seen improvements in their game play, and the areas where great opportunity for development existed. I've always found this reflective process very effective, as I think it is vital for players to come to training sessions with a clear understanding of the purpose, aligned to the strategic objectives of the team. What was interesting to note was the girls talking about their positioning on the field, and being available when in possession of the ball, in order to transfer the knowledge that had been developed in the passing games from session one. The girls recognised that they needed to do more work in defence as the other teams they played were able to get the ball to the goal quite quickly. They also recognised that their fitness probably played a role in their ability to stay with the play. Based on this observation, we commenced the session with a game of tag, where girls had to try and steal a tag tucked into others shorts while dribbling their own soccer ball. This activity created much laughter and frustration as they attempted to challenge their movement and peripheral awareness. Following the warm-up, we commenced with a game extended from four passes, which is moving towards four versus three soccer.

The girls were split into four teams of four, with two games being played simultaneously with the aim of the game being to score goals with the defensive team rotating a goalie. They took a bit of time to develop the concept of the rotating goalie, and I had to focus on tactical questions in order to connect their understanding of the game and further development of game play. I questioned the attacking team about how they can speed up their attack once the ball is turned over, and the type of tactics they could apply to score a goal when a goalie is in place. As defence was a real focus for this team, my questioning asked the girls to consider their field position and what needed to be considered when there was a turnover in possession. This prompted deeper discussion about how to manage this in a game, and we talked about how they would respond, in order to maintain possession.

Throughout the questioning, I praised their responses and asked for higher order questions encouraging deeper learning. Understanding and feeling comfortable to contribute is a key component of the positive pedagogy process. I noticed that the girl's confidence improved as they started to put forward a range of thoughts and ideas in response to prompting questions. I've always been guide in my questioning by the notion that there is no wrong answer, they are all ideas to be considered, which allows for creativity and a sense of contributing to a group objective. A strength-based approach instils a sense of achievement as ideas are integrated into the session, and the game is allowed to evolve in ways that often the coach does not anticipate. A key factor is giving players ownership of the game, and I could see the change in the girls when they went back into the game with increased motivation, to test their ideas. As a coach, this is very rewarding to see the social and emotional connection enhanced while developing their skills and awareness of game play.

When designing a session, the PPed coach typically includes games or activities beginning with high success rates but increasing the challenge in a progression toward more demanding games and activities. A key indicator of when to move on to the next activity relies on the coach observing the level of engagement, under-standing whole person experience and being able to judge how well the players are handling the challenge of the game or activity. With the in-game design for coaching sessions, we cannot predict the time allocated and have to be tuned in to learning and engagement, shaped by the conversation and questioning that take place. I determined it was time to move to the next activity which was four v four triangle soccer and felt this game would further develop direction toward a goal, while providing an additional challenge of adapting to a different space, therefore changing the focus of attack.

In this game, three goals are set up in a triangular pattern, and the objective is for each team of four to score as many goals as possible, when the ball is passed through any of the three goals from either direction. This game really challenged the girls, as it was fast-paced and did not sit within their traditional concepts of a soccer training session. I stopped the game to focus on asking each team what they could do to anticipate and prepare for maintaining possession and trying to score the next goal. I asked them how they determined which goal to attack next and asked them to consider when they were defending, what was their strategy to stop the opposition scoring. This led to the question of anticipation, aligning to their matches about how the opposition attacks and what they need to do to respond. I then asked the girls to have a team talk to determine their strategy. I always find this to be a valuable process to create strong team play where all players have a clear direction of the objective and their role. The teams went back into the game, and I was intrigued by the difference I could see after they'd had the time to think tactically and define their game strategy. After a few minutes, the girls asked for a timeout so they could have another team talk and I think an opportunity for a breather, and this was a good indicator of their engagement.

They went back into game play for a few more minutes and then asked if they could play one of the other teams. This resulted in them having to consider different tactics and strategies because each team comes with a different approach and responses to play have to be adapted. It was at this point the girls indicated they wanted to move into a bigger proper game and apply the tactics they'd been focusing on. This is an important learning that takes place particularly when young people start to connect to what they are actually trying to achieve, and the focus on tactic and strategy. You can see the lightbulb moment in some players when they are encouraged through questioning to think beyond trying to get the ball to their goal. The deeper learning that takes place in the how and the why within an environment of encouragement and the promoting of risk taking to formulate and test their ideas.

We moved to a game of eight-on-eight, with the girls starting with a team talk to determine their action plan. As the girls played, Jess and I reflected on individual players, and the importance of promoting their strengths and the role they play in the team, with the intention of the value this would provide for the girls understanding of the team as a whole. I was really proud of the girls' enthusiasm for trying new things in the game and greater peer encouragement was evident. We were looking forward to watching Sunday's game to see the transfer of knowledge that we'd hoped would be visible.

The girls approached the game with enthusiasm and were keen to talk about their game plan action before kick-off which they led. Jess had traditionally been a very directive coach, and as is common in game-based literature, it is a challenge for some coaches to move to athlete centred coaching approaches. They played really well and both Jess and I could see the improvement in positioning and their control of the ball when in possession. Their defence was better, but fitness was still a challenge on a large playing field with only one training session per week but at this level I believe time is better spent on improving game understanding and performance.

Reflections and Assessment

From my interaction with Jess, I felt she gained a deeper understanding of game-based coaching, and the value created through applying a strength-based approach to coaching. The transition from player to coach is a challenging one, particularly when many players have been coached in the traditional approach, which is very skill and drill focused, with the coach directing the player's movements and positioning. Jess commented that she felt the girls were more engaged and receptive to the activities at training sessions, and really liked the opportunity to contribute. Jess worked hard to reduce the coach centred nature of her coaching, but this will need more work to undo after so many years of exposure to, and experience of, traditional coaching.

The girls were competitive among very strong teams in the competition but the greater outcome for me was the improvement in the team dynamic through the development of a culture of valuing each other, the strengths each player brings and the trust that was created over the course of the season. This was a team that potentially was not going to go ahead because there were not enough players. Some girls had stopped playing and new players had been brought along by existing players, and there was no coach to begin with. What resulted was the coming together of a team who were committed to training and games, and a community coach who was willing to challenge their own beliefs about coaching, in order to provide positive experiences for a group of teenage girls while at the same time developing their soccer playing skills.

References

Light, R. L. (2013) *Game Sense: Pedagogy for performance, participation and enjoyment*, London and New York: Routledge.

Rebar, A. L., Stanton, R., Geard, D., Short, C., Duncan, M. J. and Vandelanotte, C. (2015) 'A meta-meta-analysis of the effect of physical activity on depression and anxiety in non-clinical adult populations', *Health Psychology Review*, 9(3), 366–378. doi:10.1080/17437199.2015.1022901

Robertson, J., Eime, R. and Westerbeek, H. (2018) 'Community sports clubs: are they only about playing sport, or do they have broader health promotion and social responsibilities?' *Annals of Leisure Research*. doi:10. 1080/11745398.2018.1430598

8

USING POSITIVE PEDAGOGY IN STRIKING AND FIELDING GAMES

Nick Hill

My understanding and use of Positive Pedagogy for sport coaching originates in my experience as a rugby coach and my introduction to game-based approaches (GBA). I started my coaching journey in 1999 at my old school where I taught and coached, very much the way I was taught and coached. I used direct instructions and drills, and only played a game at the end of a lesson/session which is an approach synonymous with a 'traditional' model of teaching. I began to develop my ideas on player-centred coaching as Director of Rugby at Denstone College (UK) from 2005 to 2013 due to the influence of my main professional coaching mentor, Brian Ashton.

As well as developing my rugby coaching, I taught physical education lessons in badminton, basketball and tennis using a GBA in the UK and when I was coaching in Chile from 2013 to 2016, I further developed my GBA by teaching softball and cricket in physical education. My teaching of individual sports such as athletics, swimming and gymnastics in physical education was also influenced by GBA even though they are not games. I did not know that my approach had a name but, after reading about Athlete-centred coaching (see Kidman, 2005), I thought that what I was doing lined up well with it. I later read Light's (2013) *Game Sense: Pedagogy for performance, participation and enjoyment* book, and again, felt good alignment with my own coaching approach.

My exposure to Positive Pedagogy for sport coaching (PPed) began through reading journal articles (see Light and Harvey, 2017) and the first and second editions of PPed (Light, 2017; Light and Harvey, 2019). On reading these articles and books, I had some initial interactions on email and then via skype with Professor Stephen Harvey. As Stephen and I chatted and I shared some of my work and ideas on teaching and coaching, I realized that a lot of what I was doing was synonymous with the ideas that underpin PPed. In 2018 I had a great opportunity to see just how well my approach lined up with PPed when asked to deliver a practical session at the Ohio University's Global Coaching Symposium and talk to masters' students. I did a practical session on using PPed in striking and fielding games, which I repeated when I visited again in 2019 and is what this chapter focuses on.

Context

As part of the Masters in Coaching Education program that is delivered online, the Global Coaching Symposium is an intense, five-day period of learning attended by masters' students from all over the US. In the two symposia I was invited to, the students were provided with lecture-based content from three experts in PPed, which was supplemented by on-field demonstrations by these same experts before the students conducted a micro-coaching session in their own sport based on the previously experienced content.

For my practical session, I chose cricket, a sport from the striking and fielding classification of games, as the vehicle for teaching PPed principles to the students in the teaching sessions' part of the symposium. I chose cricket because the students had little to no knowledge of the sport, which offered me an opportunity to showcase the flexibility of PPed. It also offered me the chance to show how tactical problems and solutions are shared among striking and fielding games such as baseball and cricket. I assumed they could develop game appreciation, cricket skills and understanding through me using PPed to highlight how they could transfer skills from the already familiar sports of baseball and softball. I felt this would also emphasize the point that they could be successful at something that they have never done before.

The PPed features I used throughout the session were: a) designing physical learning environment or experience for student engagement, b) asking questions that generate dialogue and thinking instead of telling the students what to do, c), providing a supportive socio-moral environment on which making mistakes was accepted as an essential part of learning, and d) adopting an inquiry approach to learning where the students became active learners and took responsibility for their learning through the collaborative formation of ideas/solutions to the problems that arise in games. The 60 students were split into three groups of approximately twenty each to work with each expert and experienced each one for 40 minutes each time after which they rotated. I recorded my session using my GoPro camera, which I strapped to my chest harness so that I could reflect on my session and recall interactions I had with the students for the writing of this chapter.

The Session

My main objective of the session was for the students in each group to be able to play cricket and understand the key tactical problems that underpin the game through PPed. At the start of the session, I asked the following questions to see what prior knowledge and understanding the students already had and thus build on their already existing knowledge from playing and/or watching American striking and fielding games such as baseball and/or softball and help them make sense of cricket: 'What are the main tactical problems associated with a striking and fielding games?' The two key tactical problems of cricket boil down to: a) how to score for the batting side and b) how to prevent or impede scoring as the bowling and fielding side. These are the same for baseball and softball which meant that teaching via the tactical problems of the game highlighted how easy it is to transfer knowledge from one game (such as baseball) to a game they have never played before. Based on their answers to the previous tactical problems question, I then asked these basic two questions: 'What is the aim of a batting team?' and 'What are the aims of the bowlers and fielders?' while also asking supplementary questions to guide them toward the answers I was looking for. I used this guided discovery type questioning to help them understand that: 1) the aim of the batter is to score runs by creating and finding space and time, and to not get out and that 2) the aim of the bowler is to get the batsman out or to reduce the chances of them scoring runs by reducing their space and time, as is the aim of fielders. In their answers, many of the students used terminology from baseball and softball, and all I had to then do was translate that to what it is in cricket, e.g. 'pitcher' to 'bowler'.

I then moved from questioning their prior knowledge of striking and fielding games to implementing game-based scenarios to enhance their learning experience. I split the group into two teams by asking them to get in pairs and do one game of rock, paper, scissors to randomly assign the two teams. One team would bowl and field on one of the pitches and they would then bat on the other pitch. This helped me form two small-sided games to ensure as many students as possible were active. I split the playing area into two via a line of cones down the middle to separate them.

In each small-sided game I had one set of wickets, which were two, big cones for the batter's end and one big cone for the bowler's end about 15 yards apart, creating a vertical field (narrow and long), and the other set creating a horizontal field (wide width and short). The two wickets were parallel and about and created very different challenges for the batters. I left a pile of different types and sizes of balls at the bowler's wicket end of each wicket and a couple of bats at each end, one being a tennis racket and one being a thick plastic racket.

The rules were that, as a batter, if you hit the ball, both batters (one at either end) had to run but if you hit the ball past the midline of cones that separated the two fields you were out. For the bowler, the ball had to bounce on the floor at least once and every four balls s/he had to change with a teammate. Every two balls, the fielders had to move around to the next marker on the floor (the markers were evenly spread out, with three or four on each side (offside/legside) of the wicket, and about 10–15 yards from the wickets). During this first five-minute set, all I did was reinforce the rules, ask the students questions about the rules, and/or demonstrate how to perform specific skills like bowling.

I had the students play this basic game of cricket for around five minutes and after this first five-minute game, I called the students in and asked them to raise their hand along a sliding scale to dictate the level to which they felt they know what was going on in the game (if they had no idea being what was going on they had to hold their hand all the way up). This was aimed at giving the students a chance for self-reflection and for me to reflect, while empowering the students to take some ownership of their learning by being able to express their feelings/thoughts/understanding in an easy, open and non-threatening way. Most of the students raised their hands all the way up, which was where I expected them to be and indicted the level of challenge for them.

To explore where the students were at in more depth, I asked more questions through what could be termed a 'reflective toss' episode (van Zee and Minstrell, 1997):

ME: What is the objective of the bowler?
STUDENT 1: Hit the wicket.
ME: How do you do that?
STUDENT 1: Bowling the ball.
ME: What can you do when you bowl the ball to achieve this objective?
STUDENT 2: You can shorten the bounce.
ME: Where were you aiming? (asking Student 3)
STUDENT 3: Right before the wicket so that it would be low so they couldn't really hit it.
ME: What's the second thing I'm trying to do as a bowler?
STUDENT 4: Stop them from scoring.
ME: What else?
STUDENT 4: You can spin it. You can curve it.
STUDENT 2: You can kind of bowl it at the batsman, so they have to manoeuvre or adjust.

After this, I put them back into the same game but swapped the fields they were playing on so that they were batting within different constraints and had to adapt their fielding tactics to a different space. I walked around the two fields again observing different students in action and at when I thought it was necessary, I asked them individual questions unless they asked me about something in the game that had just happened or not happened to seek understanding or clarification. When they did this, I responded by saying, 'Try and figure it out first'. I did, however, offer praise to students when they did things well, and, when needed, I reminded them of the rules I had put on the game. For example, I said the fielders: 'What do we do after every two balls?'

After playing this game for a while, I called the group back in and, again, asked them to give me a gauge of their level of confusion. I followed this up by asking them what things that had helped them develop their understanding of the game. The most common responses were, 'communication', 'peer teaching and coaching', and 'asking questions to you and my peers to clarify the rules of the game'. Some students said that the repetition of play helped them while others liked experiencing and adapting skill and tactics to the different limits and opportunities provided by the different shapes of the two wickets.

For the final bout of play, I told them to tally their individual runs so that we could add up the teams' totals at the end of the play and see which team won the game. The students then had to work together to develop a simple scoring system and decide on things like whether or not they could get batsman out at both ends. I empowered them to change the rules of the game as they felt they needed so that they took ownership of their game. I walked between the two games reinforcing the conditions on the game, e.g. every four balls you change bowler, every two balls you move around, Fielders on the markers. Plus continue to give positive feedback/reinforcement of good things they were doing.

At the end of the session, I asked the students to indicate the level to which they felt they know what was going on in the game by raising their hands, as I had at the beginning of the session.

This time, they either did not put their hand up at all, or only raised it up to halfway. I then asked them how long they had been playing cricket for, which they replied, 'around 30 minutes'. I emphasized the impact and power of PPed could have on a group of novices in a new sport in what was relatively, a very short length of time. By the end of the third bout of game play, all the students were playing cricket, being competitive and having fun!

Reflection

It was great for me to see people pick up a new game so quickly. I was pleased to see how they understood the basic principles and concepts of cricket, particularly when they had never played the game before. What made the experience challenging for me was the different dynamics within each of the small-sided teams, the rate at which they picked up the different skills and tactical knowledge and the different constraints/rules I had to put on their games at different times to help them achieve the objective of the session. The three groups I worked with over the afternoon got to the same end point of understanding the game as indicated by their ability to play this modified game of cricket.

Using PPed helped me create a very positive learning environment and the students enjoyed themselves because there was no 'fear of failure' as I did not dwell on, or highlight, mistakes. The hit and run rule for the batsman created lots of opportunities to bat because, even when anyone might get out first ball, s/he did not have too long a wait to bat again. Within a traditional session that one 'at bat' might be the only opportunity for that batsman and they would have to wait till the next session to have another bat.

Moreover, I felt I was able to get the game, and the challenges it presented for them, right for the students by adapting and modifying it to suit the understanding and skill of the students. For example, I took away some of the difficult skills associated with cricket such as overarm bowling by just giving the students a rule that the ball has to bounce at least once before it could be played by the batter. This helped get around the time it would have taken to learn to bowl which is a very unnatural movement and to focus more on understanding the whole game and on tactical awareness and knowledge. I also reduced the distance between stumps so that the bowler was not bowling lots of no-balls and/or wides. As the students gained more confidence, I would then have been able to lengthen the distance to that an appropriate amount of challenge was present to create a productive amount of struggle for the bowler. This highlights the need to get a game going and adjust the pace of learning to the development of understanding and skill develop. This reinforces the need to be tuned in to athlete learning in a more humanistic way than in traditional approaches, and the able to adjust and adapt activities and their demands in PPed. With the fielders, I deliberately moved them around into different fielding positions every two balls so that they could stay involved in the game and begin to learn the tactical and technical skills associated with fielding in the different positions. For me personally, I see this form of rotation of positions as a key component of PPed and other athlete-centered coaching.

Another positive aspect of this session was how students experienced the interconnectivity of tactical knowledge, technical skill execution and decision making by playing the actual game and not doing isolated technical skill drills as is the case with any GBA. The different shape of the two wickets created different challenges they had to adapt to by hitting different types of shots in different directions with different amounts of force. For example, on the long pitch they could hit the ball back over the head of the bowler really hard to create time to score runs whereas but on the short pitch this same shot would be out because the ball would travel past the midline of cones between the two fields.

I was happy with my questioning in these sessions. I asked some questions aimed at getting an answer I was after, and open-ended questions that generated dialogue between myself and the students and/or between the students themselves. There was very little, if any direct instruction, and if there was any it only occurred when I had to re-iterate the rules of the game. To build a positive and supportive environment, I avoided saying that the students were wrong. This was the case even if they did actually do some wrong things, because they were brand new to the game and things like swinging and missing at the ball as a batter, and misfields were going to occur quite frequently. I used individual and collective questioning and promoted 'team meetings' for discussions on tactics.

The use of a very foreign sport for the students in this session blows the notion right out of the ballpark (pun included) that you have to reach a certain level of technical skill competence before you can play the game. PPed has a positive focus on what the learners can do and creates opportunities for interaction within the context of the game between the batter, bowler and fielders but it must create the right level of challenge for all involved and if this is just right it can encourage a state of flow, or at least to establish flow of the session.

References

Kidman, L. (2005) *Athlete-centred coaching: Developing inspired and inspiring people*, Christchurch, NZ: Innovative Print Communications Ltd.

Light, R. (2013) *Game Sense: Pedagogy for performance, participation and enjoyment*, London and New York: Routledge.

Light, R. (2017) *Positive Pedagogy for sport coaching: Athlete-centred coaching for individual sports*, London and New York, Routledge.

Light, R. L. and Harvey, S. (2017) 'Positive Pedagogy for sport coaching,' *Sport, Education and Society*, 22(2), 271–287.

Light, R. and Harvey, S. (2019) *Positive Pedagogy for sport coaching* (2nd edn), London and New York, Routledge.

van Zee, E. and Minstrell, J. (1997) 'Using questioning to guide student thinking,' *Journal of the Learning Sciences*, 6(2), 227–269.

PART II
Individual Sports

9

THE INFLUENCE OF A PPED COURSE ON COACHING PRACTICE

Richard Light and Mohammad Shah Razak

This chapter is a little different to the others in the book because it focuses on the experiences of six coaches enrolled in a Bachelor of Sport Coaching program instead of on an individual coach's experiences. While this means it does not offer the same subjective insights into coaching that the other chapters do, it does provide some understanding of how coaches in the early stages of their careers can interpret and apply PPed, and work through the challenges involved. Although attracting growing attention from researchers and practitioners, athlete-centred approaches' challenge to the dominance of coach-centred traditional approaches has been limited (see Kidman 2005; Pill 2011, 2018), which is largely due to the reproductive influence of experience on coaches' beliefs and practice (coaching how they were coached) and the comparative ineffectiveness of formal coach education programs (see, Cushion, Amour and Jones 2003; Reid, 2015).

Growth in university sport coaching programs offers opportunity for promoting athlete-centred approaches but the extent to which these programs influence the coaching of their graduates has not been explored. This chapter redresses this oversight by drawing on a study that inquired into the influence of student-centred, inquiry-based higher education teaching in a course on Positive Pedagogy for sport coaching in individual sports. It briefly looks at the effectiveness of using the same pedagogy promoted in PPed before moving on to focus on the experiences of six coaches who completed the course of applying it to their coaching.

The Study

The study adopted constructivist grounded theory (Charmaz 2006) methodology to focus on six, final year undergraduates in a course on athlete-centred coaching for individual sport and who had completed another course on athlete-centred coaching for team sports the year before. It aimed to answer the central research question of

'How effective is the pedagogy used in the course in positively influencing *sport coaching students' coaching practice and why?*' It was conducted over the six months following completion of the course to reduce any possible influence on the interview data by the students' concerns with how their responses might affect their grades.

Data Generation

Data were generated through two stages, which were: 1) a single, retrospective/reflective interview focused on their experiences of the course within three weeks of its completion, and 2) three, one-on-one interviews that focused on the influence of the course on their practice over the six months following completion of the course.

Analysis

We developed theory from the data through initial, and then focussed, coding, then developed categories through a process of memoing and constant comparison to conceptualise data (Charmaz 2006). Through memo writing we developed strong substantive codes that we elevated to theoretical codes as an example of, 'how the substantive codes may relate to each other as hypotheses to be integrated into a theory' (Glaser, 1978, p. 72).

The Context

In the design of this course we drew on the work of Dewey (1916; 1938) to place physical experience at the centre of learning for the course with lectures, practical sessions and assessment structured around it. This was aimed at grounding learning in practice and encouraging the development of knowledge and understanding of the course content at a non-conscious level by the students that we brought to consciousness through the use of language. Delivered over one semester (12 weeks of teaching) the course comprised a one-hour lecture and a two-hour workshop each week and focused on individual sports. Over the workshops during the first six weeks, the students experienced being athletes/learners with us using a PPed approach to coach them in coaching team sport skills, 4 x 100m relay baton changeovers, swimming, karate punching and throwing the javelin. Assessment for this half of the course was an essay in which the students reflected upon their experiences on how it felt, how it compared to previous experiences and how effective they felt it was. Over the second six weeks, they formed small coaching teams of two or three to design and implement a twenty-minute coaching session using the Positive Pedagogy for sport coaching framework (Light, 2017; Light and Harvey, 2019) for an individual sport of their choice, but with two groups choosing to coach a single, specific technique or skill from a team sport. For their assessment, the coaching teams presented an analysis of, and critical reflection on, their coaching to their peers. This approach was aimed at providing the experience of PPed as an athlete to encourage understanding and empathy with how learners experience the approach and to be critically reflective as coaches.

After briefly looking at how the students felt they learned, this chapter looks at how the coaches applied and adapted PPed to their coaching needs and situations over the six months following their completion of the course.

Findings

How They Learned

We arrived at three dominant themes explaining how the participants felt they learned and which reflect much of PPed. In order of importance, they were: 1) the experiential pedagogy used, 2) meeting the challenges they faced and, 3) their enjoyment of the course. In this section we briefly focus on the main influence on their beliefs and practice, which was the experiential pedagogy used but we focus on how all three influenced their coaching practice in the following section.

All six participants emphasised the central importance of their experience as learners and in peer coaching teams in developing and an understanding of PPed that was more focused on the experience of the workshops but also recognized the role played by reflection. This lent support to Dewey's (see, 1916/97) contention that we learn through both the experience of doing and the (second) experience of reflecting upon it. The participants felt that experience was central to their learning and occurred in three stages, which are:

1. The first-hand experience of being an athlete coached using PPed in the workshops and the formal reflection on it during these sessions and after them as well as through the assessment task, which was a reflective essay.
2. The 'hands on' experience of working with a small team to design and implement a coaching session using the PPed approach and then formally reflect on it and critically analysis it in a formal presentation as the assessment task.
3. The experience of applying the PPed approach to their coaching and having to adapt it, which required critical reflection.

Applying PPed to Practice

Here we begin with a general discussion of the six coaches' dispositions toward PPed and the ways in which they applied and adapted PPed to their coaching situations. We then focus on the two strongest themes among them over this period which were, the challenge of questioning and how they met it, and their belief in the need for athlete enjoyment.

The coaches chose to use PPed in their coaching and were able to adapt it to the challenges of day-to-day coaching, which was facilitated by their ability and inclination to learn and solve problems. They enjoyed being challenged during their university course to think deeply and critically about their own coaching beliefs and practice during the course. James said that it, 'helped me step out of my comfort zone to develop sessions'. They understood what they were asked to do and felt that they could manage the challenge of applying PPed to their coaching by drawing on existing knowledge, reflection and the ability to find, understand and apply knowledge. This suggests that they experienced the *knowledgeability* and *manageability* that Antonovsky (1996) suggests contributes to wellbeing. They also felt that understanding the big ideas and concepts of specific sports helped them understand what they were doing and why. They all enjoyed the way PPed challenged the 'status quo' of traditional coaching where the coach tells the athletes what to do and makes all decisions and came to like the idea of being critically reflective and open to learning.

As a surf instructor, Sam had been unable to put his learning into action in practice but the other five had all decided to apply some of what they had learned in the course to their practice as coaches. Max said he liked the PPed approach but coached at a secondary school where he was initially anxious about applying it due to the 'real-life behavioural and cognitive issues' he said he had to deal with, but decided to try it out. The low decile school he was in was plagued by behavioural issues and low academic achievement but instead of being a problem for him he said that PPed provided flexibility and helped him learn to adapt it to the demands of the situations in which he coached:

> After doing it (PPed) for a while you can see, 'Oh that might need some direct coaching'. That was why I was able to sit back and check on positive stuff and questioning more. That kind of coaching was more like gaining experiences (for me) especially in looking at what athletes were like during the coaching and responding to the Positive Pedagogy.
>
> *(Max, interview 3, November 2016)*

Questioning

The coaches applied what they learned through being challenged in their university course to meet the challenges they faced in attempting to change their practice. For the five coaches who applied PPed to their coaching, developing skill in questioning was the most challenging aspect of PPed in their peer coaching during the university course. It was also the biggest challenge for them when using PPed in their coaching outside university and is a common problem for coaches learning to use athlete- centred approaches (see Forrest 2014; Roberts, 2011). Over the semester at university, they began to develop their ability to set, manage and meet appropriate levels of challenge for athletes and improved this over the six months following the completion of the course, as self-directed learners. They took on the challenge of accommodating a PPed approach into their way of coaching and meeting the more specific challenge of developing effective questioning. Meeting these challenges gave them confidence and a better understanding of PPed as Tom, who was a basketball coach, suggests:

> [The] part I find difficult is questioning but it comes with practice. Trains you into looking through different lenses of coaching as well. Not just about the technical skills it is also about the feel and the experience of the sport itself like

in the karate session. This new coaching approach has deepened my under-standing of sport as more than just the game and more than just skills.

(Tom, interview 2, August 2016)

Indiana coached badminton and decided to try PPed with secondary school students whose previous coach had been very coach-centred. This meant that his students were very much accustomed to being told what to do and would, 'sometimes just look at me in astonishment' when he asked them questions. He said that they found it difficult to adjust to his PPed influenced coaching style and being asked questions instead of being told what to do (see also Roberts 2011) but he felt that what he saw as the more humanistic approach he took, and the different relationships this developed, was very helpful for his coaching. He felt that being more 'tuned in' to his athletes, caring about them, and trying to empathise with them helped him implement a PPed approach as he saw them begin to change:

They were used to being told what to do and having coaches making all the decisions. This transition is tough, both on coaches and athletes. However, over time these athletes started to open up and decided to think and figure out on their own.

(Indiana, interview 1, June 2016)

Indiana adjusted his coaching to suit the needs of the group and to make learning more meaningful for them by linking the detailed foci of activities he used to the end aims of the session and the season to make them meaningful for his athletes. He felt that this helped his students develop as independent learners who were more able to solve problems themselves instead of always relying on him to tell them what to do:

For these athletes, I decided to put them into smaller groups and assisted them by providing suggestions when they were stuck and questioned them about their decision supportively. This process took at least a couple of months before they were able to do these on their own and was rather effective when it happened. After a while, their reliance on me began to decrease significantly and they were able to discuss with their team. My role as the coach changed but still remained the same in terms of constantly challenging them to improve.

(Indiana, interview 3, November 2016)

This development of PPed through reflection on experience and being able to identify and find solutions for the problems that arose in their coaching, suggests the coaches' inclination toward being critically reflective coaches, developing good relationships with their athletes/students and moving toward a humanistic approach.

Enjoyment through Flow

The coaches' enjoyment of the university course motivated them, and they wanted to provide the same experience for their young athletes. They emphasized the central role they felt enjoyment played in their learning about PPed and developing a positive disposition toward it. They all mentioned the positive emotions that they felt during the workshops and particularly in regard to the swimming and karate workshops where they had felt some apprehension prior to the sessions because of them not having had experience in these sports and believing that they could only be coached using traditional approaches:

> For individual sports, you can't really play a game like team based games but the activities like karate and swimming were cool and they were interesting and most enjoyable. The athlete-centred way of coaching certainly made it more enjoyable and beneficial. Especially in swimming, swimming coaches just put on the board and tell you to jump and just swim, but you don't get one-on-one coaching like Positive Pedagogy which was so beneficial. Fun course and cool.
>
> *(Sam, interview 3, November 2016)*

The coaches' enjoyment of the course arose from positive experiences of doing, reflecting and interacting, which are the learning experiences they wanted to provide for their athletes. The three with backgrounds in team sports were a little anxious when they had to coach and do a presentation on an individual sport in their course at university, but they were able to use PPed to coach a specific skill or technique from a team sport. They invariably mentioned how they felt the emphasis on athletes responding to challenges and having an empathetic understanding of athlete learning and experience in PPed helped them coach in ways that made practice fun for their athletes:

> You want athletes to take on a challenge that tests them and helps them realise how good they are and not to be worried about failing. Then you get them feeling like they have achieved something that they worked for. If they can feel some flow then that should be enjoyable for them and motivate them.
>
> *(James, interview 3, November, 2016)*

The coaches in the study wanted to provide similar positive experiences for athletes they coached to what they had experienced in the course workshops over the first six weeks and the notion of flow and how to promote it in coaching resonated with them all. This was something they said they used to help their athletes enjoy practice by setting and adjusting the level of challenge to achieve optimal experience and learning (see Csikszentmihalyi, 1990). Most of them believed that having a flow of coaching activities that moved from high success rates to being really challenged and having to commit to meet the challenge made practice enjoyable for athletes. They also wanted to provide the flow experiences Csikszentmihalyi (1990) refers to, where athletes are lost in the flow of games as what he sees as optimal performance by establishing the right 'challenge–skill balance'. This is a difficult task for young coaches just learning about this special state of being and, not surprisingly, they struggled to meet their own expectations:

> I find it difficult to get a good level of challenge for my athletes and more difficult to keep it going and be able to adjust it, but I think that watching them closely and knowing how they are going helps. Being positive about how they are going also helps them feel positive.
>
> *(Indiana, interview 3, November 2016)*

Reflection and Evaluation

For us, this chapter provides some useful understanding of young coaches' experiences of learning about, and using, PPed and how they adapted it to their practice and particular situations. The challenge of developing effective questioning is a common problem for coaches taking up athlete-centred coaching approaches (see Forrest, 2014; Harvey, Cushion and Massa-Gonzalez, 2010; Roberts 2011). It is also evident in many of the other chapters in this book but the ways in which the coaches in this study responded to this challenge is enlightening. It suggests how important it is for coaches interested in taking up a PPed or any other athlete-centred approach to be critically reflective, thoughtful, have the ability to learn, and to have a positive disposition toward, learning and adapting to the situation at hand. These young coaches were open to learning through critical reflection as independent learners who were able to find, interpret and adapt knowledge to help them do what they were trying to do.

As a result of their experiences of the workshops in their university course, the six coaches in this study believed in the importance of athlete enjoyment and having positive experiences of learning. In addition to finding ways of developing their questioning the coaches wanted to make their sessions more enjoyable and provide positive experiences of learning. They tried to achieve this mainly through trying to establish and maintain their athletes' 'challenge–skill balance' but also by being positive in their comments and creating a supportive environment. This is a big challenge for any coach moving to a PPed approach. Adjusting and managing the challenge–skill balance of sessions is an advanced coaching skill and building a supportive environment takes time. For these reasons progress seems to have been slow, but the coaches were positive about it and felt they were moving in the right direction.

References

Antonovsky, A. (1996) 'The salutogenic model as a theory to guide health promotion', *Health Promotion International*, 11(1): 11–17.

Charmaz, K. (2006) *Constructing grounded theory: A practical guide through qualitative analysis*, London, UK: Sage.

Csikszentmihalyi, M. (1990) *The psychology of optimum experience*, New York: Harper and Row.

Cushion, C. J., Amour, K. M. and Jones, R. L. (2003) 'Coach education and continuing professional development: Experience and learning to coach', *Quest*, 55(3): 215–230. doi:10.1080/00336297.2003.10491800

Dewey, J. (1916) *Democracy in education*, New York: Free Press.

Dewey, J. (1938) *Experience in education*, New York: Touchstone.

Forrest, G. (2014) 'Questions and answers: Understanding the connection between questioning and knowledge in games-centred approaches', in R. Light, J. Quay, S. Harvey and A. Mooney (eds) *Contemporary development in games teaching*, London: Routledge, 167–177.

Glaser, B. (1978) *Theoretical sensitivity: Advances in the methodology of grounded theory*, San Francisco: University of California Press.

Harvey, S., Cushion, C. and Massa-Gonzalez, A. (2010) 'Learning a new method: Teaching Games for Understanding in the coaches' eyes', *Physical Education and Sport Pedagogy*, 15 (4): 361–382.

Kidman, L. (ed.) (2005) *Athlete centered coaching: Developing inspired and inspiring people*, Christchurch: Innovative Print Communications.

Light, R. (2017) *Positive Pedagogy for sport coaching: Athlete-centred coaching for individual sports*, London and New York, Routledge.

Light, R. L. and Harvey, S. (2017) 'Positive Pedagogy for sport coaching', *Sport, Education and Society*, 22(2): 271–287. doi:10.1080/13573322.2015.1015977

Light, R. L. and Harvey, S. (2019) *Positive Pedagogy for sport coaching* (2nd edn), London and New York: Routledge.

Maslow, A. H. (1968) *Toward a psychology of being*. New York: D. van Nostrand Company.

Pill, S. (2011) 'Teacher engagement with games for understanding – game sense in physical education', *Journal of Physical Education and Sport*, 11(2): 115–123.

Pill, S. (ed.) (2018) *Perspectives on athlete centred coaching*, London and New York: Routledge. doi:10.4324/9781315102450

Reid, P. (2015) 'The interpretation and misinterpretation of Game Sense in its implementation by the RFU' in R. Light, S. Harvey, J. Evans and R. Hassanin (eds) *Advances in rugby coaching: An holistic approach*, London and New York: Routledge, 142–155.

Roberts, S. J. (2011) 'Teaching Games for Understanding: The difficulties and challenges experienced by participation cricket coaches', *Physical Education and Sport Pedagogy*, 16(1): 33–48. doi:10.1080/17408980903273824

Seligman, M. E. P. (2012) *Flourish: A visionary new understanding of happiness and wellbeing*, Sydney: Random House.

10

SWIMMING

Second Kick in Butterfly

Richard Light

This chapter recounts my teaching of a swimming session in which I focused on a very technical aspect of the kick in butterfly to provide an example of how Positive Pedagogy for sport coaching (PPed) can be used to coach technical aspects of sport. Although there is a tactical element in most swimming events, technique is of pivotal importance and has to form the main focus when coaching young swimmers in particular, but mechanistic coaching is not the only way to do this. Learning to swim efficiently at any level from learn-to-swim classes to the most elite competitive levels is more complex than traditional, directive coaching suggests it is and there is much to gain from the use of inquiry-based, athlete-centred pedagogy such as Positive Pedagogy for sport coaching (Light, 2017; Light and Wallian, 2008; Light and Harvey, 2019; Magias, 2018).

For swimmers of any age, learning (improving) swimming technique is not merely a process of reproducing standardized movements but instead, is one of interpretation, reinterpretation and adaptation (Light and Wallian, 2008; Light, 2014). It is a process through which the swimmer's personal interpretation of technique and whole-person experience of it within a literally fluid environment, leads to learning as an 'unfolding from within' (Dewey, 1916, p. 68). Similar language and conceptions of learning characterize contemporary approaches to learning that recognize, and strive to account for, complexity (see, Davis and Sumara, 1997) and which have been applied to physical education and sport (see Ovens, Hopper and Butler, 2013).

Official rules set by the international swimming organization (FINA) and the ongoing development of the most bio-mechanically efficient movements limit variation in the different strokes, but techniques are not completely standardized, and uniform and learning technique is not merely a process of reproduction. It involves interpretation and adaptation on an individual basis that can benefit from coaching that moves beyond the limitations of direct instruction and the pursuit of one 'ideal' way of performing technique through the correction of errors aimed at moving closer to the correct way of executing the skill. This more humanistic and holistic view of swimming efficiently requires coaching approaches that eschew an objective view of it as a linear process of replication.

Underpinned by the philosophic positions of humanism and holism, PPed provides one way of coaching that can account for the complexity of swimming with this chapter providing an example of its use in swim coaching. In it I recount and reflect upon my own 'one off' experience of coaching junior swimmers in the UK where I adopted a *Positive Pedagogy for sport coaching* approach for teaching the second kick in butterfly.

The Context

Here I reflect on a swimming session that I have written on previously (Light, 2017) but for which I provide more detail here. I am not a swimming coach, but I have a daughter who was an elite level junior swimmer performing at a level where she won silver medals in the Australian schools and British age group championships. As both a father supporting his daughter and a curious academic working in sport coaching, I was drawn into the world of children's and youth swimming over a twelve-year period. Over this time, I learned a great deal from watching coaches at work and interacting with them from learn-to-swim level to Olympic level coaches in Australia, France and the UK. I also had a coach in Australia work with my undergraduate physical education students at The University of Sydney to explore possibilities for developing athlete-centred swim coaching. To develop my ideas on this approach I drew on what I had seen my daughter's coaches do, knowledge developed through conversations with them and my academic understanding of learning and pedagogy. I also drew on the insights into personal experience that my research on young swimmers, conducted across different cultural settings such as Australia, France and Germany, have provided for me (see Light and Lémonie, 2012; Light, Harvey and Memmert, 2013).

In this session I recount how I worked with six competitive age group swimmers in the UK aged 12 to 16 as part of a postgraduate summer school on sport and physical education pedagogy that I had organized. As one of the six presenters I delivered a one-hour lecture on my athlete-centred approach to coaching individual sports that, as is the case in Chapter 16, I was developing but had not yet named Positive Pedagogy for sport coaching. I then conducted a ninety-minute demonstration using swimming as an example that was followed by a one-hour tutorial for discussion about what the postgraduate students has seen and listened to. For the practical demonstration, I used my connections with the local swimming club to invite six, age-group swimmers, aged 12 to 16 years who had qualified for the British national age-group championships. I chose to focus on improving the second kick in butterfly as a very technical aspect of the stroke to highlight the ways in which athlete-centred pedagogy could be used in technique-intensive sports. The aim of the session was to develop the swimmers' awareness of this part of the kick and assist them in understanding how it fits into the whole stroke and to improve its contribution to their stroke.

The Session

In the session I focus on here I wanted to relate technical detail to 'feel' and the fundamental concept of maximizing thrust/propulsion, with the other being reducing resistance. When swimmers develop a deep understanding of these two fundamental principles, they can draw on this knowledge base to interpret instruction on technique from the coach and adapt it to their ways of swimming. My session plan aimed at enhancing the swimmers' embodied and reflective understanding of how performance of the technique influences propulsion as part of the complex act of swimming. This understanding of this core principle is not limited to the conscious knowledge expressed through articulation, but also includes the corporeal learning and feel they developed through their experiences in the pool that I planned for.

I strove to develop the swimmers' understanding and knowledge-in-action through a 'conversation' between the non-reflective learning arising from experiences of engagement *in* action and the conscious, reflective learning *about* action (Light and Fawns, 2003). In the session I recount here, this perspective sees non-reflective learning occurring through the swimmer's adaptation to the (enabling) constraint (Davis and Sumara, 1997) imposed on them by having them perform butterfly with one arm. This experience involves rational, conscious learning occurring through the swimmer's individual and collective reflections after and during experience.

After a warm-up I asked the swimmers to swim one-armed butterfly but to breathe facing forward rather than turning their heads to the side as is sometimes done to make breathing without taking in water easier. I did this to help accentuate the relationship between the timing of the second kick and breathing with the primary function of the second kick being to provide drive when the head is elevated to inhale. After they had swum a few laps I stopped them to ask them, as a group, how it felt and what particular problems they encountered. I asked them, 'How was that?' but did not wait for an answer. Then I asked them, 'How did that feel compared to normal fly?' and paused to invite an answer. I listened to a couple of responses and then asked, 'Can you identify any particular problem or difficulty that swimming with one arm created for you?'.

After a few more questions from me, one swimmer said that he was swallowing a little water, so I asked the others whether or not they experienced the same problem with general agreement in their responses. I then focused my questions on breathing by asking, 'How do you think you can compensate for the lack of propulsion that is creating breathing problems for you?' The answer was immediate with one of the girls suggesting that kicking more effectively could compensate for the reduction in propulsion created by only being able to use one arm. This is a logical and obvious response, but I wanted them to think about the two kicks in butterfly per stroke so asked: 'How many kicks do you usually perform for each stroke?' After two swimmers answered that there were two kicks per stroke, I asked, 'Which kick would be better – first or second?' There was a short pause while they thought about it with only a couple of tentative responses offered that I did not follow up because I wanted them to discover the answer through experience, reflection and dialogue.

To provide opportunity to learn through reflection on experience and interaction I asked the six swimmers to form three pairs. I then asked them to discuss the issue of which kick would most help provide thrust to keep their mouth above the water and allow unimpeded breathing, after which I asked them to formulate ideas for using their kick to provide enough thrust to assist breathing. When they had done this, I asked them to refine their technique by doing some reciprocal teaching (Mosston and Ashworth, 1986). This involved one acting as coach and the other as athlete and then swapping roles (reciprocating). It provided them with the experience of doing, watching their partner do it, thinking about it as they 'coach' him/her and talking about it.

I then called in the pairs to form one group, which is much like the GBA approach to coaching team sport when the coach calls in all the group playing small sided games for a discussion before transitioning into the next game, or at the end of a session. We formed a circle to briefly discuss what they had learned, and I asked one from each pair, one at a time, to demonstrate their technique to the group doing one-arm butterfly. After this I led a discussion and collective reflection among the six swimmers who I asked to draw on objective (watching) and subjective (doing) perspectives. This then expanded what could be seen from a constructivist perspective as distributed thinking/cognition (Bruner, 1990) across the entire group emphasizing the social nature of learning and the greater capacity for learning in a social group over that at an individual level.

We finished off by removing the constraint, which is usually very enjoyable for the athletes, as is evident in Chapter 16 on beach sprint starts. I asked them to all get in the pool and practise the technique that we had agreed was most effective for five minutes but free of the constraint, allowing them to work the second kick technique into the full stroke as one whole action. The session was conducted in front of the postgraduate students attending the symposium that I talked to after the session. Some with swimming experience suggested that they could see improvements in the way that the swimmers swam butterfly before and after the one-hour or so duration of the demonstration. Probably more importantly, some of the swimmers said that they *felt* an improvement over the session and an improved awareness of their bodies when swimming. Indeed, one thirteen-year old boy, who was a national finalist in the 100-metre butterfly for his age group, told his father that he had discovered something very important. His father later told me that his son had been so excited and stimulated by being asked to think and problem solve in swimming and having someone care about him and being interested in what he thinks that he wanted to know why Richard could not be his coach. His father suggested he felt a sense of liberation and empowerment arising from the joy of discovery.

Clearly, one such session is unlikely to make a lasting difference to the technique of the swimmers and this approach can be relatively time consuming but, it could be done early in the season and probably only once to provide foundational knowledge and experience that could be drawn on over the season for more autonomous learning. If, in subsequent practice sessions, the coach were to help the swimmers make connections between the conceptual understandings they developed in such a session and technique it could help them develop their technique in more physically demanding training later in the season while they adapt the technique to how they swim in race conditions. As is the case with technique in team sport, the swimmers will be empowered by not only knowing *how* to perform technique but also *why*. Like Teaching Games for Understanding (TGfU) for team sports, the contrast of a PPed approach to teaching swimming with traditional coaching suggests how little emphasis coaches typically place on athlete understanding. Development of a conscious and embodied understanding of the link between technique and the fundamental principles of increasing thrust and reducing resistance that underpin all swimming empowers swimmers and increases their capacity to be autonomous learners.

Reflection and Discussion

The coaching session I reflect on in this chapter aimed to provide opportunities for learning through doing, individual and collective reflection on experience and dialogue. I made some notes on my experience at the time and have written a little on it so am able to recall how I felt, how I thought the session had gone, how well it went and how and what I thought the swimmers had learned. I only had six swimmers and knew them all, which made it easier to take this approach than it would be for most swim coaches due to the numbers that they typically have in their squads. On the other hand, I had limited experience as a swim coach, had never tried this session plan before and it was the first and only time I coached these swimmers. I remember feeling both relieved and happy about the progress of the session and the responses of the swimmers. I took a risk by trying this at a postgraduate symposium for the first time and was a little anxious about how it would work out, but it had good flow, energy and athlete engagement. I provided experiences designed to present a particular problem through the use of a constraint, which was swimming butterfly using one arm. I used this constraint to develop awareness of the second kick in butterfly and its function and to improve the timing and thrust/propulsion of this kick.

One armed 'fly' is a drill commonly used by swim coaches and is not something I created. When Australian Olympic coach Rohan Taylor was visiting the UK, I talked with him about the dangers of overtraining and in particular, about the relationship between conditioning and technique. When talking about butterfly he suggested to me that, 'you never do bad fly'. He told me that coaches have to use a range of drills as variations on butterfly (or any other stroke) and use freestyle to build race fitness but without compromising good technique. He warned that continuing to swim with poor technique due to fatigue embedded bad and inefficient technique and nominated one-armed fly as a possible drill to use in developing fitness. The challenge of drills like one-armed fly are initially met at a non-conscious level as the swimmer adjusts to the constraint and I suspect that if I had left the swimmers alone to make adjustments on their own, and uncoached, they may have made similar progress over time. Indeed, when coaches have their swimmers do drills like this and developing feel in breast-stroke by just sculling with no kick (see Light and Harvey, 2019), there is no intended pedagogy involved. They just learn by doing and adapting.

During this session I asked questions that, although they were designed to lead to the discovery of pre-determined knowledge, can still be what Freire (1970) describes as liberatory and can lead to the joy of discovery. I used questions to stimulate dialogue and bring the embodied, non-conscious learning occurring as the swimmer adapts to the constraint imposed to consciousness for rational consideration. I have also used this emphasis on reflection and dialogue in my university teaching in New Zealand and Japan to enhance learning as opposed to the dominance of monologue in swim coaching. In this session in the UK I recount, I tried to link the activities and questioning I used to the core concept of increasing propulsion that Fosnot (1996) calls the 'big idea', in reference to constructivist learning theory. Understanding how technique relates to the core concepts of 1) maximizing thrust and 2) reducing resistance can liberate swimmers and empower them to interpret what the coach tells them and to understand why technique is executed in a certain way. It can also make swimming training a more positive experience by providing *comprehensibility, manageability* and *meaning* for them. My swim coaching is now limited to my undergraduate teaching in New Zealand for one or two sessions a year and sometimes in Japan when I visit as an Invited Professor. It is also usually limited to a single session but I am always pleased with student/athlete learning and their enjoyment of discovery. Learning to swim better is a complex process that cannot be reduced to the repetition of discrete components and which requires a more holistic approach.

The session I write about in this chapter focused on a specific aspect of technique that is inseparable from the whole stroke and the experience of swimming as a phenomenon that includes the swimmer and his/her connection with the water. The approach I took aimed to give this part of the stroke meaning for the learner and to help him/her understand swimming as a whole-body experience. I tried to promote active learning that provided the swimmers with a challenge that extended them but which they were able to meet by drawing on their individual and collective resources. I am confident that they not only developed awareness of the function of the second kick in butterfly and improved its efficiency, but also took a tiny step toward being independent learners. However, I was most pleased with the positive learning experiences they had that can enhanced learning and learning how to learn.

References

Bruner, J. (1990) *Acts of meaning*, Cambridge, MA: Harvard University Press.
Davis, B. and Sumara, D. (1997) 'Cognition, complexity and teacher education', *Harvard Education Review*, 67(1): 105–125.
Dewey, J. (1916) *Democracy and education*, New York: Free Press.

Fosnot, C. T. (1996) 'Constructivism: A psychological theory of learning', in C. T. Fosnot (ed.) *Constructivism: Theory, perspectives and practice*, New York and London: Teachers College Columbia University, 103–119.

Freire, P. (1970) *Pedagogy of the oppressed*, New York: Continuum.

Light, R. L. (2017) *Positive Pedagogy for sport coaching: Athlete centred coaching for individual sports*, London and New York: Routledge. Available at: www.routledge.com/Positive-Pedagogy-for-Sport-Coaching-Athlete-centred-coaching-for-individual/Light/p/book/9781138215597

Light, R. L. (2014) 'Learner-centred pedagogy for swim coaching: A complex learning theory informed approach', *Asia-Pacific Journal of Health, Sport and Physical Education*, 5(2): 167–180. doi:10.1080/18377122.2014.906056

Light, R. and Fawns, R. (2003) 'Knowing the game: Integrating speech and action through TGfU', *Quest*, 55: 161–177.

Light, R. and Harvey, S. (2019) *Positive Pedagogy for coaching team and individual sports* (2nd edn), London and New York: Routledge.

Light, R. L., Harvey, S. and Memmert, D. (2013) 'Why children join and stay in sports clubs: Case studies in Australian, French and German swimming clubs', *Sport Education and Society*, 18(4): 550–566.

Light, R. L. and Lémonie, Y. (2012) 'Constructivisme et pédagogie dans l'enseignement de la natation [Constructivism and pedagogy for coaching in swimming]', *eJRIEPS*, 26: 34–52.

Light, R. and Wallian, N. (2008) 'A constructivist approach to teaching swimming', *Quest*, 60(3), 387–404.

Magias, T. (2018) 'Athlete-centred coaching in swimming: An autoethnography', in S. Pill (ed.) *Perspectives on Athlete-Centred Coaching*, London and New York: Routledge.

Mosston, M. and Ashworth, S. (1986) *Teaching physical education* (3rd edn), Columbus, OH: Merrill.

Ovens, A., Hopper, T. and Butler J. (2013) *Complexity thinking in physical education: Reframing curriculum, pedagogy and research*, London and New York: Routledge.

11

PERFORMING IN CHAOS

Coaching Transition for Young Triathletes Using Positive Pedagogy

Juliet Paterson and Kass Gibson

This chapter provides insight into the first author's experiences of using *Positive Pedagogy for Sport Coaching* (Light and Harvey, 2019) as part of an empirical study conducted in part-fulfilment of her Sport Coaching: Children and Young People Master's Degree, at a University in the UK. During this study she was supervised by Dr Kass Gibson, who is co-author of this chapter, even though it is written in the first person from the introduction on. The purpose of the study was to evaluate the effectiveness of Positive Pedagogy for sport coaching (PPed) in facilitating a holistic, child-centred approach for coaching children and young people in triathlon clubs. During the study, Juliet's coaching considerations in planning, delivery and reflection were structured by the PPed framework (Light and Harvey, 2019) to inform and advance her own coaching practice.

In this chapter Juliet reflects on a session she coached on transition. After setting the context briefly and explaining the study, we provide detail on its planning and delivery that Juliet reflects on. It was a training session aimed at improving awareness and decision-making during transition. Moreover, Juliet reflects on her continued use and refinement of PPed when working with young athletes of differing ages, abilities and experiences, at various stages along the competitive regional pathway and on how this framework has guided her in her role as British Triathlon's South West Regional Lead for 'Skills School' as the national initiative supporting the development of coaches working with children and young people in triathlon clubs and school settings.

The Context

I began my Masters' studies with a belief that, at grass roots level and in primary school education, sporting experiences are powerful. I have personally witnessed and experienced the incredible influence that excellent and effective coaching can have in guiding improvements, in the physical, technical and tactical performances of young people. This can also influence the future personal, social and emotional and cognitive development of each child and young person in our care. Therefore, my professional focus has always been to ensure children experience the positive power of sport, which necessitates holistic and humanistic approaches to coaching.

Throughout my early professional experiences in clubs and schools, working as a swimming and athletics teacher/coach and subsequently a developer of primary school teacher swimming practice, I advanced by evaluating and applying the effective practice of my own coaches, tutors and colleagues. My early experiences highlighted how effective coaching meets the child's individual and developmental needs as well as their aspirations. It is child-centred, prioritises early positive experiences and always considers the child as a person first and performer second. This was further highlighted as excellent practice when I embarked on my primary school teaching career, where I supported the development of PE as lead for the subject in three schools. During my teaching career my colleagues and ongoing professional development opportunities were again the main point of reference for guiding improvements in my practice. Therefore, I had not based my practice on a single pedagogical model but rather been involved in a successful cyclical process whereby I adapted with an intricate knowledge of what the children in my class needed to develop successfully for their life ahead.

During the initial stages of my Master's studies I evaluated 'what is excellent and effective coaching of children and young people in sport?' which reinforced these priorities as key to ensuring the holistic development of young participants. I reviewed the application and impact that athlete/student-centred coaching/teaching such as 'Teaching Games for Understanding' (Bunker and Thorpe, 1982) and 'Games Based Approaches' (GBAs) like 'Game Sense' (Light, 2013) were having upon the coaching practices of team games' coaches and their influence on participant's learning, performance improvements and positive experiences. I was particularly interested in how these approaches seemed to be able to develop participants holistically so decided to attempt to implement them in triathlon, which was a challenging and time-consuming task.

Positive Pedagogy for Sport Coaching (Light, 2017) offered specific support to guide technical improvements within triathlon, from a holistic as well as humanist philosophical position. Not only did it focus on individual sports but also aligned with my own personal philosophy as a teacher, coach and educator. Furthermore, I saw an opportunity, beyond advancing my own personal knowledge, to apply – *and* evaluate – PPed in my club settings. In conjunction with other pedagogical frameworks that prioritise learning over performance, PPed has supported me in developing coaching practice across the South West region, for British Triathlon. Indeed, as part of broader shifts in coaching British Triathlon Federation conceived 'Skills School' (2016a; 2016b), an initiative designed to support coaches in moving away from a reliance on traditional, reductionist coaching methods common place in its subsidiary disciplines, particularly swimming and athletics. Instead, encouraging coaches to use 'Guided Challenge and Discovery' methods which promote the use of exploration, questioning and creative, engaging coaching methods as valuable tools for enhancing young athlete skill development and continued engagement with specifically triathlon but also sport in general.

Although triathlon is a rapidly growing sport, it originates from mainly adult participatory foundations, which means it is still continuing to evolve and adapt to the needs of new participatory groups, such as children and young people. The requirements of my studies, my own professional development, and the broader changes in coach education mentioned above, combined with PPed as a newly articulated approach to coaching presented a need for applied practitioner research to better understand how children and young people can be coached to enable maximum improvement in performance alongside promotion of early positive experiences (Paterson, 2018). PPed appeared to provide a great opportunity to address the research gap by providing a highly effective, evidenced approach.

Triathlon

Traditionally triathlon coaching focuses on physiological training principles and technical competence to enable the efficiency and economy in movement required to meet the ever-increasing physical demands of training as determined by race intensity and distance. However, triathletes must also be psychologically, tactically and cognitively prepared and be able to adapt to race conditions and situations that arise because formats of triathlon courses vary hugely. Such variations include, but are not limited to, swimming locations (e.g., pools, lakes or sea); starts (wave or time-trial); bike terrains (e.g., tarmac, grass, track); regulations (e.g., draft legal/non-drafting), weather conditions, course topography and technicality. Furthermore, discipline-specific demands are complex. For example, in open water swimming, wetsuit/non-wetsuit requirements necessitate adaptions to stroke; starts vary between deep water starts, beach/shallow entry starts and dive starts; tactical considerations differ with regards to positioning at the start; confidence is required when swimming in close proximity to other swimmers; competence in performing buoy turns; adaptions to the stroke when sighting, drafting or due to environmental conditions, such as waves.

All told, this is indicative of the importance of continuous decision-making in triathlon and the need to be thinking athletes. For triathlon coaches wishing to guide the development of athletes as independent decision-makers, the emphasis of PPed on inquiry-based learning that fosters 'curiosity, thinking and reflection' makes it an ideal approach for developing adaptable athletes as self-regulating learners.

The Study

For this study we used a Practitioner Action Research (PAR) approach to evaluate the experiences of children and young people in triathlon clubs, coached using PPed. PAR offered us the opportunity to address calls for more practice-based, theory-driven, context and domain specific research of pedagogical approaches for coaching (Kirk, 2005; Oslin and Mitchell, 2006). I adopted PAR to provide a thorough understanding of how PPed influenced my coaching practice and the learning of the triathletes I coached, which I hope is evident in this chapter. The sessions I report on took place in junior triathlon clubs, with a total of 36 junior triathletes, aged 10–17 years. I coached these triathletes at two clubs, over a period of 15 weeks, during pre- (Spring) and mid- (Summer) race season in the UK.

The unit and weekly coaching plans that I designed, focussed on employing the PPed core features (see Light and Harvey, 2019). I created the weekly plans to be appropriately challenging and provide progression across sport-specific skills out-lined in the *The 4Es Guidance Matrix: Skills Development* (British Triathlon Federa-tion, 2020a). Furthermore, I used Fosnot's (1996) 'Big ideas' to provide the core concepts that PPed aims to link questioning and its inquiry-based approach to. In the case of triathlon, this includes understanding how to maintain momentum by focussing on efficiency and economy of movements to empower learners. This combination allowed me to draw sessions together to encourage 'flow' *within* and *between* sessions, aiming to increase the depth of learning (Light and Harvey, 2019).

As coach and researcher, I recorded my own reflections of applying PPed and my perceptions of impact, in a coach's field journal. Additionally, I used the field journal to record the triathletes' immediate responses and reactions to the sessions I had delivered. Considering the triathletes' reflections of prime importance in guiding my practice, their reflections were gathered during post–unit group inter-views and within written reflective logs, which they completed at home, some of which are shared in this chapter.

The Session Design

Here I reflect upon a session focussed on transition that I designed and coached around the pedagogical features of PPed. With appropriate adjustments, I have successfully implemented this session with young triathletes of differing ages, experiences and at various points along the regional competitive pathway in both club and young athlete development settings. I have also used this as an exemplar of best practice when working in my development role with triathlon coaches and teachers across the region.

Creating the Learning Environment

For me, a key consideration for understanding and applying PPed, was its emphasis on *learning* within the performance-focussed culture of sport and the construction of a supportive environment to encourage inquiry, risk-taking and creativity. To create this environment, I considered the triathletes' main reasons for attendance which were, principally for enjoyment, improving performance and developing new skills. The young triathletes in the study also expressed a desire to join triathlon clubs because of the unique experience they provide that is distinct from that provided at athletics and swimming clubs. To meet their needs and provide a positive experience I tried to create an engaging and explorative environment for them by designing activities to encourage experimentation, strategy creation and problem solving. This planning was detailed, complex, and required dedication and commitment to a constant cycle of reading, adaption and re-reading of PPed. As Light and Harvey (2019) suggest, the relaxed demeanour of a PPed coach typically belies the hard work involved in planning that is not visible.

During this session and others like it, I encouraged the young triathletes to explore and critically reflect on their 'known knowledge' and current processes, aiming to facilitate development of 'new knowledge' (Light, 2017). I did this by:

1. Considering their current individual practice
2. Considering other options and choices available for developing this practice through collaboration with fellow triathletes
3. Experimenting with these other options
4. Devising solutions, thus finding a preference that suited them.

When applied to individual sports for technical improvement, PPed often involves creating a problem to be solved through a discovery, or guided discovery approach (Light, 2017). In my sessions I focussed on the following three areas:

1. Exploration of technique, for example: exploring changes in the streamlined position from the pool wall (minimising resistance); cycling cornering technique (maximising propulsion); the arm action in running (maximising efficiency and running economy).
2. Exploration of tactical scenarios, such as: positioning during an open water start; exploring pack positioning when riding in draft-legal races; experimenting with running strategies according to terrain/topography demands.
3. Exploration of physical intensity, for example: exploring the notion of 'pacing'; using ratings of perceived exertion to guide personal physical application; using negative splits to reduce onset of fatigue in running.

The session I reflect on in this chapter focussed on improving performance on approach to, during and on leaving transition.

Transition (the so-called fourth discipline) is unique to triathlon and involves entering a designated area to transition from the swim phase to cycling or cycling to running. Transition can be chaotic and triathletes have to be able to adapt to and make good decisions in this chaos. Indeed, British Triathlon recognises the importance of having to negotiate such chaotic conditions and promotes the use of a coaching method dubbed 'choreographed chaos' (British Triathlon Federation, 2016; 2020b). Here coaches provide opportunities that require triathletes to adapt to a given situation or scenario, introducing triathletes to chaotic conditions, by choreographing this carefully. While a (young) triathlete can plan ahead to be prepared and set up ideally to execute the fastest transition time, the ability to be aware of what is happening and make appropriate decisions independently throughout transition is crucial.

I designed this session to develop awareness of the options open to the triathletes in transitions and give them opportunities to make decisions and reflect on them as well as being aware of others in transition. I wanted to increase their confidence and support them in independently responding to others as well as changes that may occur while mounting and dismounting the bike. First, I created an area which necessitated riding, mounting, and dismounting bikes in close proximity to others. Through careful consideration of spatial constraints, I prepared an oval of yellow cones, approximately 25m x 15m. Inside this oval, I placed approximately 10 mount gates (2 red marker cones 1m apart) and 10 dismount gates (2 blue marker cones 1m apart) randomly (Figure 11.1).

To emulate 'chaos', all children were simultaneously active. While I had planned in detail, the understanding was that the plan was not set in stone, but rather 'written in the sand' and ready to be adjusted according to my observations, analysis and subsequent judgements of progress in learning. This required me to be comfortable with constantly adapting but also highlighted a need for me to have a detailed knowledge of the progressions available to appropriately adjust to the triathletes' needs.

Coaching the Session

Introduction

A significant accomplishment for me, across all the clubs I coached in, has been the fine tuning of the introduction. The phrase 'start as you mean to go on' eloquently describes the importance of a well-considered introduction that leads fluidly into and reflects my pedagogical approach for the main part of the session. So, in consideration of the PPed core features, I began each unit with a big idea such as maintaining momentum. I would begin by saying, 'Over the next five weeks we're thinking about how we can maintain momentum during each phase of a triathlon, specifically enabling us to race through transition effectively'. At the beginning of each session I then created a session focus, linked to the big idea of maintaining momentum such as by saying that, 'Today we are going to explore how we may need to adapt our mounting/dismounting technique and our transition plan,

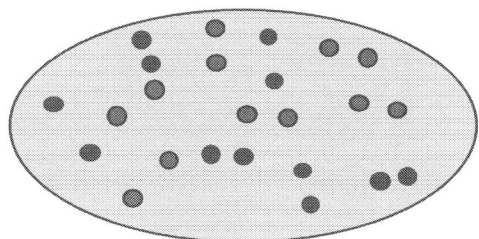

FIGURE 11.1 Transition oval

depending on the actions of other triathletes, to maintain race momentum'. On this occasion, the focus was received with considered nods and immediate athlete engagement, noted by maintenance of eye contact, alert body posture and eagerness to begin.

Main Activity

After the introduction I gave an instruction to provide minimal structure, reinforcing the idea of independent exploration. I asked them to explore the on/off challenge which involved pushing their bikes towards the red cones, where they mounted their bikes, cycled towards two blue cones and dismounted at them. They repeated this for three minutes, going in any direction and approaching gates in any order they wanted to. They were all immediately surprised when I explained this challenge, looking at each other, laughing in disbelief and checking with me to make sure they had understood what I wanted them to do. They asked me, 'We do this altogether?' and 'In any direction?' to which I replied: 'That's the challenge!' Again, laughter followed, with some asking, 'Can we start?'

I noticed older and more confident riders charged into the oval, while less confident and experienced riders were initially more tentative, taking time out to observe the others and then joining the activity in their own time, challenging themselves without my prompting, just 'having a go'. For a few minutes I provided them the opportunity to become accustomed with the task and environment and used this time to take note of proficiency levels and decide how to adapt to these. This approach worked well, and I could see triathletes of all abilities, developmental stages, and levels of experience engaged in the activity. Crucially, this approach accommodated the diversity which is evident in most junior sessions and often exacerbated by the 'drop in' nature of the participating triathlon clubs.

After this, we regrouped and I encouraged them to consider their initial feelings, using 'skinny' questions. These questions served as reminders of the 'rules' of transition I had set, such as where they should mount the bike. More importantly, they increased subsequent opportunities for self-reflection on the *how* such as, 'How did you mount your bike?' I then repeated the on/off challenge and asked them, 'This time think about what you are doing to adjust your mounts and dismounts when riding in close proximity to others'. Some children more used to being told what to do, asked for clarification while others relished the freedom. Challenging them to critically reflect on what they had been doing stimulated immersion in the task and they seemed both grounded and attentive.

Usually, each practice session was followed by discussion and reflection but to provide more children with the opportunity to share I varied how I did this. For example, at times I used the technique of paired reflection, 'Think, pair, share'. Here I used 'fat' questions to probe triathlete consideration of any adjustments made. This probing of changes in practice enhanced triathlete levels of cognitive and physical engagement, advanced opportunities for corporeal learning and was evident throughout this and all sessions. On occasion, I also needed to teach discussion and diplomacy skills (Slade et al, 2019) to the group and felt that this encouraged them to engage in dialogue and confidently justify the decisions they made. The open and supportive environment I had been building seemed to encourage the triathletes to contribute to discussions and debates with questions acting as 'invitations for dialogue' (Light, 2017: 68).

To provide multiple opportunities for practice I set another challenge, aiming to enrich their understanding by facilitating experiences of *in the moment* reflection. I asked them to try different solution to any problems they might have and to consider trying one their partner shared with them. To encourage meaningful sharing and debates, I used 'Question starters' (Kracl, 2012 in Harvey and Light, 2015) with small groups of triathletes. At first, the younger triathletes took offence if directly disagreed with but, through explanation and repeated attention to teaching diplomacy skills, I encouraged the triathletes to begin to see others' opinions as non-threatening and increasingly valuable.

Pleased with progress, I then raised the level of challenge. I repeated the 'on/off' challenge, but asked all riders to push their bikes around the circumference of the yellow circle and on hearing my call of 'transition!', push their bike to any red gate, mount, cycle and dismount at the blue gate, and repeat it. I also asked them to count how many dismounts they could perform in 30 seconds and, on completion, I used questions to encourage quiet reflection. For example, I said to them, 'Have a minute to think about how adding a competitive challenge impacted on your technique and/or preferred strategy' followed up with, 'Now adjust something to help improve your score'. I then asked them to repeat the activity, but with the challenge of having to 'beat your own score'. This was followed with discussion as a whole group of the positive changes they found aided their performance to direct attention towards not only to *how* to perform skills efficiently but also *when* to apply them, *where* and crucially, *why* (Light, 2017; Light and Harvey, 2019).

Session Conclusion

For the final activity I asked all the triathletes to race through a more traditional, linear transition area, aligning with competitive race environments. I then drew the group together and asked them to share ideas, solutions and improvements with a partner as is common practice in PPed. I then asked them more general and open questions such as, 'What have you learnt or become more aware of today? Is there anything you have improved today? What have you identified you want to work on more?' As a result of this session and based on my observations and questioning I felt my triathletes developed improved awareness of others in approach to, during and on leaving transition. They also seemed to gain an appreciation of the many possibilities for performing the same task, due to sharing and sampling a multitude of strategies aiming to aid independence in adaption, specifically valuable for maintaining momentum through transition. At this session and sessions at other clubs the triathletes responded more positively to questioning each week, 'warming up' to the method and increasingly empowered by the process, as one said to me, 'I like to be challenged in thinking if I am doing something correct or not, rather than being told'.

Reflection and Evaluation

Over the past two years, I have found applying the PPed approach in junior triathlon club and young athlete development settings a beneficial and enjoyable experience, advancing my own performance as an effective coach with positive responses by the triathletes I coached. They also reported improvements in engagement, increased perceptions of competence, increased confidence and connectedness. Importantly, the development of positive character traits and independent decision-making abilities were also evident in their reflections (Paterson, 2018). The PPed framework has been a comprehensive point of reference for me – informing both my coaching and my role as a coach developer. This has been particularly valuable when guiding coaches' creation and maintenance of learning and learner-centred, inquiry-based environments to enable increased understanding of the significance of adopting humanist and holistic approaches to learning and experiences for triathletes of varying ages, ability and levels of experience.

The PPed core features offered me clarity in planning questions to advance understanding of the *how, what, where* and crucially the *why*, not often recognised as valuable with athletes of such a young age. As such I modified my practice, subsequently improved the quality of learning experiences and the impact I have had upon the individual development and performances of the triathletes I work with. More specifically, as evidenced throughout this chapter, PPed has informed and enhanced my questioning, which has consistently guided improvements in triathlete learning, the creation of an effective inquiry-based environment and, critically, their development as independent, adaptable decision-makers. This has only been possible through me designing a range of questions and questioning strategies that go beyond traditional focus on *how* and *when* to perform certain skills. During planning I create a range of questions to elicit understanding of *where* and *why* such skills and adaptions are beneficial. This shift in practice ensures contextualised understanding and meaningful experience by developing cognitive reasoning and empowering triathletes to be in active in *their own* learning process.

Developing a repertoire of questioning skills has been time consuming and improving the influence of questioning on learning required me to educate the participants in how to respond, discuss and listen in discussions. This necessitated considering my own behaviours carefully. For example, how I should respond to and reflect on the answers that children offered, to open up opportunities for purposeful debate to enhance divergent thinking capabilities? Critically though, throughout this I have focused on maintaining balance in the sessions, appreciating that while questioning is valuable, there is also a place for constructive, specific and individual feedback. As Cushion (2013: 66) suggests, a coach must 'learn when to ask and when to tell'. For me, PPed has not been a case of developing technical coaching skills such as questioning, but of focusing on learning and increased the depth of this learning to create socially-supportive environment. When aiming to sustain engagement, ensure meaningfulness, and support continuation in triathlon, and other sports, the creation of such environments – in this case through the use of PPed – is critical for nurturing the development of positive, supportive relationships and concomitantly meaningful learning.

References

British Triathlon Federation (2016a) *Skills School. Be your best – A Framework for young triathlete development in Britain.* September 2016. British Triathlon Federation.

British Triathlon Federation (2016b) *Skills School. Coaches playbook.* September 2016. British Triathlon Federation.

British Triathlon Federation (2020a) *The 4Es Guidance Matrix: Skill Development.* British Triathlon Federation.

British Triathlon Federation (2020b) *Skills Framework. Children's Coach Development. A Framework guiding young triathlete development in Britain.* British Triathlon Federation.

Bunker, D. and Thorpe, R. (1982) 'A model for teaching games in secondary school', *Bulletin of Physical Education*, 10: 9–16.

Cushion, C. J. (2013) 'Applying game centred approaches in coaching: a critical analysis of the "dilemmas of practice" impacting change', *Sports Coaching Review*, 2: 61–76.

Fosnot, C. T. (ed.) (1996) *Constructivism: Theory, perspectives and practice.* New York and London: Teachers College, Columbia University.

Harvey, S. and Light, R. L. (2015) 'Questioning for learning in game-based approaches to teaching and coaching', *Asia-Pacific Journal of Health, Sport and Physical Education*, 6(2): 175–190.

Kirk, D. (2005) 'Physical education, youth sport and lifelong participation: the importance of early learning experiences', *European Physical Education Review*, 11(3): 239–255.

Light, R. L. (2013) *Game Sense: Pedagogy for performance, participation and enjoyment*, London and New York: Routledge.

Light, R. L. (2017) *Positive Pedagogy for sport coaching: Athlete-centred coaching for individual sports*, London and New York: Routledge.

Light, R. L. and Harvey, S. (2019) *Positive Pedagogy for coaching* (2nd edn). London and New York: Routledge.

Oslin, J. and Mitchell, S. (2006) '*Games Centred Approaches to teaching physical education*', in D. Kirk, D. MacDonald and M. O'Sullivan (eds) *The Handbook of Physical Education.* London: Sage Publications.

Paterson, J. (2018) *The Positive Pedagogy Approach for Coaching: Young Triathlete and Coach Experiences of Practice.* Unpublished MA research. Plymouth Marjon University.

Slade, D. G., Martin, A. J. and Watson, G. (2019) 'Developing a game and learning-centred flexible teaching model for transforming play', *Physical Education and Sport Pedagogy*, 24(5): 434–446.

12

TEACHING JAVELIN IN A SINGAPORE SCHOOL

Richard Light

I have a coaching background in school sports as a teacher and in rugby and martial arts at high performance levels but what is most relevant to this chapter is my experience as a teacher in Australia and Japan. I have been a general primary (elementary) and secondary school teacher in Australia and taught at secondary level in Japan. While coaching rugby in Japan at professional level I worked during my mornings teaching at a sport high school in Osaka. Later, I worked full time as an English teacher at an elite level academic school in Osaka where I was also the school's rugby coach.

My teaching experience is relevant to this chapter because it is a reflection on my experiences of teaching classes of fourteen-year old students in a Singapore secondary school as part of a seminar I delivered on PPed for Singaporean physical education teachers in 2019. I recognise there are differences between coaching sport (even in a school setting) and physical education that includes the motivation of students, the variation in skills and experience among the learners and the aims or learning objectives. However, as Armour (2014) suggests in her collection of case studies in youth sport and sport coaching, there are significant similarities.

In my books on Game Sense (see Light, 2013) and Positive Pedagogy for sport coaching (see Light and Harvey, 2019) I emphasize the importance of the context the coach works in and how s/he must be aware of, and be able adapt to, context. I have conducted research on the influence of context on coaching, teaching and learning with an emphasis on culture across a range of cultures (see, Hassanin and Light, 2014; Light and Yasaki, 2016). This chapter offers an example of how coaches and teachers need to be aware of, and account for, the influence of institutional and cultural context with the experience I reflect on occurring in August 2019. It provided me a great learning experience that generated improved understanding of the challenges facing coaches and teachers when implementing PPed and GBA, and the need to do it gradually.

The Context

I planned the four-day seminar around the delivery of a one-hour lecture followed by a practical workshop of about 90 minutes duration, teacher discussions about the lecture and workshop during which they developed questions for me in a Q and A session at the end of each day. Based on my experiences of working with teachers around the globe (Australia, New Zealand, Macau, Japan, Canada and the UK) I feel that they make the most sense of ideas when put into action in real classes. For this reason, the organizer of the seminar asked me to teach classes in the school to demonstrate PPed, but I was only able to teach three classes due to the gym being unavailable one day. I taught basketball and football to classes of 40 students with equal numbers for boys and girls and taught javelin throwing to a 'difficult class' of 30 students with only five girls.

The students had very little, if any, experience of being taught using student-centred and/or inquiry-based pedagogy, which meant that my approach was foreign to them. When teachers or coaches want to begin using contemporary pedagogy like PPed with teams, squads or classes like this, I always advise them to make changes gradually and wait for the learners to adapt before implementing the approach more fully. This is because it can be a shock for athletes or students who are accustomed to being told and being passive participants in learning, to be empowered and expected to be responsible and accountable. However, this was not an option for me on this occasion because I had only an hour and a half in each lesson to demonstrate the PPed approach to the teachers. I have had experience in teaching 'difficult classes' as a casual teacher in Sydney, the NSW Far North Coast and Brisbane for a total of ten years and am familiar with the challenges of teaching classes where I don't know the students and they don't know me. Going in 'cold' to teaching any new class is a challenge but adopting a radically different pedagogy at the same time makes it much more difficult.

In the two classes I taught prior to the javelin class, the students were very reluctant to answer question in a whole class setting and this was not because they did not know the answer. During my discussions with teachers after a class, one teacher told me that when I asked a question in the whole-class circle, a boy turned to his classmate and told him the answer that I was looking for but was not prepared to tell me in front of his classmates. The challenges for me that I describe above were not limited to students being disinclined to answer questions. Owing to how the students had been taught, the lack of a relationship between the class and me, the nature of Singaporean society and the way I taught unsettled the students to varying degrees and particularly early in the lessons. This included some minor behaviour problems that seemed to arise from the freedom given to them in contrast to the tight control they were normally under in highly structured lessons. On the first day, this was noted as something of concern to a couple of teachers but was not mentioned again after that as their understanding of PPed and the situation I was in developed from our daily group discussions.

To provide an example, I briefly reflect on the football session which was my second practical workshop. My starting point was a little 'off' in the football lesson due to lack of skill among the students and my lack of knowledge of their abilities. I started with a game of 'keepings-off' or 'piggy in the middle' in which teams of four had to keep the ball away from the 'piggy' but few of them had the skill required to make this work – no matter how I played with the numbers and ratio of players. Owing to the fact that I planned for this activity to lead into the next and more complex activity, it required some changes 'on the run'. I would also normally have spent much more time with each activity to raise performance of it before being able to transition up to more complex and testing activities/games, but I wanted to show something of the games that the beginning activities would lead to for the teachers. This meant that, in terms of skill, knowledge and confidence, the students were not really ready to play the end game of four-goal soccer with no keeper and for this reason it did not start well. However, as they adapted and responded to my questioning (even without answers) the quality of play, engagement, motivation and enjoyment improved and enable finishing on a positive note.

Teaching classes of 40 students requires good organisational skills but this was not a problem for me because I have taught similar sized classes in Japanese schools where I taught part time in a sports high school for three years and full time in an elite academic school for two years in Osaka. More recently, I ran two Game Sense workshops in a Tokyo university and in 2019 I did a PPed workshop in a women's university in Amagazaki, Japan, which I was very happy with because of the flow and energy of the session and the extent the girls all enjoyed it.

The Session

The javelin class was my third and most difficult lesson, and I had been warned by teachers about 'challenging' student behaviour. It was smaller than the first two classes I taught with about 30 students and only five girls. The class had been told to sit down in lines by their regular teacher before I was introduced and my first action was to ask them to stand up and form a large circle in the middle of the gym, as I had done with the other two classes. This simple task alerted me to some likely challenges for the lesson in terms of some students' behaviour. Once they were reasonably settled and I had their attention, I explained that the class would be on javelin throwing and that my focus would be on having them think about how they could develop the best technique for throwing the javelin as far as possible. I told them that with all their throwing they should aim to release at a 45 degree angle and that if they did then the speed of release would determine the distance of the throw with the aim of the lesson being to develop the best technique to achieve maximum velocity at release. I then explained what the progression of activities would be and how we would finish the lesson.

Activity 1

In the first activity, and with the behaviour of the class in mind, I started off with a very structured approach. I had them form 10 groups of three lined behind cones at one end of the gym with one medicine ball for each group of three with their task being to work out how to throw the medicine ball as far as possible. I started at one end with the first group and with the student at the front of the line throwing a 3kg medicine ball as far as possible on my command and told them all that they should aim to release at a 45-degree angle. Then, on the sound of my whistle, they were to run to retrieve the medicine ball, take it to the next thrower and go to the back of the line. After each student had a throw I asked them to discuss in their groups of three how they could throw the medicine ball as far as possible during which, I was pleasantly surprised at how much they engaged in this discussion and collaboration, which made me feel more positive about how the lesson would develop they all then had two more throws each to test their ideas. I had been wary at the beginning of the lesson but felt pleased about this engagement.

Activity 2

For the next activity I asked the class to stay in their groups of three, find a safe space in the gym where they could practise throwing the medicine ball, and develop their technique during which, I moved about the groups monitoring progress, asking questions and making positive remarks about their ideas and technique where justifiable. After a few minutes a small number of students became bored and began to drift off task, but the majority of the class stayed on task and made good progress. I then blew my whistle and called them in to form a large circle where I asked them to share what they did to improve their throwing, asking one from each group to demonstrate the technique they had developed. My aim here was to identify the four principles of throwing I outlined in the introduction which where, 1) transferring weight from the back to the front foot, 2) the movement of joints from flexion to extension, 3) moving the body from low to high and 4) transferring power generated from the lower body through rotation of the hips with a lag between hip and upper body rotation and release.

This class had no previous experience of student–centred teaching and the teacher questioning involved. From my experience of teaching the two previous lessons, I knew that getting the answers I was after would be difficult and could slow down the little momentum I had managed to build. So, instead of asking questions about the technique that was being demonstrated I commented on the demonstration to identify relevant features. I did ask a few questions that I did not get any answers to but gave them time to think about it. For example, 'That is great! What is happening with his weight? which foot is it on – back or front? Look at where his weight is when he starts and where it is when he releases (weight transfer)'. When focused on flexing and then extending joints I asked the demonstrating student to do one throw. I then asked him/her to throw again but before s/he did I asked the class to,

'Watch his knees and his elbows when he throws again and tell me what is happening'. At the end of this sharing of ideas and identifying of the four principles of throwing I reinforced the importance of them in any throwing and explained how we would now apply these ideas to throwing the javelin. The javelins were actually 'Turbo-javs' which are the same weight as a normal javelin but made of plastic with a rounded rubber tip and much shorter.

Activity 3

For the next activity I asked the class to form groups of five and return to the lines behind cones at the end of the gym where we had been for activity 1. I only had six javelins that I brought with me from New Zealand so divided the class into groups of five with one javelin per group. I gave basic technical instruction on how to throw the javelin and how to hold it and related this to the four principles they had discovered. As I had done with the medicine balls, I asked the students to throw one at a time. When happy with how this was going, I asked every student at the front of the line with a javelin to all throw at once on my command. Then, when I blew the whistle, the ones who had thrown the javelins would retrieve them. give them to the next student in line and join at back of line. after each round of five throws I asked the groups to discuss and develop their technique and did a total of three rounds.

At the end of the lesson I had the class form a big circle to discuss the session and reinforce the role that the four principles we had discovered played in throwing the javelin. These were: 1) transferring weight from the back to the front foot, 2) the movement of joints from flexion to extension, 3) moving the body from low to high and 4) generating power from the lower body that is transferred through rotation of the hips with a lag between hip, upper body rotation and release.

Reflection and Evaluation

Across the basketball, football and javelin classes I was initially challenged by the lack of student willingness to provide answers and how slow I felt they were to adapt to a different approach to teaching. I dealt with this by being patient and adjusting my expectations and 'lesson plan' to the skills, attitude and behaviour of the class. While there were challenges for me in each class there were also many moments of satisfaction and a sense of achievement for me with significant engagement in most of all these classes after shaky beginnings, which were due to my lack of knowledge of the class. In the basketball and football classes, the girls were initially more reluctant than the boys to engage but, as we worked through to 'team talks' and working as groups through interaction, their enthusiasm, enjoyment and engagement grew very quickly to surpass that of the boys but with so few in the javelin class this was not evident. In the basketball and football classes, the girls seemed to respond very well to the more complex games and activities that required team talks than the boys and this was noted in discussions with three teachers who were pleasantly surprised as the engagement and enthusiasm of the girls, who they said normally did not engage physically.

Owing to the potential for behavioural problems in the class I tried to keep a balance between control and the freedom to explore, inquire and discover by gradually releasing control and letting the class taste some student-centred learning. I began with ten groups of three throwing medicine balls one at a time with the little discussions some of them had about technique providing more freedom to inquire for them. I then gave more room to experiment, interact and gain a little control of their learning by allowing them to work in groups to develop their technique. Some flourished, others participated with limited enthusiasm and some quickly lost interest, so I pulled them back into a big circle. I used this to identify the four principles of throwing that underpinned the lesson and asked the students to apply them to the javelin by beginning with strong control but loosening it as I saw fit and finishing with the big circle to go back over what we had done and what they should have learned. As I adapted to the demands of my situation, I implemented an approach that opened and closed as we moved through the learning experience. This centred around the big, whole-class circle as a way of communicating, guiding and facilitating their learning of, and about, the four throwing principles as the core of my learning objectives.

I knew I was in for a challenge teaching the javelin class so did not expect too much but was happy with the progress of the lesson and the engagement of most students. I had to sit out several students due to disruptive behaviour but, overall, and considering the challenge I was faced with, I felt the lesson went well. The reluctance of most students to answer questions was no surprise for me but, instead of seeing this as too much of challenge, it might suggest how much the students actually need an approach like this in PE because of how it can contribute to their development and broader learning. The experience certainly gave me valuable insight into what it is like for a teacher or coach when trying to implement PPed or any other athlete, or student-centred, approach too quickly in an environment that works against the student-centred, inquiry-based nature of Positive Pedagogy for sport coaching.

It had been a very long time since I had last taught junior high school classes before these lessons in Singapore and I felt significantly challenged but was equally satisfied with the three lessons. I am also pleased that I had the opportunity to teach like this and to keep in touch with teaching in schools and to get some useful insight into teachers' experiences of adopting innovation such as PPed. If I were to do these classes again, with the same students, I would make some small changes, but I think it is important to note here that this was different to teaching a class under normal conditions. To demonstrate PPed in action, I felt obliged to do more activities and transition more quickly than I would if not using the lesson to demonstrate PPed. For me, this reinforced the importance of gradual change and the need to be well tuned into learning progress and the nature of the experience for the students, which is facilitated with a humanistic approach (Light and Harvey, 2019).

References

Armour, K. (ed.) (2014) *Pedagogical case studies in physical education and youth sport* (1st edn), London and New York: Routledge.

Hassanin, R. and Light, R. L. (2014) 'Culture, experience and the construction of views on coaching: Implications for the uptake of Game Sense', *University of Sydney Papers in Human Movement, Health and Coach Education – Special Games Sense Edition*, 51–65. Retrieved from www.sydney.edu.au/edsw/hmhce-journal

Light, R. L. (2013) *Game Sense: Pedagogy for performance, participation and enjoyment.* London and New York: Routledge.

Light, R. and Harvey, S. (2019) *Positive Pedagogy for coaching team and individual sports*, London and New York: Routledge.

Light, R. L. and Yasaki, W. (2016) 'The nature of experience and learning for Japanese girls in a high school basketball club', in O. Vors, and D. Kirk (eds) Special issue on '*L'écologie de la classe: approches contextualisées en éducation physique et en sport* [The ecology of the class: Contextualised approaches in physical education and sport]'. *Recherches & Educations*, 15, June, 51–68.

13

TEACHING FOR MOTIVATION AND AWARENESS IN CHILDREN'S AND YOUTH GYMNASTICS

Bianca Couto de Aguiar

I have been in the gymnastics field for 23 years, initially as a gymnast and for the last ten years, as a gymnastics coach with the last four in New Zealand. I feel like I had a particular way of coaching since very early on in my coaching career but I have never really thought about that until recently. Writing the chapter "Gymnastics: Enhancing thought, awareness and positive experiences" for the first Positive Pedagogy book (Light, 2017) encouraged me to deeply and honestly reflect on my coaching, which led me to realise how my approach aligned with features of Positive Pedagogy (PPed). It also led me to think that my coaching approach was probably a much more creative, discovery-based way of coaching gymnastics than I had thought it had been. Through this process of reflection, I understood that my main goal as a coach has always been to foster gymnasts' enjoyment, motivation and awareness rather than seeking perfection in technique through highly repetitive drills.

During my development as a coach, I have always been very proud of the connection and trust I have developed with all my gymnasts. As I reflected on the chapter I wrote in the first edition of PPed (Light, 2017), I felt that my approach to coaching didn't resemble the strict, result oriented way of coaching that is commonly seen in gymnastics. Through fostering learning as discovery and self-awareness in a positive environment, I could feel my gymnasts' joy, motivation and confidence when trying new skills. In my eyes, they seemed happier when compared with gymnasts who had very strict, traditional coaches.

As it has been shown in the literature, and recently articulated by Light and Harvey (2019, p. 15), "traditional approaches tend to feature direct instruction, feedback and demonstrations based upon the assumption that the more the coach intervenes, the more the athletes will improve". While I believe in the importance of the constant interaction between the coach and the athlete, when reflecting on my practice, I see this constant intervention as being through continuous stimulation of the gymnasts' thinking and problem-solving ability instead of directly telling them what to do.

Not only my experience as a gymnastics coach, but also as a physical education teacher, led me to have a more humanistic approach to coaching which is a feature of PPed. I realised that each one of my gymnasts is an individual being and that they are so much more than what I can see and in a gymnastics session. This has made me plan and adapt my activities according with their level, respecting their pace and challenging them as they needed. Over the last ten years as a coach, I became aware that stimulus is possible and the challenges better received by the gymnasts when there is a close relationship between them and coach, and when they feel that the coach understands them.

In a demanding and complex sport such as gymnastics, my gymnasts, like any other gymnast, were sometimes afraid of performing a new skill. However, they were never afraid of failing nor afraid of what I could say because of the good relationship, positive, encouraging environment we have created and, which is emphasised in PPed.

The Context

Since writing my chapter in the first edition of *Positive Pedagogy for Sport Coaching* (Light, 2017), I have been much more aware of my own practice. After realising that my practice had many features of PPed, it was fascinating to understand how much more there was to learn and reflect on in relation to my own approach than I thought. For the past two and a half years, I have noticed that my coaching approach varies according with the age group I am coaching and the level of understanding of each gymnast. Also, I have realised that I have been able to change and adapt the strict lesson plans I had to follow in my gym in order to meet my gymnasts' needs.

While in New Zealand, I coached pre-school classes (2–4 years old), recreational classes (5–7 years old – Recreation; 8–12 years old – Advanced Recreation), school groups (5–13 years old depending on their school grade), and regional competitive squads (7–14 years old). I had a wide range of gymnasts in different stages of motor and cognitive development, and more importantly, with different goals and expectations regarding gymnastics. I had groups that came to the gym just to have fun all the way to competitive squads. Every class had its own dynamics and I realised that I had to adapt my coaching to each one of them and what their goals were. I can say that, while keeping the same enthusiasm and still fostering body awareness and understanding through a discovery-based approach, I realised that I was almost a different coach for each one of those groups regarding my interaction and feedback to them. While reflecting on my practice, it was interesting to notice that even when all these groups had the same skills to learn or practice, my coaching approach was different according with their level and their age group.

In this chapter, I reflect on my coaching experience while in New Zealand. I contemplate how my practice was guided by features of PPed and how I adapted my approach according with the distinct groups I had while coaching there. I will give examples of this through identifying differences and/or similarities in my approach, and the tools and/or cues I used for each group in order to help them throughout their learning process. I will give particular emphasis on how my interaction and feedback would be for each group according with their level of understanding. Moreover, I will pay attention to what I believe my gymnasts' response was in terms of their learning, motivation, and feelings (for example, frustration, pleasure, engagement etc.).

The Sessions

In a typical day at the gym in New Zealand I would coach three different groups: school groups; recreational classes (divided in Recreation and Advanced Recreation) and competitive squads. Each class had an average age gap between the gymnasts of three years. Before giving an example of one skill (jumps on the beam), and how I would coach it in each class, it is important to reflect on one of the main challenges I had to face while coaching in New Zealand over the four-year period, and how I had to adapt and set achievable goals not only for me as a coach, but more importantly, for my gymnasts.

Making a Plan Fit Different Needs

During the time I coached in New Zealand, I had a lesson plan for the recreational classes and for the school groups that was made by the manager (the person responsible for the programme), and that was meant to be followed by all the coaches. I believe this was to guarantee that all the gymnasts were learning the same content and that at the end of each term all the skills had been taught. Each class had a very strict structured, and at first this was very hard for me to adapt to. Each class had around forty gymnasts and four coaches. Besides the warm up and stretches, each coach would only interact with their own group that had been assign to them for the entire term. It was only for the competitive squads that coaches had the opportunity to do their own plan and run the class as they wanted and/or see fit.

Having to follow a strict plan, represented the first big challenge I had to face in my career as it was the first time I had to follow someone else's plan. A plan that resembled very much a structured, traditional way of coaching. From the warm-up until the end of the session everything was set up, timed and written down on paper. My question was: How can I adapt their plan to my coaching approach and my group's needs, and at the same time strictly follow their plan?

For a while, I felt a little bit trapped as the strict way they coached was completely opposite to my developing approach. To me, the gym policy and how they were trying to develop their gymnasts looked like 'mass production'.

The groups we had assign for one term could change in the following term which, once again, challenge my vision of continuity and being able to follow my gymnasts' progress and growth. Even though I was initially disappointed, I quickly realised that I was able to at least provide them with positive experiences and a good foundation that they could use later on, so I set that as my short-term goal for all my classes apart from my competitive squads.

Each recreational class and each school group would come to the gym once a week for one or one hour and a half. Every class was divided in warm up and stretch (20–25 minutes) and four rotations (beam, bar, floor and vault or a conditioning station) (10–15 minutes). As a way of circumvent their rigid structure, I started going to the gym fifteen minutes before each class to see the set up they had and how could I adapt that to my group. Slowly but surely, I started grabbing extra equipment such as mats, slopes, dots, hoops, bean bags, ropes, anything I could find really, and place them on the side of the stations I was going to be at in order to help my gymnasts if needed. Even though I couldn't change the plan, I realise that through using different equipment, questioning and feedback to help them learn and understand a skill, I was using features of Positive Pedagogy to help manage learning and have the right level of challenge for each group and individual.

Skill: Jumps on Beam – Losing Momentary Contact with the Apparatus

For each class apart the competitive squads, every session, I would have to coach all four events (beam, bar, floor and vault). Beam was always the most challenging apparatus across all groups, and for that reason, the most challenging to coach as well. The gymnasts had mixed emotions when doing beam. Some of them would consider beam as their favourite apparatus, while others hated being on top of it and were truly afraid.

As a gymnast, I had a love-hate relationship with the beam. Until something went wrong, for example falling off the beam, I would love it, but I realise that learning new skills was not really enjoyable. Reflecting on this, I understood that since early on in my coaching career, I have tried to make the drills fun to help my gymnasts get comfortable on beam and enjoy learning and trying new skills regardless the failure that it would be inevitable during skill acquisition. Here, I describe how I would coach jumps drills (that usually have high rates of failure) in three different classes (school groups, advanced recreation, and competitive squads), and how my emphasis was on motivation, awareness and the right amount of challenge.

School Group (1st Grade – 5–7 years old)

Each school group would usually come to the gym once a week for six weeks. For school groups, within a variety of jumps that are possible to do on the beam, I had mainly to coach straight jumps. This is not a skill with a high level of difficulty but scary enough for the majority of new gymnasts.

I had always the students start on the low beam. I wanted them to experience and try the skill without having the fear of falling from a high beam. Having high rates of success on the first try was always good to develop their confidence. Even though, with this group, achieving the correct technique was not my main focus, I wanted them to understand and be aware of their body in relation to the beam when doing a jump. For this reason, most of the times I would use a ladder pattern with the beams (from the lowest beam to the higher beam), and would let them choose in which beam they wanted to try the skill. Giving them the power to choose made them feel more comfortable in trying, and gave them confidence and motivation to challenge themselves. It was possible to see that they were enjoying learning the skill and getting better, and that there was a healthy and positive level of competition between the gymnasts. They wanted to see how far they could go, how high they could jump, and compare results with their friends. Another strategy I used when coaching straight jumps was to use extra equipment to help them understand how to execute the skill and adapt to their level. For example, I would use chalk to draw lines along the beam so the students could jump over them, or, for more advanced students, bean bags to add some height and raise the challenge.

As in school groups, most of the students were not actually gymnasts, more than correcting their technique I would encourage them throughout the drill and would use the equipment (as in the example above) to generate body awareness, adapt to their levels, and in turn, increase their success rates and enjoyment. For these groups, I would set as my immediate goal, generate a positive environment that could foster learning, and second, I would aim to help them improve their skills as much as possible over a course of six weeks.

Even though sometimes I had to resort to a more direct instruction to help them understand what I wanted from them, most of their learning was fostered through experience, trial and error. Reflecting on how I coached this group, making learning a positive experience while challenging each individual was the priority which I believe aligns with the features of PPed.

Advanced Recreation (8–12 years old)

Advanced recreation was a class for gymnasts that wanted to learn gymnastics just for fun as they didn't want to compete. In this class, the gymnasts already had some experience or were too old to be in a class with five-year-olds. Like in the school groups, jumps were also part of the plan for this class. However, after trying the same approach I have tried with the school groups (adding equipment to make the drill more fun and challenging), I realised that having the same approach would not suit this group, so I had to adapt. The girls were almost teenagers and felt ridiculed when doing the same drills as the younger gymnasts did. I soon realised that giving feedback and just guiding them through the exercise was the best way of helping them improve. Their level of understanding was definitely higher than the younger gymnasts but their level of execution not always matched. Because of this disparity, questioning became one of the main tools I used to enhance their understanding as well as their awareness. As we discussed and they figured out what they needed to do to execute jumps on beam successfully, they felt they were part of their learning process and became more motivated to try harder jumps. I started coaching different drills and variations of the straight jump such as straight jump swapping feet, tuck jumps, split jumps, or even letting them connect two jumps, everything to meet their needs and keep them motivated and challenged. As they enjoyed being part of a group and had fun learning new skills, the social part of gymnastics and sense of belonging became much more relevant and evident.

Reflecting on how I coached this group, I realised that even though my short-term goal for them was still having fun and enjoy learning, I had higher expectations regarding their improvement. While I still wanted to generate positive experiences and challenge them, I paid more attention to how the skills were executed and gave more emphasis in helping them understand and discover how to perform the jumps through questioning.

Competitive Squad (7–14 years old)

Opposite to the other classes, that trained once a week for one/one hour and a half, the competitive squads would train at least twice a week for four hours and their ultimate goal was to be prepared for competitions. Here, technique and results mattered. Repetition for this class was somehow important so their bodies could automate the movement and be prepared to execute the skills under pressure (for example, during competitions). Even though they were performing at a higher level, these squads would also work on some of the same skills as the other classes and jumps on beam were one of them. However, the way I coached was different. Because the girls worked long hours on the same skills, my approach to keep them motivated and committed was to give them almost 100% control of their learning so they felt accountable for their growth and success. As a coach, I acted as a facilitator, helped them through discovery, and managed the level of challenge so they could improve.

The gymnasts would start by having a routine with a straight jump, for example, as it is the jump with the lowest level of difficulty. As they mastered the straight jump I would suggest changing to a jump with a higher difficulty, for example, split jump, in order to increase the difficulty and give them a better shot at having higher scores in competitions. There are a lot of little details that the gymnasts have to pay attention to when doing a jump (a split jump, for example) – the height of the jump, the amplitude of the split, the landing, if the legs are straight, if the feet are pointed, among other things. While coaching them, correcting every little mistake, in a way that they were able to understand and make the changes that were needed, was very challenging. For this reason, I decided to use questioning, and ask the girls how they felt when executing the skill and what they thought they could do to improve it. They were not always able to recognise what was wrong in order to modify it, so with this group I used a lot of video. They would film each other doing a skill, and, as a group or individually, would analyse it and comment on what they thought was wrong and how it could be improved.

I found that by giving my gymnasts the power to be in control of their learning, they were much more motivated and had fun learning. It allowed me to be not only a coach but a friend they trusted. Having this relationship with them also allowed me to easily manage their level of challenge as they were open to it.

Reflection and Evaluation

Reflecting on my practice through the lens of PPed has helped me identify how fostering learning through self-discovery has been my main goal since I became a coach. Writing about my teaching in New Zealand has reminded me how I have always encouraged my gymnasts to seek answers to, and solve, problems by themselves or as a group in what can be seen as an inquiry-based approach to teaching. After completing a PhD on physical education teachers' and school-based coaches' beliefs about games teaching, I now pay close attention to the way I coach, and to how my practice influences my gymnasts' performance and learning process. Over the past four years, I realised that I have set *short-term goals, continuous goals and long-term* goals for my gymnasts that were different from gymnast to gymnast and are influenced by what their goals are.

While writing this chapter and sharing my experience, I have come to understand that the main *short-term goal* for all my gymnasts, regardless their age or level, was for them to have fun and enjoy what they do with me drawing on PPed's use of Positive Psychology and Antonovsky's work (1996) to achieve this aim. I believe that positive experiences of learning and positive emotions like fun and joy formed the base for the development of my gymnasts' passion for the sport and set the tone for their level of commitment to the sport.

As a *continuous goal* I set improvement. I would always work and help them toward getting better in each session and throughout the season. I would try to find the right tools to help my gymnasts improve regardless of how big the improvement was, or how fast each kid would improve. This aligns with Positive Pedagogy's principal focus which "is on creating conditions that will maximise learning (improvement) and help athletes learn how to learn" (Light and Harvey, 2019, p. 61). Finding strategies to help my gymnasts gain awareness and understand the movement in a way that empowers them though comprehensive understanding was always my goal, and I have found PPed very helpful in achieving this aim.

Finally, *long-term goals*. In my opinion, performance and the ability to self-manage the learning process are important and was one of my goals, mainly for my competitive squads. In a demanding sport such as gymnasts, performance is always important, even though I do not consider it to be the most important. When the gymnasts are passionate about what they do and take it seriously, at a certain point, more than I do, they will feel the need (they will want) to show results. This is the pinnacle and the culmination of all the short term and continuous goals that, I believe, I have worked with them prior to seeking performance. Using features of PPed here helped me coach them how to self-manage their learning, using an inquiry approach and questioning.

While focusing on working toward each goal, I have also been committed to developing a good relationship with my gymnasts. Having them trust me and not be afraid of asking me questions or expressing what they feel and what their fears are was very important for me and reflects the philosophic position of humanism that underpins PPed. This reflects the emphasis in PPed on humanistic coaching and developing empathy and deep understanding of students or athletes. I have placed great emphasis on this especially at the beginning of each season as new athletes get to know me and the group they will be working with for the first time.

Concluding Thoughts

Reflecting on my coaching approach for gymnastics, I think that, although I have features of PPed in my coaching, I applied them according to the level and needs of each group I coached, such as with the use of questioning. My intention for all the groups was always to create a drill or experience designed to achieve learning outcomes and manage learning to establish and sustain the right level of challenge. When the focal point is the development of each gymnast, and what he or she needs from their coach to improve, I believe that there is often a fine line between traditional and more contemporary approaches to coaching in gymnastics. While writing this chapter, I have come to think that coaching does not necessarily have to involve using PPed or traditional approaches to coaching. It can vary at an individual level but I think that instead of athlete-centred and traditional directive coaching opposing each other they should be used in tandem to contribute to the athlete's development at the same time, while fostering motivation, positive experiences and enjoyment.

References

Antonovsky, A. (1996) 'The salutogenic model as a theory to guide health promotion', *Health Promotion International*, 11 (1): 11–18.

Light, R. (2017) *Positive Pedagogy for sport coaching: Athlete-centred coaching for individual sports*, London and New York: Routledge.

Light, R. and Harvey, S. (2019) *Positive Pedagogy for sport coaching* (2nd edn), London and New York: Routledge.

14

BOXING TECHNIQUE

Richard Light

I trained in karate for over 30 years, during which I earned a living teaching karate for eight years and spent six years training in Japan where I was graded to fifth dan black belt by the founder of Hayashi Ha Shito Ryu Kai Karate, the late Soke Hanshi (master), Hayashi Teruo. This background in karate encouraged me to teach karate technique such as *gyakuzuki* (reverse punch – see Light 2017) to my undergraduate students in a course on athlete-centred coaching for individual sports. It provided a great way of showing how to use PPed to teach or coach technique, but the culturally shaped use of the body in karate presented a challenge for my New Zealand students. In particular, maintaining a low centre of gravity throughout movement by keeping the hips low and generating power from the lower half of the body was foreign to them.

In 2018 I added teaching how to punch in boxing to the activities I used for workshops and drew on my own experiences of boxing and kickboxing. This involves similar generation of power to karate from the feet and lower body that is transferred through hip rotation to the upper body and the fist on impact but is less pronounced and physically less challenging for Western bodies and awareness. In boxing there are four main punches, which are the jab, cross, hook and uppercut. The rip to the body is also used but is less common with the jab being the punch that is most frequently thrown in a bout and which boxers must most commonly avoid or deal with in defence. A right-handed boxer throws a jab with his/her left (lead) hand and with the left foot forward.

For the first session on boxing in 2018 at The University of Canterbury I taught the jab and the right cross in semester one (Feb–June). I focused on feel and using kinesthetic feedback to adjust and improve technique with my use of the term kinesthetic referring to awareness of the body's movement through sensory organs in the body. Not long after teaching my first class on boxing technique, I presented two keynote addresses and ran a workshop at the 2018 Global Coaching Symposium at The University of Ohio, USA. For my workshop in Ohio I again taught the boxing jab and cross, using the opportunity to develop my teaching and improve student experience in this course. Of course, tactics are very important in boxing but there is a lot of drilling technique separate to the contest in the ring and I wanted to show students how PPed can be used even when there is a very technical focus (Light and Harvey, 2019). The following year (2019) when I taught boxing again in my athlete-centred coaching classes, at The University of Canterbury, I used what I had learned from my sessions in the US in a process of continuing reflection and improvement that I think all coaches need to constantly engage in.

Tactics, awareness and decision-making are important in boxing when sparring or competing but the focus of the session I recount in this chapter was purely technical and aimed at learners with the participants having no, or very little, knowledge or experience of this sport. This is why I used it as an example of PPed coaching for technique as an alternative to coach-centred, direct instruction. Boxing is a sport with a long history that can be traced as far back as the 688BC Olympic Games in ancient Greece and has a long history as a combat sport but is also used for conditioning across a range of sports. It is also an excellent way of developing high levels of general fitness.

The Session

My aim for this session was to help the students feel and understand the connection between the feet and fists on impact and how punching is a whole-body skill that is not restricted to the upper body. As is the case in karate (Light, 2017), power for the boxing punch originates from the balls of the feet and I wanted them to feel the connection between feet and fists when they progressed to hitting pads. I also wanted them to understand how power is generated from the lower body and transferred through the upper body into the moment of impact.

As I often do when teaching or coaching technique, I began using direct instruction. I had the class facing me in two lines to punch in the air at an imaginary target with me facing them to demonstrate the technique for each punch and tell them the main technical points that I wanted them to think about and focus on. This was important for the reciprocal teaching they would engage in later in the session because it gave them things to focus on. While demonstrating, I explained how the jab and cross were used in boxing and showed them the stance they should adopt. I asked them to press against the floor with the balls of their feet to encourage awareness of this part of the body and the connection between the ball of the foot and fist on impact when punching. I explained how power is generated from the balls of the feet up through lower and then upper body and that this is what I wanted them to develop. I told them I wanted them to feel the ball of the foot pressing against the floor on the same side as the hand they were punching with when they punched.

Next, I asked them form pairs by having the students in the front line turn around to face a partner in the rear line. I had one student hold the hit pads and the other put on boxing mitts to hit the pads. I started with the jab, which is used to unsettle, distract and move an opponent and asked them to keep in mind that it is a snappy punch and not a knockout punch. I asked them to feel the ball of the front foot when the jab makes sharp contact with the hit pad. I told them that when they get it right and hit the pad with 'snap' they would feel it, like hitting the 'sweet spot' in cricket or baseball when batting and hear it due to the sound that a good punch makes. I focused their attention on this kinesthetic feedback because I wanted this to be their measure of an efficient punch as something they would use to adjust and refine their technique. Their aim was to feel and hear the result of good technique. My aim here was to use subjective experience of hitting the pad as feedback to develop efficiency. I also asked the person holding the pads to watch and provide objective feedback based on the main points I had talked about earlier.

Once all in the class were punching well enough, I asked the holder of the pads to take a short step back when the puncher moved toward them and then showed the puncher how to move forward to jab while retaining posture. When doing this most students overreached, which meant they could not generate power because their legs were too far away from the target. I stopped the class and told them that they needed to retain alignment of their upper and lower body and move their whole body forward to get within range of their target – to get their hips close to the target. I probably could have let them do stationary punching while over-reaching and with body alignment to compare and understand but was aware of the need to not lose the pace of the session but did not. I asked the punchers to think about this and pay attention to it as well as asking the pad holders to watch for this in particular and to alert their partner if they noticed them overreaching. I then had the pairs change roles and repeated the same sequence of activities.

After the jab I asked them to hit a pad using a cross with the dominant hand. This is a powerful punch that can be used to knock down an opponent with its power originating from the rear foot and increasing as it passes through the hips, shoulders, arm and fist. For this punch I asked them to feel the connection between the moment of impact on the pad and pressure on the ball of the foot on the floor on impact. Some were too heavy and deliberate, which I responded to with a brief comment on it to the whole group and by asking the partner holding the pads to analyze what the puncher was doing and make suggestions to him/her for improvement. Another issue that arose was with tightening up before throwing the punch. I briefly told them that they needed to stay relaxed, 'start from 0' and let the power generated from the lower body to flow through to impact. Again, I asked the person holding the pads to pay attention to tightening up and remind the hitter to relax. Across all sports from golf to boxing it is important to relax to generate power. I reiterated how they needed to be aware of how impact felt and sounded, and to use this as feedback on how well they were executing the technique. Extrinsic feedback also came from comments made by their partners. I noted things to be aware of, asked the one holding the pads to look for how the puncher could improve technique and used questioning and verbal encouragement to stimulate interaction and dialogue.

After working on the jab and cross separately I asked the class to do a drill that combined the two techniques but before doing this asked them to swap partners. I then asked them to combine the two punches to do jab-jab-cross with a slight pause after the first jab, to develop some rhythm with this combination and to step in to throw the cross because the jab is thrown from further away (jab...jab-cross) and the puncher must bridge the gap to get close enough to unleash an effective cross. I then asked them to run though the same progression they had used when working on the single techniques of the jab and the cross. When they had completed this activity, I called them all in to form a semi-circle for the first group 'debate of ideas' (Grehaigne, Richard and Griffin, 2005) for the session. I asked questions of the whole group like, 'What can you share with us all about what you have learned so far and how you think you learned it?' Through this we collectively developed some basic ideas to focus on in the next activity in which I added an objective observer to each pair.

Next, I had them form groups of three with one punching, one holding the pads and one observing to increase interaction and dialogue to increase dialogue, observation and reflection. They repeated the same routine we had just completed (jab-jab-cross) but with a little more movement, more speed of combinations and a pause between them. After each 'round' I would stop and ask for a three-way conversation focused on where the puncher could make improvements on his/her technique and then have them rotate. After rotating all three through the activity once, I called them in for a second 'debate of ideas' (Grehaigne et al. 2005) in which they again shared ideas about what they thought they had learned. This produced more dialogue than the first all-group discussion and generated more knowledge due to the contribution that taking the role of observer made to the participants' construction of knowledge. I then asked them to repeat the activity and apply the ideas we had discussed as a whole class in their groups of three and for the observers to look to encourage the puncher take up these ideas but to ensure they were positive with their comments. This addition of a third person as an observer worked well at the Global Symposium in Ohio the year before (2018) and worked just as well in my undergraduate class (2019) by increasing interaction.

The final segment of the session was the debriefing, or collective reflection, at the end of the session. It is common practice in athlete-centred coaching and particularly with game based approaches (GBA) like, Teaching Games for Understanding (TGfU – Bunker and Thorpe, 1982), Game Sense (Light, 2013), Tactical Games (Mitchell, Oslin and Griffin, 2006) and Play Practice (Launder and Piltz, 2013). It is something that I do almost without exception. I knew these students and they knew me and, although a session on boxing technique was completely new to them all, they were familiar with the PPed approach. They enjoyed the session but without the same level of energy that I have been used to feeling when exposing new learners to this approach, such as in Ohio the year before. I began my questioning by asking them about their sensory experiences of the session when punching and when holding the pads, such as, 'What did a really good hit feel like?' 'What did it sound like?' and 'What made it a good hit?' I then asked them, 'When you hit the pad well do you remember what you were doing well?' 'What connection was there between the balls of your feet and your fist on impact?' This questioning was aimed at making connections between efficiency and sensory experience. More specifically, they were aimed at reliving, or at least reflecting on, the whole-body experience of a good punch, and the connection between the ball of the foot and the fist on impact. The session and my questioning at the end focused on the efficient use of the body and core considerations for delivering any punch efficiently in boxing.

Reflections

Teaching my own students halfway through semester meant that I did not have any major problems or challenges with this group. The students were positively disposed toward PPed and athlete-centred coaching more broadly, and I did not have to convince them about what PPed had to offer. However, reflecting on the session, I identified an aspect of it that I thought I could probably improve on.

As I often do when teaching or coaching individual sport, I began this session by using direct instruction but gradually moved toward athlete-centred coaching and active learning as the session progressed (see also Chapter 16). I achieved this by adopting two strategies. One was by having the puncher focus on the sensory experience of executing an effective punch, as kinesthetic feedback, and adjusting technique to feel this as often as possible. The other was to increasingly promote dialogue, reflection, collaboration and the strength of relationships between athletes as they moved through the activities in the session that involved moving from working alone, into working in pairs and then in groups of three.

As was the case in the previous year when I did a similar session in the US, taking time out for whole group sharing and discussion made an important contribution to learning for all the students. Moving into groups of three worked well in terms of promoting interaction and dialogue but in this session, it seemed to slow the pace and flow of the session. On reflection, I think this might have been because only one of the three was wholly engaged, physically, mentally and emotionally, and was 'on task'. I could have attended to this by rotating more often or by picking up the pace a little and raising the level of challenge. Perhaps I could have done this by pushing the puncher to put in more physical effort, pick up the speed of the combinations and by having the pad holder moving more. This would have aligned better with the PPed emphasis on establishing and maintaining an appropriate level of challenge for the athletes and I will keep this in mind next time I do this session. I also have to consider the context when comparing this class to my session in the US. In New Zealand, I was working with undergraduates for whom this pedagogical approach was nothing really new. In the US the learners were post graduate students who were older, were practising coaches (many full time), and were motivated enough to travel from widespread places across the US such as California and Georgia to attend the event. There was also a real 'buzz' over the duration of the symposium due to the learning arising from such an intense program and excitement about being taught by overseas academics and coaches.

Many of the reflections that I write on my experiences of using PPed are with learners who I do not know because they are on workshops I have done in different parts of the world. In these cases, I do not know their abilities, dispositions or knowledge of PPed and similar approaches like TGfU but in the session I reflect on here, In the session I recount here, I knew the students well. They were already well-disposed toward athlete-centred coaching such as PPed, had good knowledge of athlete-centred coaching and were well-motivated, which made it relatively problem free for me. The session went well, and I was happy with it, but without being elated or excited and I think this might have been due to not quite creating the energy and flow that a good PPed sessions should have (Light and Harvey, 2019).

Team sports like basketball and football (soccer) lend themselves to generating energy and building flow as the session complexity, intensity and athlete engagement levels build. There is a PPed framework, but it is flexible with no real formula for using PPed for individual sports, which can make it a more challenging task for coaches than it is in team sports. Indeed, whether working in team sports or individual sports, the PPed approach is more challenging than traditional direct instruction and repetitive skill drills, but the effort is worth it because it can produce far more effective and enjoyable learning and improvement for the athlete(s) as is evident in the range of coach experiences and reflections this book. Sometimes it involves using some type of constraint to create a problem to be solved (see Chapter 10) or to promote awareness of something such as in Chapter 16 on the beach sprint start but, other times it does not involve any constraint.

When appropriate, the coach can use a constraint but it in other instances, he or she does not. In Chapters 10 and 16 I use physical constraints but in this chapter I do not. This requires thinking and understanding instead of following a formulaic, step by step model, and I think this is a reasonable expectation of a coach, whether using PPed or not. PPed typically requires deep thinking and creativity by the coach who must be prepared to experiment and willing to take a few risks at practice. Like the athletes, s/he must also think. Including the observer in the training pairs in this boxing session was not risky and the problem I identify in this reflection is very minor but being positively disposed to critical reflection is beneficial for any coach and very important when drawing on PPed, even if only to a limited extent.

References

Bunker, D. and Thorpe, R. (1982) 'A model for teaching games in secondary school', *Bulletin of Physical Education*, 10: 9–16.

Grehaigne, J.-F., Richard, J.-F. and Griffin, I. L. (2005) *Teaching and learning team sports and games*, London and New York: Routledge.

Launder, A. and Piltz, W. (2013) *Play practice: Engaging and developing skilled players from beginner to elite*, Champaign, IL: Human Kinetics.

Light, R. (2013) *Game Sense: Pedagogy for performance, participation and enjoyment*, London and New York: Routledge.

Light, R. L. (2017) *Positive Pedagogy for sport coaching: Athlete centred coaching for individual sports*, London and New York: Routledge. Available at: www.routledge.com/Positive-Pedagogy-for-Sport-Coaching-Athlete-centred-coaching-for-individual/Light/p/book/9781138215597

Light, R. and Harvey, S. (2019) *Positive Pedagogy for sport coaching* (2nd edn), London and New York: Routledge.

Mitchell, S., Oslin, J. and Griffith, L. L. (2006) *Teaching sport concepts and skills: A tactical games approach*, Champaign IL: Human Kinetics.

15

POSITIVE PEDAGOGY FOR STRENGTH AND CONDITIONING IN WOMEN'S SOCCER

Letitia Price

My coaching career in strength and conditioning (S&C) began when I was accepted into an S&C internship program in 2014 at my undergraduate *alma mater*, Sheffield Hallam University. The internship was spearheaded by a renowned S&C coach in the United Kingdom and was regarded as one of the best programs for developing new S&C coaches. I was excited to be offered this internship and learned a great deal about S&C, but the gender inequality that permeated it concerned me significantly. It epitomized the wider challenge faced by females across the entire S&C coaching domain (O'Malley and Greenwood, 2018) and motivated me to critically assess S&C as an arena dominated by male hegemony; an inequality visible in most athletic environments (Medlin-Silver, Lampard and Bunsell, 2017; O'Malley and Greenwood, 2018). Within the program, male hegemony was evident in the low representation of female S&C coaches, the comparatively less S&C provision for female college teams than for male teams and, disempowering attitudes towards female physical aptitude. This experience motivated me to embark on a journey toward delivering S&C coaching in a way that redressed this gender inequality.

I wanted to challenge coaching that created environments that marginalize all but a handful of male athletes, and I regarded athlete-centered approaches as a way of doing this. Placing each individual at the center of their own development (Light, 2016) empowers athletes, and female athletes in particular; with the holistic and humanistic nature of PPed (Light and Harvey, 2019) also appealing to me. This motivation and philosophy toward S&C protocols resulted in my appointment to two Head of S&C roles in women's soccer, one of which was for a leading professional women's team competing in the top tier of the women's division. The other role was with a semi-professional team with great potential to secure promotion within England's women professional soccer league. In this chapter, I focus on how I drew on PPed in S&C during my time coaching this team, that I refer to using the pseudonym Dynamo FC.

Context

Having just finished my second season with one of north England's leading women's professional soccer teams, I was approached by the manager of Dynamo FC. Her ambitions were clear, she was assembling a team of support staff with the aspiration of becoming the first regional team to be promoted to the Women's Super League (WSL). In 2014, women's soccer in the U.K. had undergone significant restructuring (Dunn, 2016). The English Football Association (EFA), had created two new professional leagues, WSL 1 & WSL 2. WSL 1 had been characterized as the 'fully professional league' and WSL 2 as the 'semi-professional league'. To ensure competitiveness and excitement, two teams would be relegated from WSL 1 into WSL 2 and two teams would be promoted from WSL 2 into WSL 1 (Dunn, 2016). To secure the correct number of teams for WSL 2, the FA concluded that one team would need to be promoted from the national regional leagues below the WSL leagues.

Dynamo FC was a regional team, based in a passionate soccer city in with an excellent history of recruiting either ex-professional/international players, or players that had high potential in their youth. The team consisted of a strong 18-player roster, with ages ranging from 17 to 35 and from mixed socio-economic backgrounds. There was a strong club culture with team cohesion and camaraderie, and the team had been very successful, but started the season with extensive injuries. The culture surrounding physical preparation was based upon the archaic protocols of 1950s soccer and it was not well founded on S&C. At my first team meeting I was told by the team's top goal scorer that, 'We are here to just play soccer, not become Olympic weightlifters'. I felt that I faced an insurmountable challenge in overhauling years of deeply embedded detrimental practices in physical preparation for soccer.

To achieve the aim of being the first team promoted to the WSL, I adopted a PPed approach but focused on creating a positive, supportive learning environment that fostered empowerment (Light and Harvey, 2019) to develop independent learners (Light, 2014) and improve the overall team culture surrounding physical preparation and wellbeing. Table 15.1 shows how this approach was implemented for Dynamo FC using the following PPed. These were also presented to the coaching staff prior to the start of the season to ensure collaborative support.

The Season

Motivating Meaningfulness

'Meaningfulness refers to how much the individual feels that life makes sense and that its challenges merit commitment.' (Light and Harvey, 2019, p. 17). Motivating meaningfulness became one of the leading PPed features within Dynamo FC's S&C programming. My first priority was to give S&C meaning and relevance for

TABLE 15.1 Table highlighting how PPed features were applied to Dynamo FC's S&C

PPed feature	Aims for Dynamo FC's S&C
Comprehensibility	Empower the team's comprehension of the importance of S&C
Manageability	Create team-driven S&C culture; Visuals for team goals, Music playlists, Phrases/Hashtags
Meaningfulness	Create soccer specific S&C on the soccer field
Positive Psychology	Implementing Performance Lifestyle components such as Life Wheel Assessments (Rogers, 2012, pp. 149)
Inquiry-Based Coaching	Online Team Group Chat – used for S&C based dialect regarding; clarifications, suggestions and ideas
Empowering the Learning Environment	Player pairing for S&C Training, team-led monitoring, team-led objectives and on-field S&C

the team. I understood that this would require meticulous planning to establish effective learning opportunities. My first team contact was a scheduled meeting, where the theme of the session was inquiry-based. I divided the players into small groups, ensuring a mixture of ages and positions. The groups were tasked to collaboratively answer the following questions: Does physical preparation matter to us now? Can you explain your answers? What should our next steps be?

Each group presented their responses, with all group members contributing. I chose purposely to sit at the back of the room to eliminate my presence within the discussions. The session lasted for no more than 1 hour, from which very fruitful discussions emerged and the team naturally devised two of their own S&C goals. These were to: a) be the 'beastiest' team by the time they reach the WSL and, b) be able to 'run for days without feeling older than time'. While these goals were far removed from the formal structuring of SMART goals (specific, measurable, attainable, realistic and time-bound), the most important outcome from this session was that the team was transforming its detrimental predispositions towards S&C into positive attitudes that had greater meaning for everyone.

Following this meeting, I asked the team to come up with a way to reinforce their new goals. They had mentioned that 'changing room music' was an important part of their match preparation. I therefore suggested that they create a playlist of songs for S&C that could be played at every physical preparation session. In addition, they had decided they wanted to have their goals written out on a large whiteboard that would be brought to every session to serve as a visual reminder. Within 24 hours the team had collaborated to create a music playlist and purchased a portable speaker. These two factors became highly important in increasing positivity and meaningfulness for the team. It allowed them to take ownership of their practices and sparked positive group energy, which then transcended into positive attitudes towards S&C sessions. Many of the players began to look forward to the sessions, highlighting that the memories, jokes and laughter that they had created in them would remain with them for life.

Conscious of the earlier remark from the team's top forward, that the players just wanted to play soccer, I decided for the first time in my S&C career to complete their warm-ups with a ball. Prior to my arrival at Dynamo FC, the team's warm-up consisted of a light jog, followed by some inconsequential static stretches, stationary movements and conversation. Despite the ongoing debate surrounding warm-ups in youth soccer, they remain necessary in elite senior soccer due to their strong association with the concept of post-activation potentiation (PAP) and injury prevention (Sanchez-Sanchez et al., 2018). These two elements were highly important for Dynamo FC, particularly considering the team's injury history.

The adapted FIFA 11+ warm-up consisted of mobility exercises, dynamic movements, resistance band exercises, proprioceptive neuromuscular facilitation (PNF) and sprint production conditioning (Sadigursky et al., 2017). Each of these exercises were performed with a soccer ball at their feet, on one half of a soccer pitch, encouraging movement in and around the space. In between sets of warm-up exercises I would encourage players to pass, move and exchange soccer balls with their teammates. Importantly, the coaches utilized the same half of the pitch for the following technical session, meaning that the warm-up environment replicated the setup of the soccer specific training. This was a significant factor in enhancing the meaningfulness behind S&C practices for the players, as it allowed the team to recognize how S&C practices can be easily embedded into soccer practices, and as an entity integral to the game itself.

Throughout these warm-ups, the players were having fun and identifying how each of the exercises was helping them to feel more physically prepared or even overcome physical discomfort. Consequently, in combination with increasing empowerment and the development of a supportive and positive environment, they also became very inquisitive and even critical of each other's understanding and performance of the warm-up exercises. As the season continued, it became evident to me that the team valued the process of warm-ups. Players remarked on how much the process had helped them overcome physical adversities and, as the season progressed, they managed the entire warm-up by themselves. As the players took ownership of their physical preparations, I became a facilitator and source of information.

Empowering the Learners

'Learning occurs through experience in two ways: engagement with the physical learning environment; and reflection on this experience as a second experience' (Light and Harvey, 2019, p. 24). Replicating my success with the warm-up within the weight training and recovery protocols was more challenging. With only two sessions per week, the Head Coach insisted that the S&C sessions were not to reduce the time that she had to work with the team and there was concern among other coaching staff that S&C practices could cause the team too much muscle soreness and fatigue. This and other challenges such as access to facilities meant that I had to meticulously periodize how I could effectively implement a holistic S&C program for the season.

First, I created an overarching S&C periodization plan for the season which comprised various physical objectives, centered upon strength, sprint production and sprint repeatability. I had asked each player to select an S&C training partner from the team with whom they would be able to train outside of practice times, at a mutually suitable location. I recommended that the pairings consisted of a less-experienced player and a more-experienced player in terms of S&C training history. As all the players lived in close proximity within the same city, this was achievable.

To achieve the necessary monitoring of the S&C training, one player from each pairing was responsible for uploading an S&C monitoring form to a shared folder. This form included components such as; exercises completed, number of repetitions, physiological markers and various profile of mood state (POMs) questions. In addition, several senior players were delegated responsibility for the entire monitoring database, meaning I was able to simply provide indirect supervision to address any major physiological/psychological concerns.

Each week I sent the team an overview of the S&C objectives for that week, which included a basic structure for their strength sessions. For example, the objective may have been 'Leg strength', for which I recommended the number of sets, repetitions and exercises to complete. I also provided examples of good exercises to complete to achieve this. So, this did not impact their technical/tactical sessions on Tuesdays and Thursdays, the strength sessions were completed on Monday, Wednesday and Friday, within a time and environment of the pairing's choice.

The success of this approach was not only evident within the significant physical improvements across the entire team over the season, but also in the newly created culture and entire team's positive attitude towards S&C. The less-experienced players became more involved with the S&C process and eventually took up monitoring responsibilities, and the team set up a cell phone group chat specifically for S&C, which they used to anecdotally document their sessions, pose questions to each other and even to post useful knowledge-based resources. These were all signs of the players being empowered to, and taking, responsibility for their own learning.

The nature of the recovery sessions was determined exclusively by the team, who had opted for pitch-based sessions consisting of 20 minutes' deep yoga- inspired stretching, alongside the consumption of a small, nutritious recovery snack/drink. Over the season I stepped back from directing, to facilitating and providing recovery nutrition information and sources of guidance on the format of the sessions (exercises/ duration/repetitions). I had suggested that for each recovery session a player must come up with a 'campfire question' to pose to the team. Each player was required to respond accordingly and to explain their answer. An example question would be, 'What animal would you be and why?' These sessions provided great enjoyment and the opportunity to relax and rejuvenate prior to returning home. As practices finished at 10:00pm, previously, ninety percent of the players reported in their monitoring forms that they would: a) not consume any effective nutrition, and, b) get into bed between the hours of 1:00–2:00am. The recovery sessions for the season I write about in this chapter ate into time after practice, but players were now reporting that they were able to complete their necessary post-practice home tasks more efficiently because they were feeling more relaxed. This resulted in an improvement in the team's average bedtime to 11:30pm.

Furthermore, the inclusion of these recovery sessions provided an alleviation of any potential exercise-induced muscle soreness/fatigue. Players were reporting how 'alive and energetic' they felt, even though their week encompassed a greater training volume in comparison to the previous season. Additionally, the inclusion of the 'Campfire Questions' propelled the team's personal connectivity, as the discussions allowed for deepened understanding of each other. These recovery sessions guided by a PPed approach greatly improved the players' overall wellbeing and positively influenced the team's psychological climate regarding; culture, motivation and overall meaningfulness surrounding being a part of the team's new approach to achieving their overall aim.

Making History

The season came to a euphoric climax. Dynamo FC were crowned champions of their league and became the first regional team to be promoted to the professional Women's Super League (WSL). The winning goal was scored in the 92nd minute by one of Dynamo FC's oldest players, who had been with the club since it started and had consistently suffered injuries. This was the first season that this same player did not acquire any injuries that caused her to be absent from practice/matches. The team's investment in their collective training is evident in the Captain's post-match interview regarding whether the team anticipated this promotion. 'All the players know that off the pitch, we have been so well taken care of to prepare us for this moment' (Dunn, 2016, p. 56). The team had taken complete ownership over its physical preparation and development and thus, the S&C environment had become a continuous autonomous learning experience. The journey of the team was epitomized in a quote from the Club Captain's post-match interview: 'The emotion of this day is unreal. It was a difficult day – and the best day of my life so far' (Dunn, 2016, p. 56).

Evaluation and Reflection

Dynamo FC exceeded everyone's expectations, including my own. What initially seemed like an impossible challenge had become one of the most successful seasons in my coaching career, and the influence of PPed on my S&C coaching played a significant part in this success.

What Went Well

The inclusion of goal setting, visualization and the use of music, as requested by the team, encouraged it to adopt a positive psychological climate that allowed for the embedding of S&C into the team's culture and ambitions for the season. The team overcame internal doubts and developed a climate of self-belief through being helped to find the meaning and relevance of S&C for their soccer. The players were able to feel the tangible connections between S&C and their soccer performance, which further propelled the team's confidence, mental strength and reassurance in their journey towards promotion. As the team became immersed within the S&C learning environment, I was able to gradually step back and allow them to lead. This resulted in the team managing the entire S&C protocols that were introduced for their training/match warm-ups and recovery sessions. Consequentially, remarkable growth in the comprehensibility of S&C had been achieved by the team.

Promoting manageability with the S&C programming also contributed to developing a positive environment. I had ensured an effective semi-structured approach to evoke greater athlete empowerment through challenging them and helping them meet the challenge. With very limited resources and facility access I had to devise a way for the players to complete S&C sessions, with success being achieved by implementing the self-led 'Buddy-Training' format. This allowed players to take ownership of their S&C sessions, becoming responsible for their own learning and growth. This also ignited a significant sense of reflexivity across the team, as it was able to critically analyze potential mistakes they were making in the S&C sessions and would utilize these as opportunities to spark discussions on how to solve various challenges.

Finally, I want to highlight how important it was to develop great interpersonal understanding between the players and myself. By regarding my players as complex people with different feelings and needs, rather than cogs in the team's machine, I was able to utilize inquiry-based coaching to build an empowering rapport. I encouraged dialogue, interaction and thinking, to allow for authentic comprehension of the values and philosophies of each player, thus understanding the team's cultural climate.

What I Would Do Differently

If I were to do this again, I would do a few things differently. The first would be to get more tangible feedback to assess the overall team climate and monitor psychological progress. I would collect weekly feedback, as I do now from my current team that I am working with in the USA and compare this to pre-season and post-season feedback regarding the team's perspectives on the PPed climate. Second, there were very few opportunities to involve the other coaches on the team within the new S&C journey and we didn't create purposeful opportunities for a more collaborative approach. This is something I think is very important and, in my current coaching role, I ensure that the other coaches have purposeful input into my use of PPed and I discuss the players' weekly feedback on the S&C training with all coaches. This has accentuated the significant benefits of positive pedagogy, as it has allowed for us as a coaching team to further grow and develop meaningfulness, comprehensibility, manageability and positive psychology as coaching staff and leaders for the team.

Conclusion

This chapter reflects on my successful use of PPed in S&C coaching and I believe it provides a compelling example of the great successes that can be achieved by taking this approach. PPed is at first demanding to implement, but the effort is worth it. I found it an empowering approach for both the players and for myself, not simply for how it boosts performance, but also for how it can help coaches challenge male hegemony in S&C to motivate, empower and liberate female athletes to embrace S&C training. PPed offers ideas for coaches to create an empowering training environment that results in pivotal changes and long-life learning.

References

Dunn, C. (2016) *The roar of the lionesses: Women's football in England*, Durrington, UK: Pitch Publishing.

Light, R. L. (2014) 'Learner-centred pedagogy for swim coaching: A complex learning theory informed approach', *Asia-Pacific Journal of Health, Sport and Physical Education*, 5(2): 167–180.

Light, R. (2016) *Positive Pedagogy for sport coaching: Athlete-centred coaching for individual sports*, London and New York: Routledge.

Light, R. and Harvey, S. (2019) *Positive Pedagogy for sport coaching* (2nd edn), London and New York: Routledge.

Medlin-Silver, N., Lampard, P. and Bunsell, T. (2017) 'Strength in numbers: An explorative study into the experiences of female strength and conditioning coaches in the UK', in A. Milner and J. Braddock (eds) *Women in sports: Breaking barriers, facing obstacles* [2 Volumes], Santa Barbara, CA: ABC-CLIO, LLC, 125–149.

O'Malley, L. M. and Greenwood, S. (2018) 'Female coaches in strength and conditioning – Why so few?' *Strength and Conditioning Journal*, 40(6): 40–48.

Rogers, J. (2012) *Coaching skills: The definitive guide to being a coach*, London: McGraw-Hill Education.

Sadigursky, D., Braid, J. A., De Lira, D. N. L., Machado, B. A. B., Carneiro, R. J. F. and Colavolpe, P. O. (2017) 'The FIFA 11+ injury prevention program for soccer players: A systematic review', *BMC Sports Science, Medicine and Rehabilitation*, 9(1): 18.

Sanchez-Sanchez, J., Rodriguez, A., Petisco, C., Ramirez-Campillo, R., Martínez, C. and Nakamura, F. Y. (2018) 'Effects of different post-activation potentiation warmups on repeated sprint ability in soccer players from different competitive levels', *Journal of Human Kinetics*, 61(1): 189–197.

16

BEACH SPRINT STARTS

Richard Light

This chapter recounts my experiences of working as an age group manager in a 'nippers' program at a surf lifesaving club in Sydney, Australia. Nippers programs focus on educating children from five years of age to fourteen about the environment of the beach and ocean where so many Australians spend their time in summer, encouraging healthy active lifestyles, and introducing them to the culture of surf life-saving. As readers outside Australia and New Zealand may know little about the function and culture of surf lifesaving in Australia, I include a brief explanation of surf lifesaving in Australia and the aims of nippers programs to provide a context for my discussion of a Positive Pedagogy for sport coaching approach I adopted to help young nippers learn and improve their beach sprint start technique. The session I recount was very early in the season and before any interclub competitions.

Context

Beach culture is very strong in Australia with well over 10,000 beaches on the Australian coast, 85 percent of Australians living within 50 kilometres of the coast and major city beaches packed on hot summer weekends. Anyone who has watched the TV program, *Bondi Rescue* would be familiar with the beauty of Australian beaches (or at least Bondi) and the potentially fatal dangers that await swimmers ignorant of the ocean as a dynamic and constantly changing environment. Surf lifesaving clubs use nippers' programs to attract potential volunteer lifesavers (as opposed to professional lifeguards) by channelling them into their cadet program (14–18 years of age) and then into volunteer surf lifesaving but only a very small percentage of the thousands of nippers who join each year follow through to become volunteer lifesavers. This might seem disappointing, but the primary function of the nippers is to educate children about the beach and ocean so that they don't need to be rescued and to encourage active, healthy lifestyles. For five years I was a member of the North Steyne Surf Lifesaving Club which was one of three clubs on Manly beach (the one in the centre). Each Sunday over summer we had up to 500 children aged 5 to 13 turn up with around the same number at the other two clubs. This meant that around 1,500 children spent every Sunday mornings as active learners for eight months of the year on one Sydney beach.

When my family and I moved to Sydney from Melbourne I wanted my daughter to enjoy beach culture like I had growing up on Sydney's northern beaches and then Byron Bay. I had also just completed a study on a Victorian surf club and had been very impressed by the learning that the children in the club experienced. After visiting the North Steyne surf club with my daughter, she joined the nippers' program and I joined the club as an associate member. By the end of her first year in the nippers she could read the surf and point out where the rips (fast moving currents of water moving out to sea) were. By the end of her third year she, like most of her clubmates, was able to use these rips as express channels to swim out beyond the break, swim across and out of the rip around the buoys and swim back to shore in surf swim competitions.

Surf lifesaving clubs were established in response to mass drownings when a law banning public bathing was repealed in 1903. In 1907 the Surf Bathing Association of New South Wales was formed and there are currently over 100,000 members of over 300 surf clubs in Australia. There are 25,000 volunteer lifesavers patrolling over 400 beaches with over half a million rescues performed over the past half century. Surf clubs in Australia are volunteer organizations that rely on fund-raising and government grants to operate as a public service. Their primary function is to ensure safe bathing, but competition has always formed a central role in their functioning and identity. Interclub and interstate competitions help to keep lifesavers fit for their duties, attracting and maintaining members and raising the public profile of clubs to ensure adequate funding. Despite performing an important public service, there is a strong culture of competition in surf clubs. At the club where I coached beach sprints about a quarter of the children competed in interclub contests and the state championships.

Young nippers are not allowed to compete in surf swims until deemed proficient and are limited to competition in the sand and the wading race in their first couple of years. The beach events they train for and can compete in, if they want to, are the beach sprint, the beach relay, and flags. In the beach flags, competitors lying face down with feet pointing toward flags on small rods planted in the sand twenty metres away and, on the starts whistle, the explode from this prone position to turn, sprint and dive to claim a flag. There is always one fewer flag than the number of competitors who must sprint to take a flag and with the one who does get a flag, eliminated and with this process continued until there is a single winner. For more insight into the nippers, see Light, 2006.

The Session

In the beach sprint there is a clear need to develop technical proficiency and this may require some direct instruction but, even with a strong focus on technique, coaches can take a holistic and humanistic approach to help young athletes learn technique. Humanistic coaching is influenced by work in humanistic psychology over the 1960s and 70s such as that of Maslow (see 1968) and Rogers (1951) that is discussed in detail in the first and second editions of *Positive Pedagogy for sport coaching* (Light, 2017; Light and Harvey, 2019). Here, I describe a session I ran when coaching nippers in the beach sprint that was guided by the pedagogical features of *Positive Pedagogy for sport coaching* (Light, 2017; Light and Harvey, 2019) and a view of learning as an ongoing 'conversation' between pre-reflective and reflective learning, between speech and action (Light and Fawns 2003).

The beach sprint for nippers is contested over 70 metres in deep, soft sand. With only one training session a week (Sunday) over the eight-month long season I thought that focusing on starts might get the best results. I decided to focus on the use of the arms in the start and began by trying to develop awareness of the importance of the arms in sprinting. The learning activities I started with involved placing a constraint on using the arms when running to encourage awareness of the contribution arm movement makes to sprinting that were followed by exaggeration aimed at guiding the discovery of how to best use the arms for sprinting. I then asked them to apply this knowledge to improving their starts.

Arm Action

Coaching a group of eight to ten-year-old 'nippers', I began by asking them to run holding a rubber relay baton (a length of garden hose) in both hands. If you do this exercise yourself, you will appreciate how it impedes sprinting. After a couple of runs with this constraint imposed I asked them to reflect upon the experience by asking questions such as 'How did that feel?' and 'Why do you think that restricted your running so much?' to focus their attention on the feeling of running without the drive provided by the arms. Next, I removed the constraint for them to compare and contrast running when not using the arms, to running with free use of their arms. I then asked questions such as, 'Did that feel any better?' and 'How did that compare to not being able to use your arms?' to which the group responded by expressing their enjoyment of being able to run freely. I then asked, 'Do you think you have learned anything about running by running without using your arms and then using them?' to which, invariably, the answer was invariably that they learned how important the arms are for sprinting. Unlike some other examples in this book, the use of this constraint was not intended to demand a solution to a problem. Instead, it was aimed at creating awareness of the role that arm movement plays in sprinting.

After applying the constraint and removing it I playfully encouraged the group to have a little fun in guiding them toward discovering what the most efficient us of the arms is in terms of the magnitude of movement to get the best drive. I asked questions like, 'Now we know how important the arms are for sprinting but what do you think is the best way to use them?' to which there were answers such as 'Move your arms really fast' or 'Put a lot of power into your arms', that I would encourage discussion of as I narrowed the focus to the question of what the optimum range of movement might be. I then asked, 'Do you think that bigger arm movements would help you run faster?' and suggested that we should test that idea by running with 'really big' or 'huge' arm movements to see how it worked. Of course, the timing between the stride and arm action was out and felt awkward for them. It certainly looked awkward.

I then brought them in for a group reflection upon and discuss this exaggeration, which brought them to the conclusion that really big arm movements were not efficient because it threw out the timing of their arm and stride frequency. I began this collective reflection by asking them all how it felt. I asked them whether or not it seemed effective to them and then asked them to suggest why it did not work, using questions to encourage thinking about the relationship between stride and arm drive frequency. I then asked them to go to the other extreme by running with very small but rapid movements of the arms. I playfully asked, 'If big arm movements did not work for us, I wonder if using small, but very fast, arms would work?' but did not wait for an answer. I then went through the same process that I had with the exaggerated, huge arm movements with them using short, rapid arm movements over a couple of short sprints, which was followed by collective reflection on how small but fast arms worked – or didn't work.

My next step was to ask the group to do a couple of sprints using their arms in the way that they felt was most efficient after which I had them regroup for reflection and a talk on how this felt. I then put them into small groups of five or six to discuss and decide what they felt was the optimum range of movement. After this I pulled them into together for each small group to tell the whole squad what they had greed on as the best range of movement and why. As part of this process I asked one of the nippers with good technique to demonstrate for the rest of the group to comment on or analyse her technique.

Starts

Following experimenting with the magnitude and frequency of arm movement I moved the squad of nippers on to the beach sprint start to transfer learning and awareness to start technique with a focus on the arms. Beach sprint starts share similarities with track starts but there are differences due to the very different surface competitors start and sprint on. The distance between the front and rear foot is the same but very few use the crouch start, with most preferring a standing start but from a low position with hips and knees flexed and weight forward as in the crouch start. The sprinter also quickly twists and burrows his/her feet down to find firm sand that s/he can push against for an explosive start.

I began this part of the session by asking them to start with both hands held behind their back and sprint for ten metres. Then I asked them to put both hands in front of their body and sprint for ten metres. They found both these starts awkward but soon knew why by drawing on previous learning in the same session. Back on the starting line I asked them to think about which arm should be forward and which one back in relation to their feet when they first push off but did not ask for an answer. Instead, I asked them to experiment to compare how it felt with the lead hand over the lead foot with the lead hand on the side (same side as the rear foot). Over this time, I asked them to think and reflect but did not ask for an answer. I then asked them to form pairs and gave then five minutes to work together to determine which hand should be the lead one and how to best use the lead hand to develop power and execute an explosive start.

For the final activity I called them in to share what they had decided on and with all pairs recognizing that the hand opposite to the front foot had to be up in front with the other hand back and elbow up. I then asked one of the nippers in the pairs thy had been working in to start and his/her partner to watch and act as coach. This had half the group doing starts and the other half watching and advising for three starts after which I had them swap roles as a type of 'reciprocal teaching' (Mosston, 1972). I finished on a positive note by having one 'max effort' start *en masse* and let them go without the usual debrief to finish on a high.

Reflection and Evaluation

I conducted this session during the early stages of my thinking about, and development of, an athlete-centred coaching approach that could be applied to individual sports and which I later named 'Positive Pedagogy for sport coaching' (Light, 2017). Rather than follow the accepted approach of putting theory into practice or of theorizing practice (see Griffin and Butler, 2005), I used the dialectic between theory and practice as mutually-informing aspects of coaching (see Light and Wallian, 2008) to develop my ideas and in which, experiences of coaching like the one I recount here were invaluable in the development of my ideas. In this beach sprint session, I focused on using feel to understand technique as I have suggested for other individual sports (Light, 2017; Light and Harvey, 2019). The pedagogy I adopted focused on reflection on experience, dialogue and inquiry, and on providing positive experiences of learning as hallmarks of PPed. At this time of my career I was beginning to develop Positive Pedagogy for sport coaching with opportunities like coaching beach sprints in the nippers and coaching a local primary school girls relay team (Light and Harvey, 2019) being pivotal to my development of knowledge through the dialectic relationship between theory and practice that has since guided all my research and teaching. In the session I recount here, I was pleased with the positive feel of the session, how none of the children seemed to feel like they had failed and felt included, and with the apparent engagement of most of the children. I did this by adopting what can be seen as the strengths-based approach used in social work (Saleeby, 2005) that Christina Curry also refers to in Chapter 7. It focuses on the capacities, skills and knowledge that individuals have to help deal with challenges in life and is a feature of PPed (see also Antonvosky,1996).

The positive, inquiry-based approach I took meant that there were no mistakes or failures as opposed to having learners strive to reproduce 'correct' technique, through a process of constant identification of errors and their correction. There was significant variation in skill, experience and motivation among the group but, this was more of a challenge for me when asking them to apply the knowledge they had constructed about arm movement to their starts. Some worked through this activity well while others were slower, and I was tempted to just tell a few of them what to do but resisted this impulse. Reflecting on this with far more experience in this approach now, I think that what I probably needed was more effective questioning technique.

I had been using this approach before the session I refer to in this chapter at the same surf club, which meant that the nippers had experienced being empowered and being asked questions as well as feeling their answers were valued. This also contributed to their learning being positive. The approach I took for this session was one of guided discovery, which is common in PPed when used to coach technique. I had in mind what I thought was correct technique but instead of telling them how to do it and correcting mistakes, I constructed a session in which, they *discovered* it, which is much like Mosston's (1972) guided discovery teaching style for physical education. At this stage of my development I sometimes felt very tempted to tell the learners the answers because it was taking more time for them to arrive at the answers than I had expected. I also felt some pressure from parents watching the session and who had no idea what I was doing and who expecting to see a coach in control and who was strong and clear in their instruction of how to do starts. It was not a highly competitive environment but competitive enough for parents to expect visible results.

The PPed approach I took does not preclude direct instruction and in the latter stages of these sessions over the season, I would sometimes tell them what they should do in regard to the range of arm movement or other aspects of their starts and correct them but still ask how it feel but they understood why I wanted them to do what I was telling them to do. This PPed approach to coaching sprinting technique can provide comprehensive, holistic (body and mind) understanding of the principles of running and provide a foundation from which young athletes can interpret information provided by the coach and apply it in their learning. When young athletes are empowered to learn and can connect the details of technique to core concepts, they can work through the application of technical information to perform as relatively independent learners as they adapt it to their ways of running.

The session I describe and discuss in this chapter was at the beginning of the season and designed to develop deep, conceptual and embodied understanding by the nippers in the squad. As I have suggested with swimming (Light and Harvey, 2019 and in Chapter 11, this volume), progress using PPed can appear slow but the depth and meaning of what is learned provides a basis for improvement and empowerment to learn over the season. It is a good invest-ment for the season and future seasons with the disposition toward learning, thinking and interaction it promotes serving the learners well in the future and not just for sport.

References

Antonovsky, A. (1996) 'The salutogenic model as a theory to guide health promotion', *Health Promotion International*, 11(1): 11–17.

Griffin, L. L. and Butler, J. (eds) (2005) *Teaching Games for Understanding: Theory, research and practice*, Champaigne, IL: Human Kinetics.

Light, R. (2006) 'Situated learning in an Australian surf club', *Sport, Education and Society*, 11(2): 155–172.

Light, R. L. (2017) *Positive Pedagogy for sport coaching: Athlete centred coaching for individual sports*, London and New York: Routledge. Available at: www.routledge.com/Positive-Pedagogy-for-Sport-Coaching-Athlete-centred-coaching-for-individual/Light/p/book/9781138215597.

Light, R. and Fawns, R. (2003) 'Knowing the game: Integrating speech and action through TGfU', *Quest*, 55: 161–177.

Light, R. and Harvey, S. (2019) *Positive Pedagogy for sport coaching* (2nd edn), London and New York: Routledge.

Light, R. and Wallian, N. (2008) 'A constructivist approach to teaching swimming', *Quest*, 60(3), 387–404.

Maslow, A. H. (1968) *The psychology of being*, New York: D. Van Rostrand Company.

Mosston, M. (1972) *From command to discovery*, Belmore, CA: Wadsworth.

Rogers, C. (1951) *Client-centered therapy: Its current practice, implementation and theory*, London: Constable.

Saleeby, M. (2005) *The strengths perspective in social work and practice* (4th edn), Boston, MA: Allyn and Bacon.

17

TEACHING CLIMBING TECHNIQUES IN SINGAPORE

Mohammad Shah Razak

Climbing has grown in popularity and is a new sport in the coming 2020 Tokyo Olympics. In this chapter, I recount my experiences of teaching and coaching a group of primary school students aged between 10–12 years in a Co-Curricular Activity (CCA) in Singapore. The focus of the CCA was to provide rock climbers with exposure to competition at the National level while keeping fit and healthy. Here, I share my experiences of working as a coach and teacher in charge of the CCA and how I encouraged them to be better climbers through my use of a *Positive Pedagogy for sport coaching* approach to helping young climbers improve their balance and climbing techniques. This session took place in preparation for the National climbing competitions and focusses on awareness and the use of the climbers' centre of gravity.

A good climber needs to understand the central importance of balance (equilibrium) and be able to adjust it for good climbing techniques. Developing a conscious awareness of balance and being able to manipulate it is important with the awareness and ability of the climber to shift his/her centre of gravity, which is essential for climbing efficiently (Horst, 2016). The focus of this chapter is different to the chapter on rock climbing in the first edition of Positive Pedagogy (Light, 2017) that I wrote, but does follow on from that session. It recounts my teaching of young climbers in Singapore how to use an awareness, that had developed in the previous session of their centre of gravity. This session comprised two activities with the second building on the learning in the first one in a progression toward increased challenge and informed by Positive Pedagogy for sport coaching.

Activity 1 (Climbing with One Hand)

The session I focus on here built on learning in a previous session that was aimed at developing awareness of, and feel for, of the climber's centre of balance. The first activity reinforced the students' awareness of their centre of gravity and guided them toward learning how to adjust it by climbing on a 'slabby' wall (rock faces angled at less than 90 degrees or less than vertical). Slabby wall climbing played an important part in the activity because it forced the students to rely more on their feet for frictional force than on their hands and in doing so, lowered their centre of gravity. I increased he need to feel their weight on their feet by introducing a constraint that only allowed them to use one hand (either one) and two feet and any one time to climb on the rock wall. This reduced their ability to rely too much on their hands for balance.

The previous lesson had focused on developing student awareness of the centre of gravity and maintaining it when moving. For this activity, the students could only use on one hand to grip on the handhold (feature on the wall) to progress upwards, which was difficult at first as it was unnatural for them. They also had a natural tendency to compensate for this loss of the use of one hand by leaning their body against the wall to be able to climb. After their first climb, I called in the group to focus on identifying the problem, which is the first step in inquiry based learning, with questions like 'What problems are you having by only relying on one hand to touch the wall' and, 'As you moved along the wall how did you feel?' With the thinking that these simple questions promoted we were beginning to identify what Dewey called a perplexing problem and to focus clearly on it (see Schön, 1983). Some of the climbers found it difficult relying on only one hand and one identified the challenge of trying to maintain balance. At this point, I decided to be more specific and asked, 'What do you need to do in order to maintain balance with only one hand? This generated a more positive response from the climbers and after deliberating on the questions posed, one student said that the only way was 'to rely more on our feet (to try and shift their legs and, therefore, their centre of balance)' to maintain the centre of gravity due to them being handicapped by having to rely on one hand. Another student came up with the solution to flap the free hand (extend the arms and move the hand) as a counter measure in maintaining balance as they progressed in their climb. They chose these two solutions from a list as the most 'do-able' and I wanted them to experiment with them on their second climb.

In their second climb, I asked them to try out the solutions developed from what was a debate of ideas (Gréhaigne, Richard and Griffin, 2005) and most of the climbers found that by testing out these two options they progressed higher than their previous climbs. They were thus, convinced that they had chosen the right solutions to the constraint posed, with the exception of flapping the hands as it used a lot of their strength and made them tire easily. I used questions to focus them on the problems. My questions after the experience led them to identify and articulate problems such as, 'I can't stay for long on the wall with only one hand because I don't have the proper balance'. They also identified how they had adjusted to the demands of the constraint during the experience by relying on their feet as one student aptly put it: 'I had to rely only on my legs and shift the centre of my body to gain the centre of gravity because I couldn't use my hands'. Further questioning identified how they had begun to find solutions to these problems by reflecting in and on action. They reflected upon the solutions they had individually arrived through adapting to the demands of the constraints. Such as, 'I had to concentrate more on my legs and shift them to get the centre of gravity and compensate for "flapping" my free hand to have good balance' and 'I had to learn to shift my weight (gravitational force) to get good balance'. For me, this was a positive outcome because the aim of the activity was to develop greater awareness and understanding of their centre of gravity, being able to manipulate their centre of gravity to climb more efficiently and to come to understanding of its importance for climbing.

Activity 2 (Climbing with Padded Gloves)

The next activity was held on a later day and also used a guided discovery approach to continue learning how to establish and maintain a low centre of gravity by putting weight on the feet. This time the constraint involved the students wearing padded gloves to reduce their ability to use their hands whilst climbing. By using questions to promote reflection I guided them toward solving the problem by putting more weight on their feet, which lowered their centre of gravity. The impetus was on having them shift their feet to locate their centre of gravity where it was comfortable for them before executing the next move.

I started the activity by allowing the students to try and climb the wall with the padded gloves on their hands. The students found this awkward to grip on the handholds as the padding from the gloves stopped them from 'cupping' and having a firm grip on it and which ultimately affected their attempts to maintain awareness of and manipulate their centre of gravity in their climbs. With that problem in mind, I asked the students after their climb, 'How did wearing those gloves affect climbing?' and 'How did you compensate for this restriction?' I asked these questions to have them think about how shifting weight from their hands to their feet and using their centre of gravity. I asked questions like, 'When you shifted weight from your hands to your feet did anything else change' and 'What happened to your centre of gravity?' The students first had a narrow focus on their hands and mentioned how difficult it was to grip the handholds without thinking about the rest of their bodies. With a bit more questioning, intended to have them think out their centre of gravity, they also said how they now had to 'shift their feet either closer to the wall or further away to maintain their centre of gravity' to help their climbing.

I asked these questions to encourage them to make the connection between the use of the hands as temporary anchor points (as they had problem gripping), shifting weight to their feet and adjusting their centre of gravity, as learnt from the previous activity. This time, I was trying to help them recall the central importance of balance and their climbing techniques as the key concept or idea with lesser reliance of using of the arms. Most people alien to climbing might think that the arms are the most important part of climbing but in fact it's the legs or feet that are more important. Some students cited their difficulty in gripping the handhold and one said, 'I had to force the pad flat against my palms in order to do so' and others identified the reliance on using their feet to compensate for the loss of grip and balance from the hands in order to remain on the rock wall. Following their reflections on the first climb they discussed possible solutions as a group and gave pointers to each other as they 'planned their route' for their subsequent climb on the same rock surface as in Activity 1. They pointed to the wall where they would perform certain manoeuvres involving their 'reliance and shifting of their feet' as they rely more on frictional force to maintain balance on the rock surface. The next step was for them to experiment and test out their hypotheses.

After spending some time climbing and trialling with their moves and techniques, the climbers suggested that alterations to their climbing technique were required. Typically, the successful climbers suggested the key was relying on their feet and not on their hands as they could not get the full benefit of a grip from their hands. Some students also said that shifting the weight from their hands to their legs made them more stable and. in doing so, they had better awareness of their centre of gravity and the balance they needed for the next move. They would then focus on the upper limbs as temporary levers or anchor points just to get higher (reliance on feet) in their ascension of their climb.

At this stage of their learning progression, the climbers were already tuned in to shifting their feet for balance and aimed for a better climb as they had done in the preceding activity. By this stage of their learning they most seemed aware of their centre of gravity (from their previous learning) and how to keep it low to complete their manoeuvres on the wall by feeling their weight on their feet. Occasionally, I would use my better climbers who showed good climbing technique and balance to demonstrate on the wall for the rest to observe, discuss, comment on and analyse their technique. With the demonstrations of the better climbers, I asked the others to watch closely and analyse what they were doing well. I asked, 'What do you think is key to a good balance is with this climber?' and 'What is he/she doing well to have good balance and how is he/she taking advantage of this?' I then asked more general questions and for them to take what they observed with the good climbers' demonstrations and suggest what it meant for them. Characteristically, they would suggest things like, 'Your balance is important in climbing' or, 'I can adopt this to improve on my own climbing techniques'. Part of an inquiry-based approach for learning, which is a feature of Positive Pedagogy, is reflecting on experiences and engaging in dialogue with the coach and other climbers (Light and Harvey, 2017). It is an approach that encourages a learning conversation between reflection on bodily experience and the mind through speech (Light and Fawns, 2003). When teaching this session, I placed an emphasis on balance and the climber's reliance on their feet to make climbing more efficient by controlling and using their centre of gravity. I used some features of Positive Pedagogy and in writing this chapter suggest how using more of it would help in coaching rock climbing.

Discussion

In this chapter, I provide two examples of the use of PPed to develop awareness and feel for the climber's centre of gravity and how to use it to improve climbing technique with young climbers. This led them developing a greater awareness of their centre of gravity and therefore, balance, and to understand how this can contribute to more efficient climbing technique. The constraints I used encouraged the learners to experiment and discover ways of improving their performance through an inquiry-based approach to coaching. They formulated solutions that involved using their legs to absorb the gravitational pull instead of relying on their hands and upper body, which, in turn, brought their centre of gravity and awareness of it into play and I tried to use questioning to help them make the links between technique and the concept of manipulating the centre of gravity. They were then able to appreciate this learning and apply it in the next activity which enabled them to enrich their learning by building upon their previous experiences and making them more relevant and meaningful for them. Both activities emphasised the importance of taking the weight on their feet to lower their centre of gravity and feel the difference it made to their climbing. I did struggle a little bit with my questioning to have them link their discovery of effective technique to the fundamental concept of effectively manipulating, their centre of gravity when climbing without telling them but feel the two activities and the PPed approach I took worked pretty well. Eventually, they established an effective, low centre of gravity before executing their moves and maintained it while doing the moves.

My coaching of rock climbing in Singapore reflects features of Positive Pedagogy such as designing physical learning activities and environment, taking an inquiry-based approach and using questioning to stimulate thinking and interaction. I observed climbers reflecting upon experience, participating in dialogue and collectively solving problems. Initially, the questioning took the students by surprise because they were so used to being told what to do but, after some prodding and pointers from me, they began to adapt and took the questions as part and parcel of my coaching style. My support and interactions with them allowed them to think and discuss with purpose through positive and productive relationships amongst them, and between them and me.

I did initially have some problems with getting students to answer questions in front of their peers, but this improved over time with each session and activity. My questioning could also have been better, and I have been working on developing a more effective approach to questioning. If I did these sessions again, I would encourage more dialogue between the students so that they would be more collaborative in their efforts to come up with a range of possible solutions, but the response of the students was very satisfying for me. It has encouraged me to realize how I could take this learner-centred approach a little further in rock climbing while giving me ideas for coaching other individual sports, guided by PPed. Writing this chapter and my growing understanding of PPed motivates me to develop my ability to coach using this innovative approach.

References

Green, S. (2019, 9 July) '3 climbing movement drills for balance', available at: www.livea bout.com/climbing-movement-drills-for-balance-755289

Gréhaigne, J.-F., Richard, J.-F. and Griffin, L. L. (2005). *Teaching and learning team sports and games*, London: Routledge.

Harvey, S. and Light, R. L. (2015) 'Questioning for learning in game-based approaches to teaching and coaching', *Asia-Pacific Journal of Health, Sport and Physical Education*, 6(2), 175–190. doi:10.1080/18377122.2015.1051268

Horst, E. (2016) *Training for climbing: The definitive guide to improving your performance* (2nd edn), China: The Globe Pequot Press.

Light, R. and Fawns, R. (2003) 'The embodied mind: blending speech and action in games teaching through TGfU', *Quest*, 55, 161–176.

Light, R. (2008) '"Complex" learning theory in physical education: An examination of its epistemology and assumptions about how we learn', *Journal of Teaching in Physical Education*, 27(1): 21–37.

Light, R. (2017) *Positive Pedagogy for sport coaching: Athlete-centred coaching for individual sports*, London and New York: Routledge.

Light, R. L. and Harvey, S. (2017) 'Positive Pedagogy for sport coaching', *Sport, Education and Society*, 22(2): 271–287.

Razak, M. S. and Light, R. L. (2017) 'Rock climbing', in R. L. Light, *Positive Pedagogy for sport coaching: Athlete-centred coaching for individual sports*, London and New York: Routledge, 204–214.

Roberts, S. J. (2011) 'Teaching games for understanding: The difficulties and challenges experienced by participation cricket coaches', *Physical Education and Sport Pedagogy*, 16(1), 33–48. doi:10.1080/17408980903273824

Schön, D. A. (1983) *The reflective practitioner: How professionals think in action*, New York: Basic books.

Wolfgang, G. (2019, 25 November). 'AZ quotes', available at: www.azquotes.com/author/53002-Wolfgang_Gullich

18

CONCLUSIONS

Stephen Harvey

I recently argued that internal change agents faced a 'crisis of positionality':

> In this situation, internal change agents find themselves responding to, not initiating, changes. Thus, instead of being progressive change agents, they often take up the role of conservative respondents to the externally initiated change. Since educational change is not in line with their own defined missions, it is often seen as alien, unwelcome and hostile. The crisis of positionality for internal change agents is, then, that the progressive internal change agent can become the conservative, resistant and reluctant change agent of external wishes.
>
> *(Goodson, 2014, p. 12)*

As the quote above suggests, substantial change in coaches' practices involving a shift towards athlete-centred coaching approaches such as Positive Pedagogy for sport coaching must come from within and help them become progressive internal change agents. The stories of coaches' use of PPed in this volume suggest how those who are new to the approach have come to understand it through practice and, while developing their understanding of it, seem to be developing and acting as change agents. Instead of promoting a theory versus practice debate they demonstrate the dialectic between theory and practice. They help realize one of the main aims of this third book in the series on *Positive Pedagogy for Sport Coaching*, which was to establish and develop the dialectic between theory and practice in sport coaching. The practitioners that offered their narratives in the book, share insights into the flexibility of Positive Pedagogy (PPed) and how they have gradually embedded its key features into their practice. Indeed, one key different between this current edition in the series and previous volumes is the emphasis on stories of applying PPed beyond single, episodic sessions, and how PPed's features can be adopted, adapted, and embedded over, the longer-term (i.e. a coaching season). Moreover, the current edition supports an important notion outlined in the introduction and in the two previous editions of *Positive Pedagogy for Sport Coaching* book series. This is that the flexibility embedded within the loose framework of PPed allowed the practitioners to embed its features into their coaching practice at their own pace and discretion, depending on their experience, the sport they coach, and the level at which they coach. The point has been made in this volume and the two preceding it, that PPed is not a pedagogical model. The distinction made between a model *of* rather than a model *for* practice is useful for thinking about what we can make of the coaches' reflections in this volume. Models *of* practice acknowledge the potential contribution of understanding individual contexts while recognizing the commonalities within each setting (Cushion, Armour, and Jones, 2006).

Notwithstanding these key factors, I (Stephen) would like to talk more about the themes inherent in the current volume from across the practitioner's reflections on using PPed. To do this, I draw on the concepts of reflective practice and critical reflection as a way of thinking about changing behavior and practice (Gilbert, 2017). Within it, we will address the four aspects of pedagogical change addressed by Casey (2010) as a way of bringing together our own thoughts and reflections on the practitioners' stories: a) betweenness; b) becoming; c) unlearning; and, d) pedagogical fluency.

Betweenness

The betweenness has been described as a place to go when wanting to internalize the theory-practice gap. As researchers, we appreciate the challenge for practitioners when thinking about the theoretical basis of any approaches to teaching and learning and trying to represent this in their own coaching practice. an important aspect that many coaches considered was the culture of their team or program and the design of the learning environment. One of the key elements of building an effective athlete-centered program is the development of a team culture (Kidman, 2001, 2005). Within this culture there should be freedom of the development of the whole person from a technical, tactical and social-emotional standpoint, and sessions should be designed with this in mind (Light and Harvey, 2019).

What has become clear from working with the coaches in the three volumes of *Positive Pedagogy for Sport Coaching* is how the flexibility and adaptability inherent in PPed allows coaches to live in this betweenness and actually feel comfortable about being there! Many other teaching or coaching models *for* practice may not have the flexibility that models *of* practice such as PPed do. Thus, practitioners get too focused on the notion of 'doing the model' rather than focusing on the needs of the learners. The stories in this book clearly outline how PPed and its key features can be adapted across different coaching contexts including those with different cultural backgrounds (i.e., Asia, North America, Europe, etc.), sports/activities (baseball, triathlon, strength and conditioning, etc.), coaching level (collegiate, interscholastic, recreational, national governing body your programs and in a school etc.) and offer a loose framework for coaches. Consequently, coaches can integrate the features of PPed into their practice as slowly or quickly as possible, and, again, base their practice on the needs of their learners.

Becoming

The collection of coaches' narratives in this volume show that they have adopted a reflective and reflexive process to the coaching process. They understand that there is no 'quick fix' and that coaching and their own development as a coach is a process of becoming through continued reflection and practice (Gilbert, 2017; Schon, 1983). And while they may well have begun their PPed journey to address a single performance gap (reflective practice), an intended consequence has been that they, at the same time, have been reflecting on their underpinning values and philosophy (on critical reflection see Gilbert, 2017).

One key aspects of this becoming is developing an understanding of 'dealing with' the modern player/athlete and how they can be pro-active in this journey by adopting an athlete-centered and positive mindset (Pill, 2016). The coaches clearly asked questions such as 'How can I design practice sessions so that they have engagement and flow?' and, 'How is what I am doing connecting to my athletes'/ players' competitive experiences?' to enable a process of transfer of learning (Rink, 2019). For example, we see in the chapter on triathlon how the authors engaged the athletes in the learning process, thus considering much-needed affective and social-emotional skills as well as the technical-tactical skills required to manage transitions between the sport disciplines (Holt et al., 2017). Moreover, sessions should be designed with the notion task modification for individuals and small groups in mind (Rink, 2019) where coaches high impact teaching strategies such as differentiation by task, outcome, or support to meet the needs of their players/ athletes (Victoria State Government, 2018). Indeed, we saw many examples of practitioners in their chapters modifying activities in innovative ways for individual athletes' needs such as the use of analogies with the fire hose in beach sprinting, use of bean bags in gymnastics, one-arm butterfly, padded gloves in climbing (Rink, 2019). All these innovative adaptations were ways coaches managed the theory practice gap and expressed through their teaching and coaching the notions of holism and humanism as they coached using PPed.

Unlearning

One critical aspect of adopting PPed in practice is the notion of unlearning. While unlearning can be defined as putting something out of one's memory, unlearning in the context of teaching and coaching means going beyond one's own playing and previous coaching experiences. As we saw above, the coaches thought of innovative ways of designing practices. They used differentiation strategies to help athletes learn the material, and they understood the need for them as coaches to build and model an appropriate team culture (Gilbert, 2017; Kidman, 2001, 2005). It also meant they had to engage in critical reflection on their philosophy of coaching and unlearn many coaching behaviors and learn when (and how) to ask, and when to tell (Metzler, 2011). In addition, the coaches had the difficulty of managing not only their athletes learning but, at the same time, their own process of learning a 'new way of doing'. They had to develop their own sense of dealing with failure and also had to create strategies for their athletes and players to deal with this too. Jon Gordon, a leadership coach in the USA, put this well when he said that mistakes should not define you but help refine you. Many of the coaches in this volume adopted this growth mindset (Dweck, 2008) with both their athletes/players as well as themselves.

In addition, it is clear that the coaches in this volume thought about the micro and macro level influences on their coaching (de Haan and Sotiriadou, 2019) when adopting PPed and considered ways to manage the process of change. For example, not making too many changes too quickly depending on the group being coached is an interesting example, and one which resonated for me when dealing with older, more experienced, female players (see Chapter 15 on strength and conditioning; de Haan and Sotiriadou, 2019) as opposed to coaching youth. Moreover, when conducing sessions in another culture such as with Richard Light's reflections on coaching in Singapore (Chapter 12; see also Hassanin and Light, 2014) and thinking about how you might slowly integrate questioning and inquiry to help build the culture, seems to be central to success (Kidman 2001; 2005). There are also differences between team and individual sports (Light and Harvey, 2019). Finally, thinking about how to communicate your coaching philosophy to parents, and also your administration needs consideration. Writing a parent letter, for example, might be a way to introduce yourself and your philosophy and help integrate their support for what you as a coach are doing.

Pedagogical Fluency

A key aspect of the current edition of *Positive Pedagogy for Sport Coaching* shows how the coaches were not only able to espouse the language of a person-centered or athlete-centered curriculum but also embody it underpinning epistemology of humanism and holism. The chapters on a season-long process of change (e.g. Chapter 15 on strength and conditioning) demonstrated how this was a process of gradual change and required a level of commitment on behalf of both the players/ athletes as well as the coach (Kidman, 2001; 2005, Light and Harvey, 2019). The coaches also recognized how they would be in the betweenness and that the processes of becoming and unlearning were keys to the development of their pedagogical fluency or their own sense of 'slow' with using PPed. More broadly, we can also see pedagogical fluency (flow) with Richard Light now being able to adopt PPed across a range of sports both individual and team, and to coach a range of different skills and concepts. However, as he admits, this has been a long process of over 15 or more years to get to a situation of fluency with PPed, and he still faces challenges as he indicated in his various chapters, particularly in Chapter 12 on teaching javelin in a Singapore school. The good news for readers of this volume is that, unlike Richard, there were probably no similar stories of change, ideas, tips, and tricks that other coaches had shared to help accelerate learning to coach using PPed. The engaging examples in this book of a range of different coaches working with diverse groups of athletes across diverse international settings provide the deep insight into coaches use of PPed that Richard and I were after. The stories told by the coaches in this current volume should not only resonate with practitioners across the globe but also make a contribution to the development of a dialectic between theory and practice in sport coaching (Cushion et al., 2006; Light and Harvey, 2019). With the current examples in this volume, Richard and I hope that you can learn, and though doing so accelerate your own journey of learning to coach using PPed.

References

Casey, A. (2010) *Practitioner research in physical education: Teacher transformation through pedagogical and curricular change*. Unpublished PhD thesis, Leeds Metropolitan University.

Cushion, C. J., Armour, K. M. and Jones, R. L. (2006) 'Locating the coaching process in practice: Models "for" and "of" coaching', *Physical Education and Sport Pedagogy*, 11(1), 83–99.

de Haan, D. and Sotiriadou, P. (2019) 'An analysis of the multi-level factors affecting the coaching of elite women athletes', *Managing Sport and Leisure*, 24(5), 307–320.

Dweck, C. S. (2008) *Mindset: The new psychology of success*. New York, NY: Ballantine Books.

Gilbert, W. (2017) *Coaching better every season*, Champaign, IL: Human Kinetics.

Goodson, I. (2014) *Curriculum, personal narrative and the social future*, London and New York: Routledge.

Hassanin, R., and Light, R. (2014) 'The influence of cultural context on rugby coaches' beliefs about coaching', *Sports Coaching Review*, 3(2), 132–144.

Holt, N. L., Neely, K. C., Slater, L. G., Camiré, M., Côté, J., Fraser-Thomas, J., MacDonald, D., Strachan, L. and Tamminen, K. A. (2017) 'A grounded theory of positive youth development through sport based on results from a qualitative meta-study', *International Review of Sport and Exercise Psychology*, 10(1), 1–49.

Kidman, L. (2001) *Developing decision makers: An empowerment approach to coaching*, Christchurch: Innovative Print Communications.

Kidman, L. (2005) *Athlete centered coaching: Developing inspired and inspiring people*, Christchurch: Innovative Print Communications.

Light, R. and Harvey, S. (2019) *Positive Pedagogy for sport coaching* (2nd edn), London and New York: Routledge.

Metzler, M. W. (2011) *Instructional models for physical education* (3rd edn), Scottsdale, AZ: Holcomb Hathaway, Publishers.

Pill, S. (2016) 'An appreciative inquiry exploring game sense teaching in physical education', *Sport, Education and Society*, 21(2), 279–297.

Rink, J. (2019) *Teaching physical education for learning* (8th edn), New York: McGraw-Hill Education.

Schon, D. (1983) *The reflective practitioner: How professionals think in action*, London: Temple Smith.

Victoria State Government (2017) 'High impact teaching strategies: Excellence in teaching and learning', Melbourne, Victoria: Department of Education and Training. Available at: www.education.vic.gov.au/documents/school/teachers/support/highimpactteachstrat.pdf

INDEX

Page numbers in *italic* indicate figures, **bold** a table

Printed in Great Britain
by Amazon